FRACTURED GRACE:

How to Create Beauty, Peace and Healing for Yourself and the World

Julie Krull

Published by Best Seller Publishing®, Pasadena, CA
Best Seller Publishing® is a registered trademark
Printed in the United States of America.

ISBN: 978-1-076204-67-7

This publication is designed to provide accurate and authoritative information with regard to the subject matter covered. It is sold with the understanding that the publisher is not engaged in rendering legal, accounting, or other professional advice. If legal advice or other expert assistance is required, the services of a competent professional should be sought. The opinions expressed by the authors in this book are not endorsed by Best Seller Publishing® and are the sole responsibility of the author rendering the opinion.

Most Best Seller Publishing® titles are available at special quantity discounts for bulk purchases for sales promotions, premiums, fundraising, and educational use. Special versions or book excerpts can also be created to fit specific needs.

For more information, please write:
Best Seller Publishing®
1346 Walnut Street, #205
Pasadena, CA 91106
or call 1(626) 765 9750
Toll Free: 1(844) 850-3500
Visit us online at: www.BestSellerPublishing.org

Endorsements

The angels have a message for you, and Julie Krull is the messenger. Having lived a timeless, universal, archetypal journey of healing and transformation, she is doing what is asked of her - sharing her truth.

Her voice is strong, clear, and comforting; her feeling of universal oneness with everyone is an embrace of warmth that helps us feel that same truth.

Being the recipient of grace in our lives is a matter of aligning with the Divine, she says. With a loving invitation to leap forward into such a unitive consciousness, she provides the means for us to do that. In part, it is through intentional heart connection to and resonance with others.

Healing from her broken leg is an apt metaphor of how we heal from our collective wound. Our fractured world will heal only when each of us, as the cells of the collective human body, assist the natural healing of the world by creating the right conditions for a broad spectrum healing to occur. Heed her call to wholeness, and enjoy her lovely and timely message: where there is brokenness, there is also much hope, especially when all of our actions are for the good of the whole.

Robert Atkinson,
Author of *The Story of Our Time*

In her book, *Fractured Grace*, Julie Krull weaves together stories from her personal experience, inner guidance, and embodied wisdom to create a rich tapestry that is illuminating and uplifting. Her insights and probing questions for self-reflection inspire us to know ourselves as "connected, whole, and free." This book is engaging, enlightening, and highly recommended for those who are committed to making a positive contribution to the shift from self-centered to whole-centered consciousness that is so needed at this time.

~ Carolyn P Anderson, co-author of *The Co-Creator's Handbook 2.0* and co-founder of Global Family and Hummingbird Transformational Living Center

In days of ease, when love and joy flow freely, we can intuitively sense and experience the wholeness of life and existence itself. Yet in moments of difficulty, fear and pain, the separate appearance of the world, can convince us of its and our isolation. How do we re-member instead its innate unity expressed in diversity, even in the most challenging circumstances? *Fractured Grace* is based on author Julie Krull's life-long exploration of the nature of reality itself, and having along the way, experienced numerous such times of struggle. The book is a wonder-full, timely and pragmatic companion and guide to inspire and empower us, even during the most fracturing events of our lives, to 'ground the force of love as our connective tissue' and experience and embody the grace that is our divine birth-right.

~ Dr. Jude Currivan, cosmologist and author of *The Cosmic Hologram*

From the personal to the profound, from self-shame to sacred-awakening, Dr. Julie takes us on her own healing journey as a loving guide to heal ourselves and our world. If your bones or your spirit is broken, you can emerge whole and strong by engaging with the wisdom of *Fractured Grace.*

~ Marian Head, author of *Revolutionary Agreements* and founder of Agreements Institute

This is a deeply personal book. If you are one of extreme experiences and compelling vacillations between grounded scientific ways of knowing and unboundaried arenas of the mystical, this will be a significant book for you. Adventurous souls, who feel called to strip everything away and still ask question after question, will find Dr. Julie Krull a fortuitous traveling companion. It's good that seasoned travelers share how they learned to "enter through the narrow door" and discover their Healing and Wisdom. This is a complete life journey which one must believe happened for a purpose—maybe so you could read this book.

~ Kurt Johnson Ph.D., co-author of
The Coming Interspiritual Age and *Fine Lines*.

This book is presented as medicine for an ailing humanity—a way to come to our senses and reconnect with the life-force of wholeness in ourselves, in nature, and in the universe, writ large. Through the author's own personal experiences with separation and disconnection—ranging from a Near Death Experience to a bone-shattering accident—a sensitivity to life and an appreciation of its allowance, forgiveness, and vital grace is shared through an inspirational and informed narrative. By focusing on the regenerative resilience inherent in ourselves and in all of life, we are invited to draw on reserves of wisdom in and beyond ourselves, in wholeness and integral connection with a universe that fosters dynamics of coherent emergence. Appreciation and gratitude swell from this reading, inviting personal exploration of the practices involved in cultivating the competencies and sense-abilities used to connect with and create patterns of consonant emergence with the life-embracing forces of evolution.

Alexander Laszlo, Ph.D.,
President, Bertalanffy Center for the Study of Systems Science;
Director of Research, Laszlo Institute of New Paradigm Research;
57th President, International Society for the Systems Sciences

In *Fractured Grace*, Julie Krull takes the reader on a healing journey of the soul, skillfully revealing how the full and honoring experience of fracture and fragmentation is also the essence of our individual and collective medicine. Masterfully weaving her own personal story with rich inter-disciplinary knowledge and tools, she offers practical healing maps for readers to navigate their own evolutionary journey towards wholeness. The book bridges the most personal with the global and the mystical realms, inviting reflection as to the patterns that weave in parallel between these dimensions. Following the mysterious workings of Source through her own lived experience, the reader is invited to join Julie as she struggles to surrender to the challenges she encounters. It is in this relentless and resourceful pursuit of making meaning of their messages that she discovers their hidden gifts. Through this devoted, authentic encounter with her unacknowledged radiance, as well as the constriction of her own psyche, body, emotions and spirit that she is able to decipher these cryptic clues and consciously integrate more and more parts of herself. The book overflows with generosity, love, knowledge and wisdom and with an unwavering signature of service to the Good of the Whole.

~ Shelley Ostroff, Ph.D., author of *A Testament of Now* and founder of Together in Creation

Fractured Grace invites us to explore a conscious, collective healing journey through the personal experiences of a master storyteller. Visionary Julie Krull compassionately takes our hand and encourages us to dig deep within, to find our own authentic expressions, and to move from fearful vulnerabilities to courageous breakthroughs to planetary solutions. This is a must read for everyone who yearns to have hope, heal, and return to our inherent Wholeness!

~ Dr. Linda Linker Rosenthal, mentoring steward for Good of the Whole and author of *The Seven Chakra Sisters*

This treasure of a book inspires the reader to open to the grace that is always present in challenging situations. Julie intimately shares from her personal experiences, masterfully weaving her profound wisdom with the latest discoveries in multi-dimensional healing and the evolution of consciousness. She inspires the reader to take a journey of deep reflection and vulnerable honesty to discover the hidden jewel that is being gifted by the wisdom of the soul.

~ Katharine Roske, co-author of *The Co-Creator's Handbook 2.0* and co-founder of Hummingbird Community

Fractured Grace takes us through journeys within ourselves, exploring pathways to heal and be whole. Julie Krull invites all of us to inquire, connects us to many sources of learning and creates spaces for us to reflect deeply. She inspires us as she shares her own experiences and interpretations, fostering our resilience and to be our best selves.

~ Dr. Monica Sharma, author of *Radical Transformational Leadership*

Julie Krull is a brilliant storyteller as she weaves so many layers of meaning and connective wisdom in her beautiful book "Fractured Grace". This inspiring book invites you to explore the fractures of our wounded humanity in a way that is both deeply personal and at the same time finely tuned to our collective evolutionary healing right now. Julie Krull invites us into the ruptures of our dysfunctional dualistic worldview by showing us how it is precisely in those ruptures and fractured perceptions that the Light enters, to remind us of our innate wholeness and unity. This book offers wonderful narratives and essential wisdom for the birthing of a future that is waiting to be born, as we step up and into our wholeness of Being. "Fractured Grace" is a sacred gift to inspire, remember and actualise our evolutionary gifts for the Good of the Whole.

~ Anneloes Smitsman, PhD(c), author of *Love Letters from Mother Earth*, storyteller, and founder of EARTHwise Centre

Contents

Foreword

by Andrew Harvey

The time for *Fractured Grace* is NOW! The world is waiting and ready to receive this book with the necessary medicine of inspiration, resources and a reparative blueprint.

We live in dark, destructive times. With escalating political chaos, natural disasters, environmental degradation, widespread famine, species extinction, and continued catastrophic conflict in the middle east, there has been a disorienting shift that is undeniable. Many are left confused, if not hopeless and in despair. Others are angry, afraid, and anxious. Yet many others are still asleep, under the spell of denial, ignorance, false hope, and the illusion of separation. If you feel that the world has gone mad, continue reading. You have a precious resource in your hands—an antidote for the debilitating consequences of this malignant disconnection.

Death precedes birth. Sometimes things need to die and fall apart for new things to be born. During this time of unprecedented social and institutional collapse and the dismantling of the ego's stronghold, Dr. Julie invites us to remember our own divine consciousness and the sacredness of all creation as a midwife of the soul—helping us to birth something brand new in our lives and in the world. She eloquently redirects us inward as the only way through this treacherous, narrow path, which potentially can become an evolutionary birth canal.

Dr. Julie is a modern-day mystic with an evolutionary heart that's on fire. She was born for these times—pulled by the mystery and unfolding of creation. She brings a calm presence of equanimity that helps escort us through this crucial, yet dangerous, portal. In these pages, she blends intimate and personal experiences, her professional knowledge, and a grounded sense of spiritual wisdom with her mystic's heart. Her language, endearing stories, poetic prose, and piercing truths tap into our soul and take us deeper into our own journey. This down-to-earth, palatable approach invites us to explore new concepts, expand our consciousness, and heed the call to wholeness.

As an author, Dr. Julie has an uncommon ability to take big, complicated concepts and ideas, and break them into savory bite-size pieces we can comprehend, assimilate and digest. Here, we are well nourished, left craving and yearning for more with each page we turn. Unknowingly, we find ourselves in the space between words and worlds, inspired to open to our expanded potential and deepest creativity. She offers a unique synthesis of science and spirituality, the mystical and the ordinary, first-hand healing and current world events, reasoning and prophetic visioning, and painful, raw emotion mixed with tender moments of grace. We witness her continual process of turning within again and again. It reminds us of the vast treasure-trove of wisdom we all have that lies dormant until it is tapped.

My deepest hope for humanity is that everybody, all of us, wake up to the Source within. It doesn't matter what we call the Source. We must wake up to the fact that we have on the earth an immense repository of resources and simple practices from all the traditions, which are available to us right now. As we learn to access this divine Source, it's liberating. We become clearer, more compassionate, more courageous, more humble, and fierce. Finding the Source within can tune us to the truth, show us who we are, and reveal our beauty, connection and wholeness. We can see and experience the divine in everyone, everything and every situation.

Fractured Grace encourages us to develop this practice and stabilize a spacious consciousness that is not reactive, but accessible and responsive. This creates the conditions for our innate, in-born healing capacity to come forward. It is vital that we see ourselves with this inner capacity to be sourced in the divine in order to activate our deepest creativity. There are tools, there are ways forward, and there are definite ways of changing the broken systems and structures. Don't be threatened by paralysis and meaninglessness that can set in with overwhelm. Get going. Dare to be well informed, on all levels, and embrace this change as an adventure.

We cannot do this on our own. Start gathering with true colleagues, true people with whom you can have profound relationships—for companionship and mutual nourishment—but most importantly for inspired action. Create *Circles of Grace*. If you want to be happy, serve and serve together. What is more joyful than accessing our deepest creativity? What is more joyful than helping those around us in meaningful ways? What is more joyful than offering the world inspiration and hope? This global crisis is our opportunity to create lasting change. And this change is a glorious opportunity to live more splendidly, more bravely, more courageously, and more passionately. If we do this work, we will be rewarded by the wine of bliss that will be poured out directly for us by the Beloved (Rumi).

You're in for a treat. This book reads with the mystery, intrigue, and suspense usually found in a good fiction novel. The enlightened approach sprinkles the pages with medicine for the soul. Pearls of wisdom, comfort, encouragement, and sound support meet you where you are and invite you to step into real, meaningful sacred activism. The message is crucial, the voice is authentic, and the result is endearing and provocative. As many seekers reach for guidance, tools, and leadership to help make sense of a world falling apart, and to prepare for the next best steps forward, this book is one of those resources and Dr. Julie is one of those leaders.

Preface

We are more than this. We can do great things. Anything is possible.

I hope by the time you get to the last page of this book, you take these opening words to heart, and say to yourself, "I can do even greater things. Anything is possible."

I had a conversation with one of my mentors as I was finishing this manuscript. I had a list of three things I wanted to talk to her about and she added a few things of her own to the list. We had a delightful conversation that was mutually supportive and nourishing. We talked about leadership, activating our deepest greatness and creating the environment where anything is possible—where the greatness comes forward—and how we can shift into the higher consciousness that exists in everyone. We challenged each other to stretch in our vision and our agency—to manifest and do something transformative with our shared vision.

Then she asked me in what ways I was using my voice to speak the hard truth to others? She acknowledged that she believed in me and said, "Julie, you have the courage to speak truth." I was a bit taken back, but touched by her reflection. It was the second time the "courage to speak truth" was mentioned to me in two days. A colleague wrote me a note a few days earlier, saying he believed I had "the vision, the clarity and the courage to be such a voice" when it came to "leading us forward towards greater states of truth, beauty and goodness." It was a beautiful message to receive.

Inspired by these two friends, I asked myself what would I say if I really bottom-lined my message? How can I use my courage to speak truth that expands awareness, inspires change, and motivates action? These pages are full of the "expanded awareness" part. I write about my experiences and how to live connected, whole and free. Understanding the *connected* and *whole* part is a powerful prescription, a revolutionary worldview, a transformative awareness, and very liberating. Opening ourselves to expanded awareness leads to change. And that's where the message, ***"We are more than this. We can do great things. Anything is possible."*** comes from.

We live in transformative times. And change is usually preceded by crisis and chaos. It's easy to say nice things to try to inspire and uplift people. But what is the bottom line? When I thought about what inspires change and motivates me to move into action, I quickly thought about an empowering time of discovery when I was an adolescent.

In my teens, I would climb up a ladder and crawl into my loft to read, write, create and dream nearly every night before sleep. It was my private space in my small bedroom. The loft was built into the peak of our two-story house and I had a mattress on the floor up there. Think of the loft as traditional "attic space" built within the rafters of the roof, or think of it like a "tiny house" that efficiently maximizes space. There were no vertical walls, they were all angled, so there was no head room—it wasn't tall enough for me to stand up. I had to crawl in off a permanently attached ladder and crawl back out. There was a carpeted area beside the mattress with just enough space for me to sit.

Sitting there in my creative dream space, I would vision and explore. I would travel between worlds and have my lengthy conversations with God (I'll talk more about this later). I had a youth bible back then, with lots of pictures and a synopsis in the margins. I loved to dig into the New Testament, sit in my contemplative repose, and ask deep, universal questions. I spent countless hours musing. There were a handful of verses that really spoke to me. The first was in John 14 where Jesus said, "Anyone who believes in me will do the works I have been doing. In fact, they will do even greater things." *Greater works than Jesus? Wow. Was that even possible? Jesus rocked the healing and miracles thing. Anyone who believes will do greater things than this? Alright.* I was inspired.

My second favorite was in Matthew when Jesus said, "For truly I tell you, if you have faith the size of a mustard seed, you will say to this mountain, 'Move from here to there,' and it will move; and nothing will be impossible for you." *Seriously? The size of a mustard seed and the size of a mountain? Truly? Nothing will be impossible?*

That inspired me! I had a visceral knowing—a powerful remembering—deep down in my bones. I knew these two verses as if I wrote them myself. I felt them to be true. They were a guiding force that gave me courage and hope.

Jesus was an activist. He taught about consciousness and expanded awareness. He inspired great change and motivated others to move into action. When I asked myself to bottom line my own message, I began a query with myself. How can I use my voice to motivate others to move into healthy action? How can I use my courage to challenge *you* to challenge the systems and structures that don't work and don't serve the good of the whole? What can I say that would inspire you to do your part and engage in the tough work that's ahead of us? How do I clearly and confidently speak my truth and share that same message that inspired me?

We are more than this: I learned I must first have the courage to speak from my experience of non-ordinary states of consciousness and honor my non-ordinary ways of *knowing*. I do this in *Fractured Grace*. Through my personal journey, I am called to share a new narrative that demonstrates how we are so much more than we think we are. Herein, we must challenge our cultural narratives and existing worldview.

Effective social change begins with how we see ourselves and the world. It begins with our cultural narrative and the enculturation of the many influencing systems of thought—religion, education, and the media to name a few. Which then establishes our worldview... which creates our beliefs about ourselves and the world... which then influences our thoughts, ideas and values... which contributes to our felt experience and emotions... which drives our decision-making and inspired, conscious action...

What if our cultural narrative is off—even wrong? What if the dominant worldview of separation is keeping us trapped inside a belief structure that doesn't sustain life? We don't have thoughts, ideas and values outside of our fundamental beliefs. Think about it. You can't hold a thought that is different from what you believe to be true.

It's time to back up the wagon and look at the consciousness that creates our current experience. Einstein said, "No problem can be solved with the same level of consciousness that created it." As we change the cultural narrative which has shaped our fragmented worldview, we can wake to a new level of consciousness and evolve the basic belief system that supports the illusion of separation. We are more than this limited understanding. It's time to open our hearts and minds a bit so we can see the *whole* picture.

Science is helping to reconcile our understanding of the world and make sense of non-ordinary states of consciousness. New science is upgrading our fundamental beliefs and coming into alignment with the true nature of reality. This new science is creating a breakthrough in our understanding of ourselves in relation to the world and the evolutionary moment we are living in. What it means to be human is different from what the old cultural narratives have taught us. We have a co-creative influence that is beyond our imagining. Shifting the basic foundation of our cultural narrative and subsequent worldview shifts our individual and collective beliefs, values and behaviors.

Our choices now, have the potential to co-create "the more beautiful world our hearts know is possible" (Charles Eisenstein). We have the opportunity to co-create the next stage of evolution for Humanity on Earth. But we must transcend the consciousness of separation and our worldview to discover, *"We are more than this. We can do great things. Anything is possible."*

We can do great things. Today more than ever, it is imperative that we *each* find our individual and collective voices to speak truth with a clear, fierce tone of conscious wholeness, healing efficacy, and hope. It is time for us to ground the regenerative force of love and lift up our highest creative potential.

I discovered a deeply personal, transformative, living state of grace when I found the courage to speak my voice. As you read through these pages, you will see how I lost my voice in many ways and at many times throughout my life. Today's voice isn't wholly unique. It is a reflection of that "still small voice" within each and every human—within you. It echoes that of many evolutionary leaders, dedicated stewards of the earth, powerful advocates, enlightened spiritual teachers, cutting-edge scientists, awakened souls, pioneers of a new consciousness, passionate sacred activists, simple conscious beings, and as I mentioned—you.

It took me awhile to find my courage. My left-brained, perfection-addicted, ego-influenced, fear-based, thinking-mind got in the way. I expected to write from my scholarly roots—demonstrating and proving things, citing research, displaying logic and scholarly study. I wanted my words to be smart and grounded, respectful to my training in academia, counseling psychology, and integrative health and medicine, bridging science and spirituality in a coherent and intelligent conversation. My ego wanted to please and impress you;

my soul was ready to speak truth. Yet, in order to share my story, I had to transcend the old belief structure and patterning that came from fear and separation. I had to let go of wanting to be liked by everyone in order to find my voice and courageously speak my personal truth.

When I broke my leg in the fall of 2014, my authentic voice spilled out through my experience like the rush of adrenaline in a moment of crisis. And then, the *book wrote me*.

In these pages, there are only a few mentions of scientific jargon about the nature of consciousness, and no specific theological, academic, or political doctrines here. You'll find just me inside of my healing experience, finding my voice, asking questions (lots of questions!), and sharing my journey. I hope the stories I've woven throughout these pages will kindle great love, stir more kindness, and expand the heart of compassion in you, my readers, and more importantly, awaken you to your own authentic, essential wholeness—your capacity to be fully human and fully divine—and heal your wounds of separation as you move into inspired action.

For in this journey, together, we consciously and co-creatively return to our wholeness—which is always right here. We are all intuitively in touch with the pain and suffering that comes with the illusion of separation widely accepted on our planet—an outdated and erroneous worldview. Now is our time to *embody a shift into our holiness and whole-being.* I encourage you to welcome *love* into our political conversations, our healing, and the threads of our social fabric as we weave a new way of being.

This call to action isn't based in New Age nonsense or woo-woo, Pollyannaish, blind optimism. What I have to share with you is grounded in research-based science *and* ancient, spiritual and healing traditions. It's a healing prescription for our intensifying state of fractured identity and our collective wounded soul. We have the opportunity to up our game, to put our spiritual prowess into all aspects of life, imbuing compassion in all of our social forms and relationships, grounding the force of love as our connective tissue.

I invite you into a collective field of love, to return to the place within you, to discover and remember the aspects of yourself that know no separation. I invite you to experience a sense of yourself that is complete and whole, just as you are. Experience a sense of wholeness that is always there—the infinite essence of who you are—never fractured, broken, segmented, or pieced together. This personal womb of creation, your inner temple of divine wisdom and co-creative partnership, will birth what Source is calling forward in you.

As you read these pages, allow your ego to step aside, suspend judgment, and permit the mystery to flow in and fill the space between us. Shift and expand your awareness, and de-compartmentalize the sacred in your life. Unpack your soul. Enter a waking, breathing, intimate, functional relationship with the divine aspects of yourself. Take the opportunity offered to develop closeness with the benevolent, creative Source that *breathes you*. As we learn to take God out of an intellectual box or far-off place and bring the experience of the sacred into our bodies and lives, we feel ourselves as pure awareness, we experience the totality of who we really are, we find healing on many levels, and **we can do great things.**

I hope my personal experience assists you to taste, feel, see, hear, remember, and experience a higher order that operates behind the scenes and animates everything. I hope my reflections, words, and wonderments inspire you to think bigger, see farther, feel deeper, and know more.

The healing of our planet is an individual, inside job that begins with radical reconnection with Source. This important work of co-creation helps us be more effective activists—more responsive, resilient, and creative stewards. Find that fierce momma bear desire within you and be a coherent, strong force for good. This fury will continue to push you to be even more direct with relentless compassion. With a lightning-bolt-type-of-jolt that wakes us and startles us into the present moment with our hearts racing and our adrenaline-infused bodies ready to leap into action, we will do great things. If you're ready to leap, I invite you to begin with the inside journey, co-creating with the deeply creative Source within.

Anything is possible. Today, I leap forward in a state of grace and gratitude. I walk with an "enlightened" step as I navigate life, relationships, vocation, and my authentic being. I carry a new understanding—a deep sense of beauty, peace, and adventure. The peace that surpasses all understanding—the peace that can never be broken—creates even greater wholeness. I pray the still small voice and this peace will reverberate from the words on these pages, and create resonance through you, with you, and as you. May the One voice begin *to write you*, and may you live into your true beauty, peace and healing, knowing that anything is possible.

Together, we will discover that *literally* there is no separation. There is no "other" side. Let's shift our conscious awareness and co-create a new reality with no more containers, boxes, cages, boundaries, silos, or divides. This is the greatest prescription for healing our personal and collective wounds. For a balanced, peaceful, harmonious, and compassionate humanity, we must embrace our inherent unity and live into our innate oneness—our inborn, intrinsic divinity and wholeness. That begins with each and every one of us, individually.

I welcome you into my intimate healing journey as I allow my long-lost words to emerge from the dark and dance with the ineffable. I hope each chapter returns you to the home frequency within your heart, where you know yourself as "not separate." And then, know yourself as connected, whole, and free. Here, we embody the love that leads us home; the love that *creates beauty, peace and healing for ourselves and the world.*

This journey is an evolution toward something beyond what we have ever seen. Together, we are the voice of Love and undivided Wholeness. We are the song of perfect balance, beauty, and harmony. We are the poetry of healing. We are the expression of an interconnected Universe—One with all of Creation. We are the dance of integration—of intellect and intuition communing in sacred unity—of head and heart engaging in synergistic play—of masculine and feminine dancing as one—of body and spirit merging gracefully—and of you and me, inter-being as whole. We are the voice of the One. We are an expression of grace in constant motion... expanding, growing and evolving toward greater wholeness where ***anything is possible.***

Let us come together in celebration for the good of the whole, and see past all perceived and manufactured fragmentation. Transformative change occurs when we see ourselves as part of the whole and work together—contributing to and in service of a greater whole. Together, we will co-create a *whole* new world, through a *whole* new worldview, and step into a *whole* new way of being with grace. May we remember our future and return to our wholeness.

We are more than this. We can do great things. Anything is possible.

A World of Love,
Julie

How to Use This Book

FRACTURED GRACE is part personal memoir, part self-help, part educational nonfiction, and part inspiration and adventure. It is a timely prescription for individual and collective healing—a resounding call for our wholeness in today's escalating state of chaos and fear. I am sharing my intimate healing journey as an invitation for you to step out of *mass consciousness*, with its widespread fear and story of separation, and back into your natural state of wholeness and grace.

As I share my experience, you will notice text boxes sprinkled throughout the pages. Think of them as *pearls of wisdom*, small doses of soul care, or pop-up lessons. I pick out salient, helpful themes from the narrative and open a window of expanded inquiry for you. You can pause to read them or purposefully ignore them. Feel free to read through the chapter to sustain your flow, and then come back to the boxes later.

However you choose to read this book, allow the frequency and medicine of *wholeness* to imbue your consciousness and permeate your soul. Allow each chapter to be a deep inquiry and reflection into your own personal journey of being and becoming whole in this precious and holy moment of *now*. Invite the words to create the conditions for your own healing to come forward and show you where you hold your personal wounds of separation. Pause and muse into the chapter reflections.

Explore the mystery and allow yourself to experience strength, courage, and creativity. Embody greater compassion, resilience, consciousness, and love. If you choose, follow along on *www.FracturedGrace.com* for chapter meditations, deeper inquiry, support, and insights. The gift is in returning to your home frequency—your center—and co-creating a healthy resonance and coherence in your moment-to-moment creative flow. Together, we will heal our worldview and collective wounds of separation, but it all begins with us as individual, whole beings within the greater whole.

Let us begin . . .

Fractured Grace

Why not risk breaking
open, trusting
that brokenness is
the beginning of beauty
waiting to blossom.

~ Charles Gibbs

CHAPTER ONE

The Fractured Veil

In the stillness of your presence, you can feel your own formless and timeless reality as the unmanifested life that animates your physical form. You can then feel the same life deep within every other human and every other creature. You look beyond the veil of form and separation. This is the realization of oneness. This is love.

~ Eckhart Tolle

It was one of those moments. You know the kind of moment when you are fully present and witnessing an experience, when time stands still, and you know that something really, really big is happening? Yeah. It was definitely one of those moments.

At our cabin on Johnson Lake, we had a steep grass slope that led to the water. I was mindfully taking careful baby steps down the hill, as I had hundreds of times before. One quick slip, and I heard the dreadful, spine-chilling "CRACK!" I didn't cry or laugh as I normally would with a sprained ankle or a clumsy fall. Instead, I entered a hyperalert, adrenaline-induced, medical-emergency-response mode. Three hops on my right leg, and I knew I had to gracefully get myself down to the ground.

1

Everyone in the boat below and patio above heard the gruesome "CRACK!" They came running to my side. "Ice and ibuprofen," I directed when my family asked what I needed and what they could do to help. "And get those cedar planks above the washer that we grill fish on. We can use them for a splint." The ice and ibuprofen came quickly. My cedar planks were vetoed for soft, rolled-up towels and Press'n Seal plastic wrap.

The emergency room doctor was impressed with my family's creative ingenuity. Though, I still wished I had the cedar planks for more stability! After cutting off the wrap and examining my leg and ankle, he said he thought I might have broken my ankle. I said, "Maybe it's broken too, but *I know* my leg is broken—my shin bone." He touched my shin again, examining it closely, and said, "No, I don't think so. It's your ankle. We'll get some X-rays." He turned to walk away, and then he hesitated and asked, "Why do you think it's your leg?" And from that place of being *fully present and witnessing*, I replied, "I just know."

The X-rays came back, and we were both right. The imaging showed a spiral fracture on my left tibia and breaks on both sides of my ankle. They prepped me for an ambulance ride to another emergency room to be evaluated by an orthopedic surgeon. After reading the X-rays electronically, the surgeon's preliminary recommendation was surgery for at least a rod, and potentially, additional plates and screws. My sister and brother-in-law were in the waiting room as I was being prepped for the transport. I called in my healer friends and prayer warriors. I rattled off names for my sister, who had my phone, to text or call asking for prayers and healing energy: Teresa, Shelley, Nina, Sherryl, and Linda! I did not wish for surgery. I did not care to have a rod in my leg. And that was my prayer.

By the time the ambulance arrived at the second hospital, the orthopedic surgeon had changed his mind. He decided no surgery was necessary and proceeded to craft a full-leg cast with the help of two strong EMTs.

Come Dance

"How, exactly, did you do this again?" the orthopedic surgeon asked in disbelief. It was my first checkup. He was perplexed there were no bones displaced from this brutal injury with multiple fractures. He reminded me how rare and amazing it was that I didn't need surgery and reported that I was healing nicely.

A spiral fracture. I had heard of that before, but never really thought about the physics of it. It's quite interesting. The break literally moved all around my tibia in a circular spiral. In awe at the mechanics, I have imagined my foot planting on the hill, as I tried to catch myself from falling. The weight of my body, already in motion and twisting forward, created such a force as to instantly snap my bones and send that horrific sound reverberating. It was heard at least thirty feet away.

After the initial shock and trauma to my body, I settled into the new rhythm of my recovery period in a horizontal position, my leg elevated in a heavy, full-leg cast, and plenty of time to ponder. What is the meaning of this event in my life? What lessons can I glean from the experience? What is the significance of this traumatic injury? What is it about a fractured leg, and how can I create meaning from this experience?

> Look at life events for meaning and guidance. Finding meaning in life events shifts your consciousness from innocent bystander or victim of circumstances to deep listening, participation, and co-creation with life and the world around you.

Finding meaning in life's experiences has been an intriguing, but sometimes arduous part of my journey. I love to ask questions.

Why? How? What if? It started very early, when I learned to dance with the Divine. The Sufi poet Hafiz wrote:

> *Every child has known God,*
> *Not the God of names,*
> *Not the God of don'ts,*
> *Not the God who ever does anything weird,*
> *But the God who knows only four words*
> *and keeps repeating them, saying:*
> *"Come Dance with Me."*

I love the phrase, "Not the God of names." You can call the Divine anything you want— Mother, Father, God, Source, Creator, Allah, Christ, Buddha, Jesus, Great Spirit, Universal Intelligence— whatever name feels most right to you. I sometimes use Creative Source, Divine Presence, Designing Intelligence, and Creator. Often, I refer to Christ Consciousness or our Buddha Nature to teach others to embody the living presence of God. But for the most part, from my upbringing and childhood religious education, I recognized the pure, infinite field of love and creative wisdom as God—the great Spirit, magnificent power, creative force, and animating essence of Life itself. We only *experience* this essence—God—in the present moment—in the flowing presence of *now*. God is only a mental concept when we step outside of present moment awareness to think and analyze using our minds. Yet, Divine Presence is so much more—a living reality, a state of grace that exists in every moment, right here, right now.

My first dance with the ineffable that I remember occurred when I was four years old. I was lying on my parents' bed taking a nap when I heard my mother's voice, "Julie, wake up. It's time to wake up now." I observed in silence and perfect stillness as my mother's voice became more urgent and agitated as she moved around the room. "Julie (her voice rising in volume and panic), this isn't funny!" My eyes were open, following her movements, but I didn't move or speak. It was then that I left my body.

This powerful event—my first conscious experience of my dance with the Divine—taught me about trauma, cellular memory, non-ordinary states of consciousness, and the mind/body connection. I communed with the infinite mystery of Creative Source that resides beyond a thin veil.

My corporal body was scooped up, put in a car, and rushed off to the emergency room. My consciousness, however, was everywhere, and nowhere: in a beautiful, soothing realm of calm, experiencing indescribable love, expansiveness, and light. I watched everything from a distance, and yet so close, as I floated without a physical body in another realm. I remember feeling fully protected and quite comfortable, as I witnessed this lifeless, little body being placed in the backseat of the station wagon and driven to the hospital, watching the emergency unfold. Later, in the hospital after a spinal tap, I was back in my body and able to move again. I cried.

An alternative dimension or world had opened up to me, the veil between realities, lifted. I learned to walk in both worlds, commune with other realms, and dance with God.

No words exist to adequately describe the mystical realms. Even so, my childhood perception of this multidimensional reality was limited. A four year old does not have the language or cognitive function to process trauma or an out-of-body, near-death experience. And so I developed a sense of shame associated with the belief that I had been "pretending." I concluded I was being naughty and causing a lot of trouble for the adults, as I remember my mother telling me to stop pretending. Of course, I had no concept of what was happening to my mind or body. When I was told the story as a young adult, I experienced a great sense of relief. The four year old thought she'd done something horribly wrong—upsetting all the adults who were caring for her. But finally, as a young adult, I could make sense of a visceral knowing I held in my body.

I wasn't pretending. I had been critically ill.

Chronic tonsillitis had plagued me as a young child. I was supposed to have a tonsillectomy, but I am told that due to chronic infections, the surgery was continually postponed. My memory of "pretending" to be still and not cooperating when my mother told me to "Wake up!" was actually paralysis. I was not physically able to move or talk—paralyzed.

Diagnosed with septicemia, my body quickly declined into septic shock. This is an extreme consequence of bacteria in the bloodstream. Bacterial toxins, and the immune system's response to them, cause a dramatic drop in blood pressure, preventing the delivery of blood to the organs. Septic shock can lead to multiple organ failure (MOF), including respiratory failure, and may cause rapid death. I was gravely ill, and my young mind did not grasp what was happening.

Several subconscious patterns emerged from this experience in the development of my sense of self in the world. Until I learned how to do the deep-healing work necessary to liberate myself from this trauma and understand the mind/body connection, I would experience chronic issues.

Understand your subconscious patterning and conditioning. Your memories and experiences form your beliefs, habits, and behaviors. The unconscious is in constant communication with your conscious mind through your subconscious. This source provides meaning and understanding to all your interactions with the world. Everything is filtered through your unique lens that is formed by your beliefs and habits. The good news is, all of your patterns, habits, beliefs, and behaviors can be changed.

First, whenever my body was genuinely ill with symptoms, my mind thought I was pretending. Not believing I was sick, I never listened to or trusted my body in response to pain, trauma, illness, or other symptoms. Second, my neck and throat became a source of repetitive symptoms with misalignment and frequent bacterial and viral infections. And third, from the perspective that the neck and throat represent self-expression, I did not develop my *authentic voice* until much later. Quite the opposite: I fell silent and paralyzed during subsequent wounding and trauma. I became a limp rag doll that couldn't speak, couldn't move, and couldn't defend herself. Finding and claiming my voice has been an integral part of my healing journey.

> We live in a multidimensional reality. There is so much more than what we experience through our five senses and what our linear, thinking minds can understand. When we open ourselves to the true mysteries of life, we begin expanding our awareness and noticing the non-ordinary. Explore how you can develop your own practices using meditation, art, creative flow, nature, prayer, and much more.

On that day, the thin veil between worlds was fractured, and I was introduced to the mysteries of a very different reality—a spiritual realm. I learned to walk in both worlds before I consciously knew what was happening. Powerful, mystical experiences, significant visions, psychic guidance, and a keen sense of intuitive wisdom opened to me during my rag doll experience. Before I consciously understood what was happening, I learned to move between realms. With gratitude, I cherish these spiritual gifts. This different way of seeing, knowing, and experiencing the world propelled me to seek and study mysticism, spirituality, consciousness, health, healing, integral studies, ego development, and humanity's experience of our bifurcated nature. My journey guided me into intensive training, personal self-care, psycho-spiritual practices, and the art of co-creation.

What is our bifurcated nature? We are fully human and fully divine. We are expressions of the divine in human form. Often, we experience ourselves as separate, disconnected, autonomous organisms. However, as a branch of a tree bifurcates from the trunk or another branch, so we bifurcate into what appears to be an entirely separate, distinct life-form. But we are simply manifestations of consciousness, creating and playing within a unified field of consciousness. We'll talk more about this in coming chapters.

I needed Western allopathic medicine that day. It literally saved my corporal life. And I was blessed with life after a near-death experience. It expanded my awareness and activated a mystical sense of knowing (some call it clairgnosis), as well as seeing (clairvoyance), and hearing (clairaudience). Both science and spirituality have been integral pieces in the puzzle of my life and vocational expression.

I began my early career as an artist-turned-psychotherapist. I had a difficult time integrating my creative passion with my ego's perceived need for credentials and scholarly study. The right and left hemispheres of my brain were pretty strong and balanced, but I hadn't figured out how to integrate and balance my head and my heart. I started out majoring in art, but felt called to something more grounded in the helping professions. After receiving my bachelor's degree in human development and relations, I entered graduate school to get my master's degree in counseling.

My passion for art, creativity, and creative consciousness never burned out. It became an integral tool in discovering my voice, developing healing methods of creative self-expression and my spiritual practice, and exploring consciousness. I yearned to integrate creativity, consciousness, and the expressive arts into the healing process. I felt called to put the *soul* back in *psyche* and the *spirit* back in *health*. The image of a bridge was imprinted deep within my psyche as a little girl, and always, I looked for ways to integrate the disciplines and bridge the two worlds.

Creativity and creative consciousness is a powerful tool to access your deeper inner-knowing and the inherent wisdom that lies within. This is important medicine if you choose to take full responsibility for your thoughts, feelings, beliefs, habits, and behavior. If you want to begin co-creating fully with life, this is an important mastery to develop. We'll talk more about tools and practices in coming chapters.

Building the Bridge

I had a powerful dream early in my exploration of energy medicine and my Reiki practice. I was in a medical laboratory playing with high-voltage spiritual energy, and I kept blowing fuses. A little, skinny man (more like Gollum, but kind-of-like Merlin), wearing a white medical lab coat and carrying a surgical scalpel, came in and began poking and stabbing me. Picking him up, I carried him around with his body facing forward and his scrawny legs scooped over my left arm while I worked. He was happy. As long as I carried him with me, he was content, and I could play with the energy and not get hurt. But as soon as I put him down, he would come after me, continually poking and stabbing.

This dream was a perception-shifting affirmation of my need to find ways to integrate Western allopathic medicine with the ancient practices and wisdom of Eastern traditions. It directed me to ground energy, spirituality, and consciousness into the physical world through the path of non-dualistic, integral holism. It's not *either/or*. It's *and/both*. The dream rekindled my passion to bridge and unite—integrating East and West; science and spirituality; body and mind; psyche and soma; art and consciousness; Heaven and Earth.

Whenever things appear polarized, expand your aperture. Look at it from an expanded picture. There's always a third point that holds the perceived polarization in place. You can also experience the *either/or* as a continuum of a whole. It can be helpful to see the *and/both* as a dial that you can easily move between the extremes. When you hold the consciousness of the whole, you begin to see the integral elements with more acceptance and appreciation, and discover ways to integrate, elevate, and return to wholeness.

I have explored a variety of psycho-spiritual practices as well as traditional medical tools and techniques. Fascinated with the mind/body connection, I studied a plethora of alternative healing practices. I have enjoyed the teachings of Eastern and Western traditions, as well as contemporary and indigenous spirituality and medicine. I will not prescribe that any is right, wrong, good, or bad. It's all about energy and consciousness; this is a choice one needs to appropriately match with one's beliefs and level of consciousness. I choose to access multidimensional guidance and cultivate the wisdom that works for me personally, and assist my clients to do the same. I choose to blend and weave the light I see in the world through a variety of traditions into a beautiful, holistic, healing tapestry.

> Medicine and healing practices need to be matched with your beliefs and level of consciousness. What do I mean by that? There are different stages of consciousness and awareness that appear as "levels." You can look at them as developmental stages, much like your own physical, psychological, emotional, cognitive, and spiritual development. We are all on an endless journey of growing, learning, changing, and expanding. Consciousness is the same. There's a saying that when the student is ready, the teacher will appear. Medicine and healing are much the same. As you evolve your consciousness, you will begin to resonate with different energy and beliefs.

Sufi teacher, Inayat Khan, said, "No one can give spiritual knowledge to another, for this is something that is hidden within every heart. What the teacher can do is to kindle the light which is hidden in the heart." I appreciate the wisdom of this quote. I would suggest that deep healing is also an individual path. The wisdom of the mind/body is complete and whole within itself. Guiding clients to learn how to relax into resonance, communicate between the mind/body, trust the innate Divine Intelligence, and create the conditions for healing to come forward is essential. Moving into meaningful, authentic connection and unification is good medicine for any ailment.

Kelly McGonigal said, "chasing meaning is better for your health than avoiding discomfort." I am one who has chased meaning with religion and spirituality. Fumbling through a myriad of wisdom traditions, spiritual practices, and organized religions, I felt compelled to stay grounded and explore deeper and wider into the mystery, embracing both the shadow and the light. I sought to find wholeness in the mystical realms born and made incarnate within the human experience.

My search for meaning in health, healing, and spirituality was a perfect foundation for my new journey with my leg. Fractured bones . . . What was I to learn in this experience?

CHAPTER REFLECTIONS

Finding meaning in life's experiences has been an intriguing, but sometimes arduous part of my life's journey.

- We all have been conditioned to see the world as singular, three-dimensional, and finite. We see our lives in the same way. We have bodies, we are born, we live, and we die. Yet we all have moments when we deeply feel our interconnected reality. We intuitively know there is more than the material reality. Identify moments in your life when the veils were lifted. In what ways have you experienced a "oneness" with all of creation? Sense into the times you feel most "at home" or "at peace" in your life and in your body? Write about your reflections. What keeps you from welcoming this larger, more expanded awareness? How can you best create the conditions for an expanded sense of reality?

- Life presents us all with challenges and obstacles. We all have "breakdowns" that give us opportunity to pause and reflect. When that happens, take a moment and ask yourself, "What is the meaning of this life event?" Take a moment now, breathe, and reflect on your life. What are the stressors, challenges, breakdowns, wounds, and fractures you sense in your life? Look for the meaning— search for the meaning. Use these events as opportunities for growth and understanding. Look again at your current life circumstances. Where are you perceiving separation today—in this moment? Journal about the sense of fracture, separation, and lack of wholeness.

- Regardless of religion, spirituality, or faith, there is a deep sense of relationship, connection, and knowing of a Universal Life Force or Divine Intelligence that animates all of Creation. Reflect on your relationship with this Creative Force. In what ways do you dance and commune with Divine Source? In what ways do you hide behind a veil? What would create the conditions for the veil to be lifted? Muse into what keeps you from fully knowing and experiencing the presence of God. How does your head and beliefs keep you in separation? How does your heart and fear keep you divided? How does your conditioning or past wounding keep you detached? Explore the topic of divine union and communion beyond the veil of separation.

- Mind, body, and spirit have been considered "separate" by modern medicine. The holistic movement and advances in science have begun to shift that erroneous view. As we have evolved our understanding, we have moved from *alternative* medicine, to *complementary* medicine, to *integrative* medicine and *holistic* health. I wonder what we will call the next generation? Take a moment and consider your relationship with your body/mind/spirit. This is one of the foundational relationships that creates your understanding of the world. What would it mean for you to "reconnect" with your Self? In what ways do you trust the innate wisdom of your body to inform you? In what ways do you disconnect? Explore the invitation to more intimately listen to your body. How do you experience your body/mind/spirit – as a unified whole, separate entities, something else? Really feel into this. This is foundational. The *real you* is so much more than your body or your mind. My friend, Jude Currivan, says you don't have consciousness, you are consciousness. How does that phrase shift your relationship with your physical body and your sense of health?

CHAPTER TWO

Weaving Light

Doesn't it really astonish you that you are this fantastically complex thing and that you're doing all of this and you never had any education on how to do it?

~ Alan Watts

When a fracture of the bone occurs, the body leaps into action to begin the healing process. There are three important stages in the physiology of healing a fractured bone. First is the inflammatory phase, second, the reparative phase, and third, the remodeling phase.

I think the second is particularly interesting. The reparative phase begins about two weeks after the fracture occurs. In this stage, proteins begin to consolidate into what is known as *soft callus*. This soft, new bone substance eventually stiffens into a hard callus as the bone "weaves together" over a six- to twelve-week period. The bone weaves as the genius of the body takes charge to repair and heal itself. How often I sat with my leg elevated in that heavy, full-leg cast imagining and visualizing the bones weaving together. In my mind, I envisioned threads of light and bone weaving and knitting themselves into a strong material. The spiral break was an especially interesting mental picture because it began to look like Sacred Geometry and strands of DNA. It was a fascinating image to play with.

Weaving bone! As my leg was healing, the Designing Intelligence of Creation was doing its thing by assisting my body to weave bone. How stunning. How magnificent. Our human bodies have an extraordinary and complex design. And to think, Creation knows how to repair and heal itself. The same intelligence that creates the body, heals the body.

—◆—

A Foot in Both Worlds

I remember a time I had lost my faith in Creation and the magnificence of the Designing Intelligence. I was just eleven years old. As a visionary mystic in a child's life and young body, I didn't understand that not everyone saw what I saw, heard what I heard, or experienced what I experienced. My ability to walk in both worlds was rather normal to me. I belonged to a cosmic family and had the reassurance of divine companionship and connection. Innately, I learned to commune and communicate with the spirit world—at home and one with God, the spirit realm, and universal Christ Consciousness. Instead of comprehending what a gift this was at the age of eleven, I felt odd, different, separate from other humans—alone on the planet, and in my family. I experienced myself as separate from Earth and other people.

For one thing, I couldn't understand why people treat each other the way they do. My childhood was riddled with experiences of pain and separation. I endured my share of childhood abuse and trauma. I also deeply felt the impact of global issues—images and stories of corruption, greed, poverty, hunger, and war broke my heart. At eleven years old, I was a precocious young lady. I was incredibly sad about the state of the world and the circumstances in which I found myself. I grieved alone, and my heart ached for a peaceful resolution and the company of a heart-centered community, grounded in love and acceptance. I was losing faith. Where was the grace?

> Our human experience of a three-dimensional reality creates a perspective, which is just an illusion, of separation. Contemporary science is now showing us what ancient spiritual wisdom has been teaching us. We are all integral parts of one, unified whole. We are consciousness, itself, and collectively make up a unified field of consciousness.

In one of my routine, ongoing conversations with God, I walked outside into the yard, sat down on the grass, and asked, "Why? Why do humans treat each other the way they do? Why do I have to be here? Why can't I go home?" I felt so separate and alone. I longed to go home!

What I experienced in that moment influenced my understanding of consciousness, conscious evolution, our integral relationship with the planet, and my vocational purpose in meaningful and profound ways.

I was transported from my contemplative place in the grass, out of my body and into an alternative mystical reality out into space, as my consciousness expanded beyond my body. An elderly man with a long white beard, long robe, and a funny, wizard-like hat was there to escort me. He looked like Merlin. A comforting peace settled over me on this journey—a peace I'd been longing for.

We moved farther and farther away from my body, left sitting in the grass. For awhile, I could see myself down there, then I could see my neighborhood, and then the entire region, as we ascended into space. When we got up far enough, I could see our entire Earth as a planet and a beautiful, living system—a breathing organism. Earth became smaller and smaller as we continued to soar.

We settled out in space, and the earth was hovering above our hands, as if we were holding a snow globe. I felt like I was in an Earth-school laboratory. We spoke no words, but communicated very clearly. Pictures of war, violence, greed, starvation, abuse, and other tragedies played out like a movie reel in space. I saw a dark, broken world in a state of destruction. Humanity was cast under a spell of fear, all people believing they were separate and alone. My questions were being broadcast on the same reel that was playing out our human suffering, picture by picture, horror by horror. This movie depicting the story of humanity progressed through past, present, and future. It was ugly. It was dark. It was my life, my painful experiences. And it was our collective life and human experiences. Unspooled before me was the vivid display of the monstrosities of our collective brokenness and fractured sense of self.

Next, a beautiful spark of light appeared out of the cosmic abyss and ignited planet Earth. Our beautiful snow globe, Earth, exploding in sparkling glitter as if shaken, was laced in illumination, as countless dancing lights of consciousness began landing gently upon her surface. Every continent radiated with the twinkling lights. Shimmering and dancing, the lights began to grow and radiate outward. As they expanded and spread, the lights spontaneously began to leap and connect. The connections spun sublime strands of light and music, which began crisscrossing around the planet.

The luminous show continued as single strands began to weave together. I stood astounded as Earth, God, or some cosmic force was weaving light and inviting me to participate and play in the radiance.

A magnificent new matrix, grid, or web of light, hovered around Earth transmuting into a healing and unifying force field—glowing and radiating in waves of energy. When the field of light finally stabilized, the movie reel changed to images of love, compassion, trust, connectivity, harmony, and peace. Grace was returning with a gentle kiss of redemptive reconnection.

> You are invited into a new level of awareness, remembering your undivided nature and connection with Nature, God, yourself and others. You are asked to evolve consciously and engage as a conscious change agent as part of the evolving life on planet Earth.

I saw a blueprint—a template. I saw a plan and understood the destruction and breakdown as preparation for a new way of being in relationship to the Divine, Earth, and one another. I saw my life play out and felt the benevolent call to assist in the planetary healing and the evolution of consciousness. I experienced hope and, without a single word, my questions were answered. I understood deeply and directly and was given a gift that is well beyond words to describe—beyond normal comprehension.

I felt and experienced this gift as if it were part of me—weaving light within my own being.

Profound. Holy. Extraordinary. Joyful.

The next thing I knew, I was back in my body, sitting in the grass.

This mystical journey was an ineffable blessing. So much was revealed to me that day. I hold the experience as a sacred ordination. I wasn't alone anymore—I never really was. Now, as I step into my highest vocational expression, I am finding others who have shared similar experiences and visions. Everyone holds a piece of the transformative healing work on our planet, and we need all people to fulfill their part. We are weaving the light of Christ and creating heaven on earth, a beautiful, benevolent tapestry of consciousness. This is sacred work. We are threading more consciousness into matter as we birth a new, evolved, divine humanity.

Many different stories and narratives exist from ancient wisdom traditions and religions about living in unity—in Oneness. When I refer to Christ Consciousness and "weaving the light of Christ," I am not specifically talking about Jesus, but the vast Christ Consciousness, the omniscient Intelligence of God omnipresent in every part and particle of creation.

Facing Our Brokenness

We are living through the dreadful process of breakdown and fragmentation. We've forgotten our inherent unity and essential oneness. We've lost our connection to self, God, one another, and the earth. We are out of alignment and feeling the results of disharmonious relations, cultural tensions, and disconnection. The enormity of whole-systems breakdown across the global terrain is frightening and painful, and can lead one to giving in to a sense of fatalism. We are heading toward complete transformation, but fail to see our direct responsibility in the practice of transcendent alchemy and our opportunity to consciously evolve.

It is time to face our acute symptoms of brokenness, of the weight of humanity's shadow, and of the illusion that keeps us paralyzed in fear and separation. It's time to name our dysfunction and the endemic disease of a runaway ego, which creates separation consciousness and weakens our resolve, threatening our existence. It's time to diagnose the madness of individualistic, self-serving agendas and actions that are destroying us as individuals, families, and nations, as a species and as a planet.

Confronting the pathological consciousness of separation, the worldview of separation, the story of separation and brokenness, both individually and collectively, is essential to bring us hope and move us toward healing. We must remember our essential wholeness and step onto the pathway toward transformation. This process begins with the way we understand ourselves in relationship to all things—our worldview. It begins with an awakening, both individually and in community, into a soul-centric consciousness and understanding of our universal, interconnected reality.

All the modern crises and breakdowns we are experiencing in the world are symptoms of our outdated worldview and an ingrained, yet faulty, sense that makes us believe we are separate. You can look at this like upgrading your computer or cell phone. When the software and applications continue to get more and more sophisticated (the evolution of consciousness), the hardware (our current structures and systems) simply cannot keep up. An outdated computer or cell phone, built to run the current software and apps, begins to get really slow and glitchy with every upgrade we make. It simply can't keep up with the new technology and advances in programming. Sooner or later, we give in and replace the structure with the latest hardware that can keep up with the benefits and features of the advances in technology. When you understand this, you can develop inner peace and surrender as the systems and structures break down.

We are invited to remember our essential oneness with all of creation. We are invited to rise up and discover our fiery passion and eternal love. We are invited to find our individual and collective strengths, creative genius, resolve, responsibility, and resilience.

Much like my early ragdoll experience of paralysis and near-death, humanity seems to have been paralyzed in fear, unable to speak out and move forward. We must continue to rise up and cry out, "Enough!"

In these times of breakdown, we must focus on the breakthroughs, even while acknowledging our pain. We are providing hospice for the dying systems, while simultaneously midwifing a new worldview and evolved consciousness. The best medicine is empowering each and every individual to move beyond the brokenness of a fragmented worldview. As we remember our divinity, we can move through the darkness with courage and compassion to rekindle our light. As the light of higher consciousness pierces the dark, dense membrane of matter, let us be the fierce and brilliant beam of light that shines its healing power throughout all of creation, intensifying, growing, and eventually leaping into a higher order.

We are the weavers and the weaved.
We are the broken and the whole.
We are the hurting and the healed.
We are the darkness and the light.

Let us be the weavers of a peaceful existence by simply remembering the true nature of reality and being who we truly are.

Being paralyzed by fear is a real phenomenon. Fear activates a cascade of reactions and responses in your body. Both stress and fear trigger a basic survival mechanism that signals your body to respond to danger with a fight, flight, or freeze response. Fear shuts down parts of your brain and body systems to allow your energy and attention to focus solely on the threat and emergent needs of the moment—keeping your body and brain focused on staying safe until the threat is neutralized. Fear overrides conscious thought and narrows your perception and creates tunnel-like vision and hyper-focus on the problem at hand. This state isn't ideal for creative problem solving or finding long-term solutions.

CHAPTER REFLECTIONS

Creation knows how to repair and heal itself.

- We are all light weavers. Our bodies have the innate genius to heal. The powerful force that created our bodies heals our bodies. This impulse of Creation is alive and well, creating in us, through us, and as us. Yet, we are living in the midst of a predominant worldview of separation, of fragmentation—immersed in an illusion that we are separate from our own bodies. It is our time to consciously return to wholeness. Reflect on the topic of weaving light and your body's ability to weave tissue and bone. Sense into the power of this creative force. In what ways do you trust your body's own healing response? In what ways do you trust the innate impulse of Creation that is creating your life? Muse a bit deeper. Where in your life are you witnessing the miracle of this weaving? How can you best create the conditions for this magnificent force to co-creatively partner with you consciously? A wise friend, Ann, always reminds clients to claim their blessings and miracles. In what ways can you open to the expression and manifestation of your blessings and miracles?

- We are human. We are experiencing a mass shift into whole-systems transformation. Things are breaking down and old institutions are dying. We look at the news and see violence, chaos, pain, suffering, greed, war, polarization, and separation. These times are challenging us. There are times in our lives when we lose faith in Divine Order. We lose faith in ourselves and fellow humans. Pause. Breathe. Reflect on a time in your life when you wanted to give up and quit life. Journal about this experience. What happened? What were the lessons and how did the light reenter? How did you experience your light and that of the Divine? In what ways can you consciously weave light for someone else today? Look around. Where do you find others consciously weaving more light? Or others in need? I invite you to consider a personal commitment to yourself. In what ways can you join your light with the legion of other light weavers on the planet, even in the worst of times; times of great crisis, chaos and fear? How can you make this a part of your daily practice and responsibility?

- In our return to wholeness, we are evolving this fragmented worldview of separation, and more and more, we are understanding the mysteries of the universe and the quantum field (unified field). Pause and reflect on your life, gifts, strengths, and purpose. If you were to step forward and assist in shifting the worldview of separation toward a healthier worldview of unified wholeness, what would you weave into this co-creation? What is your part of the whole? What is your message and expression? What is your thread to pull through? What is your story and how can it assist others? Sense into this deeper exploration of your wider purpose.

CHAPTER THREE

Birthing the Divine Human

The Universal Human is a species capable of co-evolving with nature and co-creating with spirit.

~ **Barbara Marx Hubbard**

It's funny how life brings us signs and symbols. My broken bones happened the same year when my dad died, after three and a half years of treatment for myelodysplastic syndromes (MDS) and, in the end, acute myeloid leukemia.

MDS (formerly called *pre-leukemia*) is a type of cancer in which the bone marrow does not make enough healthy blood cells, and there are abnormal cells in the blood and/or bone marrow. In a patient with MDS, the immature blood stem cells do not become healthy red blood cells, white blood cells, or platelets. These immature blood cells, called *blasts*, do not work the way they should and die either in the bone marrow or soon after they go into the blood. This leaves less room for healthy blood cells and platelets to form in the bone marrow. When there are fewer healthy blood cells, infection, anemia, and easy bleeding may occur. MDS can turn into a fast-growing cancer of bone marrow cells called *acute myeloid leukemia*. This happens in about one out of three people with MDS, and my dad was one of the ones.

When the courageous and often-*heroic* medical treatments failed after many years, it was time to make a decision. Stay in the hospital until he died or go home on hospice care. He chose to go home. My three sisters and I went to be with him and our stepmom. Even though his health declined very rapidly, that week was a blessed time of love and healing. We took turns staying up with him at night, soaking in the unexpected gifts that came with deepening into compassion.

On Valentine's Day, I sat beside his hospital bed at 3:30 a.m. He slept restlessly through the pain in an incoherent state of tolerance. I put my hand on his hand, and without missing a beat, in his sleep, he whispered, "I love yahz." He softly winced and moaned then became quiet again. In the middle of the family room, he was bundled under layers and layers of blankets, hand-stitched quilts, and crocheted throws, with his left foot hanging out of the covers on purpose.

Perched on a folding chair next to his bed, I was wrapped with my own layers of pajamas, sweater, and vest. We were both warm and cozy, though uncomfortably so, given the circumstances. Through his irregular breathing, wincing, and moaning, whether asleep or lucid, he continued to whisper messages of love: "I love you, oh how I love you." Moans of pain, his cough, and the sweet sound of his love-whispers became a new kind of clock, marking time as it passed in the middle of the night.

He woke himself up, grimacing with a loud noise. I rested my hand on his shoulder, and he quieted down. Gently, the sound of the home oxygen concentrator and the manifest warmth of a strange, loving Presence eased him back to his shallow rest, but not before he sent out more love, "Ahhh . . . I loves ya, Jules." "I love you too, Dad," I quietly replied.

In the darkness, offset by only the dim light of my computer, I reflected on what a beautiful Valentine this was. I was soaking in the bittersweet, merciful love of sharing his last hours. I was communing in a grace-filled resonance, even as he created discordant music with his breath. This love was infinitely real and deep, though delivered in a delirious container of pain. The benevolence of this, otherwise painful, moment was so precious.

A whimper, then a loud groan, brought me back into the moment. It was time to roll over. We worked together to find a comfortable position on his left side, prop pillows in the perfect places, and rearrange the covers. "How's that, Dad?"

"Oh, it's good . . . it's good until it's not," he said and quietly drifted back into the feverish abyss of his restless reality. I chuckled at his commentary. The whispers, moans, and cough continued into the early morning hours. And time passed. He woke again with an unpleasant howl, "OH-Oooohhh-OH!" then quietly said, "I love you, honey."

"I love you too, Dad. Can I get you something for the pain?" I asked.

"Oh, no . . . I'm okay. It hurts more everywhere than anywhere." He answered in his kind, but humorous way, and then turned to me, "Why don't you go lie down in the recliner and try to get some sleep?" I replied, "I'm okay, Dad. I'm sitting here writing love letters on my computer."

"Ah . . . that's good! Real, real, good," he replied with enthusiasm. "I LOVE YOU!" he added. A tear rolled down my cheek. "I know, Dad. I love you too," I whispered in gratitude. And time passed.

As it turned out, that was the beginning of the end. Valentine's Day was his last coherent day. We had a beautiful day of celebration with his favorite meal and lots of tender memories. By 11:00 pm, the tide was turning, and the hospice staff arrived around midnight. They coached us as to what to expect, and how things would change. A few hours later the hospice nurse suggested we say our goodbyes. We entered the end-stage, which usually takes three or four hours. However, our deathbed vigil turned into an epic journey, and we were in the eleventh hour. It was such a long and laborious night for him.

—

Labor and Delivery

My memory of those moments shortly before my first child was born is keen; I felt like giving up—desperately. Not managing my pain well, I wanted the unbearable process to stop. I literally wanted to quit, pack up, and go home. However, it was a blessed event that was irreversible and forever life-changing. There was no stopping the process once it had started. The only way out was through.

> The only way out is through. Resistance and fear constricts. Avoiding pain or conflict does not resolve the issue at hand. Trust the process. The pain of holding back, resisting, and trying to change or control the situation is often greater than the perceived pain of the actual process of being fully engaged and present in the moment. Practice the art of surrender and letting go. You will become more pliable and resilient.

Contractions in my lower back, coupled with my first-time-mom fear of the unknown, made it nearly impossible to relax, do Lamaze breathing, and surrender into the experience of childbirth. After I pushed for over two hours, the doctor finally asserted he was stepping in to use forceps to assist in the delivery. A few minutes later, my son was delivered, and took his first breath.

Sitting by my father's bed, I witnessed his laboring. Cycles of shallow breathing, weakened pulse, and peaceful pauses were interrupted with what seemed like excruciating labor pains. Wincing and moaning, he journeyed through an endless rhythm of contractions as he prepared to leave his body. Then, at the moment when we thought he'd been delivered into the peaceful embrace of death, another wave of unsurrendered life sent him laboring for enough breath to get him through the next contraction.

Flashes of that moment—giving birth so long ago—grabbed my attention. I beheld my father in an arduous dance within the liminal portal—somewhere between life and death (the "death canal," if you will), managing his own labor and delivery.

I recognized myself compassionately sharing his fatigue and resistance. He had labored for hours. Fear of the unknown lingered in the room. I wanted the process to stop! In my own discomfort and pain, I prayed for a quick and easy delivery. I observed myself in the throes of self-induced suffering, not wanting him to suffer. But like birth, this was, I knew, another one of those blessed events that was irreversible and forever life-changing. And he had to go through it alone. I could choose to experience his death in a limited state, one of fear, separation, resistance, and pain or I could shift my reality and awareness to open into the expansive, *sacred knowing* of this most blessed moment.

I paused, took a deep breath, and tuned-in to the resonant field of love in the room. Calling on my higher self, I quickly discovered a cosmic harmony within the life cycle of birth and death, witnessing this eloquent process and myself within it. The mystical doors of the Universe opened, as I experienced tremendous grace and deep meaning in the Holy process. Instead of the fear, pain, resistance, and suffering that had gripped my attention, I found peace. I was handed a precious gift and consciously chose to claim and receive it. I stepped through my own limiting portal of embodied consciousness and became fully present to the mystery and miracle of life. Surrendering, I relaxed into the death process and became one with it.

Physical death was my father's lone journey now. We all wanted to be there for him—with him—to support and comfort him in his transition. We desperately desired a peaceful resolution. However, this was his delivery, and only he could labor through the process and move through the transcendent *birth/death canal*. This was work of the soul. He had to go through this narrow portal to deliver himself.

The hospice nurse, Lisa, in her palliative wisdom, intuited the same thing as I left the bedside and went to sit in a recliner several feet away. She kindly invited us to step away and rest in another room for a while, allowing my dad to fully relax into this sacred dying process. We were all there with loving intentions to support him in the transition. Yet our relationships as wife and daughters, perhaps, held him in a place of resistance and emotional attachment or interference, keeping him in his earthly embodiment as husband and father. It was time for him to release himself and give birth to the celestial role of his greater essence.

Her gentle suggestion was perfect. The short time of physical separation assisted in his ability to relax and surrender. Having us step away allowed a heavenly midwife, with divine forceps, to step in and assist. He let go, moved through the portal, and finally found peace. A few minutes later, my dad was delivered and took his last breath.

My dad birthed himself back into the mystery of his full divine nature.

I was humbled and honored to participate. After decades exploring the concept of the divine human, the emergence of infinite mind, and as some might say, the embodiment of Christ Consciousness or our Buddha Nature, I was touched by this tender moment. I have had a perpetual curiosity and passion for bringing spirit more fully into matter, bringing consciousness into life more completely. Yet I just witnessed my father slip through the ephemeral gateway in reverse. The Holy blueprint was becoming clearer. What more could this moment of grace teach me?

———

Structural Support

And now, what were the lessons in my fractured leg? Why is it that my fractured bones occurred just a few months after my father's death—one week before his birthday? And does this disease of the bone marrow have any spiritual correlation to my bone fractures? Louise Hay says that problems with the bone marrow represent our deepest beliefs about the self—how you support and care for yourself. I can definitely see how my dad, deep down, may have lacked a healthy love for himself. He definitely created challenges with his physical health, smoking, drinking, and working hard as a mechanic using toxic solvents that likely caused the MDS. When I think about my early childhood, I realize I, too, developed unhealthy beliefs about myself as a young, embodied human—neglecting physical symptoms and self-care, lacking a healthy self-love and self-compassion.

> Healthy self-love and self-compassion are critical building blocks for a healthy, whole life. The key to discovering your sustainable inner-peace begins with radical and authentic love of yourself. If you're struggling in this area, begin with the idea of loving the essence of who you really are as a unique, individualized expression of the Divine.

Louise Hay wrote a classic, evergreen book called, *Heal Your Body*. It's a guide to the mind/body connection. You look up your specific health challenge and find the probable cause for the issue and a helpful new thought pattern to overcome it. She says bones, in general, represent the structure of the Universe. Bone fractures represent rebelling against authority. As I opened to the deeper meaning of my broken bones, I wasn't quite sure about the *rebelling-against-authority* thing. But actually, there was something quite intriguing about bones representing the structure of the Universe, especially after witnessing the liminal doors briefly open as my father passed through.

I chose to let the *authority thing* be, and see what wanted to emerge. Could there be any connection to my deepest beliefs about myself, and what I know about the structure of the Universe? Yes— this was definitely a clue on my continued journey to birth the divine human.

I have always experienced the notion of the structure of the universe from a rather intuitional perspective. The "knowing" that opened to me in my childhood didn't always serve me well. I remember always questioning the truth of what I was being taught as a little girl. I vacillated between feeling like an alien and like a fraud, because I knew things that people around me didn't know; I couldn't explain how I knew—I just did. From my standpoint, my ongoing multidimensional journey and my conversations with God were where I could find ultimate truth. But how was I to explain this guidance to people? When it came to matters of consciousness, human development, and spirituality, I was at home—in my element—and I couldn't get enough.

In early adolescence, I began a private exploration into the structure of the universe through religious doctrine and teachings. From a mystic's point of view, I could see where *thinking about God* created twists and turns, arguments, separation, and profound differences in understanding and interpretation. *Thinking* about God and the universe seemed to incite a vast array of rigid or brittle ideology and dogma, whereas, *experiencing* God didn't.

Mystics and contemplatives of many faiths—almost every religion—share a rather fluid, elegant universal *experience* of the

Divine. Most people attached to thinking about God look outside for guidance to find the secret, the key, or the "right" answer. Mystics discover the Divine through connection and experience. I wish I could bottle up the mystic's experience like a potion, or write a universal recipe to share with all of humanity. I wish I could teach others how to *presence* the soul and experience the Divine. However, the path of the divine human is an individual journey, and the keys to the Kingdom are within.

> Many tools, resources, and practices exist that can teach you how to experience glimpses of the Divine. You can begin with a prayer or meditation practice and expand from there. The key is to get out of your thinking mind, connect with your breath, and go to the vast, open space within.

As with my son's birth and my father's death, birthing the divine human is something we do alone, in the dark. It's more like a remembering or an awakening. We are never *not* a divine human— most of us simply aren't consciously aware of ourselves as an integral part of this divine creation. They say an acorn has no idea there's a huge oak tree inside. And I think about a baby in the womb having no experience of itself in the world outside. The baby moves from a dark, safe space in the womb, surrounded by amniotic fluid and having all of its needs met, to life on Earth. Imagine the transition.

I think of birthing the divine human in much the same way. We are comfortable in our lives, until we are not. We avoid change. We don't know what we don't know, until we know it. We go about life from the consciousness of the finite mind—the Separate Self—with little awareness that there is so much more to be discovered. Most of the time, we feel a little impulse moving inside us like a tulip bulb ready to break open, move through the ground, stretch for the sunlight, and bloom. The Divine Intelligence of the universe moves us in perfect timing. There are many subtle invitations extended.

You don't know what you don't know, until you know it.

This is an important understanding. You didn't know how to read a book until you *knew* how to read a book. You didn't know that the sun doesn't really set or rise until you understood that the earth is rotating around the sun and a sunrise is simply the earth rotating toward the sun. Everything is impermanent, even stages and states of consciousness. Give yourself grace, forgiveness, and compassion for the times in your life when you don't know, and be open to the revelatory insights and deeper understandings of the mysteries of life.

Relaxing into Resonance

What happens when we resist the impulse to grow into our divine, higher selves? The universe may bring us a big squeeze—quite like a uterus in contraction—encouraging us to move through the *transcendent canal*. Sometimes there's that divine midwife with forceps, ready to step in and assist in our delivery. And other times, life cuts through our safe walls to deliver us like a cesarean section. Dare I say, the breaking-through process of delivering the divine human is as individual as the seven billion people on the planet, and as universal as the One consciousness that animates all of life? As the water breaks in the womb, we, too, break through that thin veil of consciousness, and there's no turning back.

We're all feeling the collective labor pains now. We're feeling the contractions—the collective squeeze. Barbara Marx Hubbard often says that breakdowns lead to breakthroughs. Could this collective squeeze in the cosmic womb be giving birth to the divine human on Earth? I do believe the breakdowns are part of the healing of our planet. We're breaking down what no longer serves the highest good: greed, war, injustice, prejudice, violence, scarcity, hunger, discrimination, inequality, oppression—all are symptoms. Every institution and structure built on a foundation of *separation consciousness* (top-down dominance and control) is breaking down.

I see that movie reel from my childhood playing out in space. We're preparing for the breakthrough, ready for the big push. It's time to leap; to break open and embrace the light; to birth ourselves into our universal selves—connected to all things; to evolve consciousness and consciously evolve. We are weaving the light of the soul and birthing a new co-creative culture.

A co-creative culture will develop when individuals and communities understand the ethos of wholeness and the art of co-creation. I will talk more about co-creation later in the book. There are a couple of different definitions of co-creation. For now, I will share the definition given by my friends at *www.livingcocreation.com:* "Conscious alignment with Spirit, Nature, and the Essence of Self and Others." Isn't that nice? Imagine developing a co-creative culture in your family, community, region, and the planet as a whole, by practicing conscious alignment. All your decisions and actions will be informed and guided by the deep values and shared practice of joining with others in resonance with Spirit, Nature, and the essence of who you really are.

But we must say goodbye, grieve, and acknowledge the death that is occurring. The breakdown of both social structures and our limiting worldview are, in fact, a real death. The evolution of consciousness and our spiritual awakening is a death/rebirth cycle. Remembering and reclaiming our wholeness is a very palpable transfiguration process. We must afford hospice to the old dying systems and parts of ourselves, while we simultaneously midwife the new emerging forms and structures. We must tend to our own personal, evolutionary metamorphosis and get our emotional attachments out of the way. As with my father's epic death vigil, we are invited to step aside, trust the Designing Intelligence, and relax into resonance with the higher plan and process. We are dying and we are birthing. We are experiencing the liminal space and may not see or know the blessing yet. Allow. Let go. Surrender.

CHAPTER REFLECTIONS

There was no stopping the process once it had started. The only way out was through.

- There is much talk about dying to our separate selves, or dying to our ego. We usually hear about the ego as a negative aspect of ourselves that we are supposed to master, conquer, or annihilate. Yet, even as adults we go through stages of development and awaken to new levels of consciousness—new levels of awareness. We are constantly birthing ourselves into our greater capacity for creativity, wisdom, love, and grace. Let's have compassion for ourselves on this human journey. We are both human and divine in our true nature. When we stabilize our divinity, the ego (Separate Self) steps back and allows our authentic, sacred, soulful self to lead. What are some of your common triggers that point to the pain of separation and cause suffering? Where in your life are you resisting the impulse to grow and express your divinity? Where does your ego get in the way, wanting to be seen, heard, and acknowledged? Are there dark tunnels, birth and death canals, or stuck places you are ready to move through—or may be resisting?

- Birthing the divine human begins with a huge dose of love, faith, and patience. Dying to a worldview of separation means surrendering into the unknown and the process of change. This can be painful. Most of us either resist the pain or cling to the old patterns and structures. This causes constriction. The life and death portal can open naturally when we relax into it. Our labor pains are humanity's labor pains. Humanity's labor pains are our labor pains. Birthing our divine selves is contributing to birthing the new consciousness. We all have to do our individual work. Reflect on yourself as a divine human. What does that mean to you? Are you in acceptance of your own individual divinity? Can you allow your divinity and humanity to coexist? Can you allow your egoic, individual, Separate Self to coexist peacefully with your divine, universal, soulful self? And finally, what is your relationship to pain? What is your pain tolerance? Do you want a natural delivery, or do you need forceps or C-section? It's your choice.

CHAPTER FOUR

Breaking through the Illusion of Separation

Precisely because there exists in all beings a common centre, scattered and separable though they are in appearance, they meet together at a deeper level. The more they perfect themselves naturally and sanctify themselves in grace, the more they come together and fuse into one, within the single, unifying Centre to which they aspire: and we may call that Centre equally well the point upon which they converge, or the ambiance in which they float. All these reachings-out that draw beings together and unify them constitute the axis of all individual and collective life.

~ Pierre Teilhard deChardin

My broken bones brought me undeniably into my body with brute force and physical pain. Recovery with a full-leg cast consisted of sitting in my reclining chair (with my leg carefully propped up) or lying flat on my back in bed (with my leg carefully propped up) for weeks. Whenever I got vertical on my crutches, gravity would pull on my heavy cast, cutting off my circulation, and my leg would begin to swell. With the increased blood flow to my healing bones, my toes would turn purple, and my leg would begin to throb from the knee down. This purple-leg thing lasted for months.

My healing journey catapulted me onto a cathartic, emotional roller coaster. The first four weeks, I would break into spontaneous tears—either crying and sobbing or laughing hysterically. I would never know when the laughing might occur, but I could count on crying every morning when my leg was swung carefully over the bed for the first time with my husband's assistance. "I'm not going to cry today; I'm not going to cry today," I would tell myself gently. However, tears would begin streaming down my cheeks in blatant disregard of my stoic intentions. I would breathe and send some love to my healing bones, and myself, as I allowed the process of cathartic release to run its course. Other times, I would end up sobbing as uncontrollably as a baby with colic. Those were times when I couldn't predict or even identify the trigger. Spontaneous waves of cathartic adventure would overtake me. There was no identifiable grief or sadness. I would just unleash raw, unbridled sobs.

On the opposite extreme, the laughter was incredible. Something would tickle my funny bone, and hysterics would erupt as quickly and violently as had the snap of my bones. The sudden attack of raucous cackling would pierce the moment, leaving me gasping for breath. A seizure-like delirium would reach clear down to my toes and initiate a healing frenzy of energy cascading throughout every cell of my being as it made its way out of my convulsing vocal cords, filling my eyes with tears. Those moments felt both sacred and insane at the same time.

This emotional catharsis began feeling like a new kind of full-body labor. I would never know when the cosmic contractions would come, but I knew they were part of some sort of clearing and deliverance. Could the unannounced, involuntary histrionics be preparing me for some sort of rebirth?

I spent a lot of time alone even though I was completely dependent for most of my care. Hours quickly turned into days, which quickly turned into weeks and months. For a while, I secretly relished this re-creative respite and called it my "surprise sabbatical without pay." Then, I began developing a self-imposed, nagging pressure to "get back to work." Nonetheless, pain and the inability to ambulate with ease continued to shatter my conditioned, unrealistic determination to return to the office. Every week, I would optimistically schedule clients for the following week, and then, be forced to cancel and surrender my intent to drive myself toward this desired outcome, retreating into my private repose. As I observed myself engaged in this relentless game, glimpses of Louise Hay's explanation of the meaning of a fractured bone crept back into my consciousness.

Was I "rebelling against authority" as I wrestled with this voice in my head? Whose voice was pressuring me to get back to work so quickly? Why did I believe that I didn't "deserve" to take this "break"—a *medical* leave? Had I begun to hear the perennial echoes of my husband's strong work ethic? Was that it? He was raised to "work hard and play hard." Or was this the same message I had adopted after my *near-death experience*—that I was somehow faking it? Or maybe it was all of the above. The voice of my ego, or "Separate Self," programed by social conditioning to work hard for approval, was definitely at play, with hints of my mother's voice exhorting me to "get up and stop pretending."

The Separate Self is what I call the personality part of us that looks at life through the small-minded, shortsighted, myopic lens of the individual, or ego—through the five senses. The ego isn't a bad thing. It's just when we see our life experiences solely through this perspective, without integrating the expansive, soulful essence—the deepest aspect of who we are—we come from a place of fear and separation. In contrast, the unified "Sacred Self" comes from a place of love, inherent unity, and connectedness—or pure consciousness. The Sacred Self can see and experience an immense, universal perspective.

Collectively, when we evolved as a species into self-reflection, we began developing the ego. Seeing ourselves as separate beings of a bifurcated nature has assisted in both our human advancement as well as our decline. We perceived ourselves as separate from God, the earth, plants, animals, and each other. This development led us to compare and contrast ourselves with others, which in turn led to competition, the impulse to conquer, and a perennial conflict with self and others. We have mastered the art of individual self-development and pushed ourselves to the brink of collective self-destruction. Not only do we strive for excellence, we quickly create conditions where we can never measure up to any standard. Perfection, as defined by the ego instead of the divine, became a minimum standard and, as we all know, our ego-ideal of perfection is impossible to achieve.

Social conditioning and pressure to keep up with these unrealistic demands are daunting. The messages we send to ourselves are, quite frankly, impossible, and perpetuate our own personal merry-go-round of insanity. Some of my own dictates arising from the ego were, "Get back to work. You should be working hard. Be responsible. Be perfect. Be *the best* at everything you do!"

Arrogantly and naively, I thought I had worked through and released those dysfunctional patterns years ago. But here was another layer of guilt surfacing, and my shadow was pushing me to get back on my feet. Not only was this premature, it was impossible. I could not meet this demand—physically. This was a time of much needed rest and recovery. It wasn't time to get back to work. So why was this fractured sense of Separate Self rearing its ugly head, demanding my attention? Maybe the stress of the situation was simply driving me into the fullest physical experience of my body, into the dense matter experienced through my senses.

> Healing and being a living expression of your wholeness is a perpetual process of layering. You never really stop growing, changing, and evolving. Your wholeness is in a continuous cycle of sprouting, blooming, wilting, and regenerating. It's never static. When you view your health and wholeness in this way, you're never really "done." Yet, you're never really *not* whole, either. You are always whole and evolving toward even greater wholeness. So, peel back those layers as they present!

Soaking up the Grace

Usually it's quite easy for me to integrate and get back to unity consciousness—that interconnected sense of being. I teach clients and audiences about their *local vs. universal selves*, the *finite vs. infinite mind*. The illusion of separation is responsible for so much anxiety, fear, depression, and unnecessary suffering in our world. But the illusion of separation is just that, an illusion. It's a story we have made up to understand our incarnation, our physical experience. We are never really separate from God/ Creator/ Source. We are not separate from Earth, and we are never separate from each other. Quite the opposite, we are interconnected, interrelated, and interdependent. Actually, we all are made of the same substance on a quantum level, playing in a quantum field of intelligence—a unified field of consciousness. Jude Currivan says we don't have consciousness, we are consciousness. We are whole beings contributing to and in service of a greater whole. The whole is within all things and all things are within the whole. There's no differentiation. We are an integral part of an interconnected, interdependent, dynamic, whole-living system— a multidimensional multiverse.

It's like our relationship to plants. All oxygen-breathing life forms take in oxygen and exhale carbon dioxide. Plants, in turn, take in the carbon dioxide and use it in their photosynthesis process, then give off oxygen. We give plants carbon dioxide to live. They give us oxygen to live. We are interdependent with one another for survival. Yet, our connection is so much more than that. We are one with the plant kingdom.

When it comes to remembering our interconnection with Source/God/Creator, some teachers use the analogy of a drop of water or a wave in the ocean to explain our bifurcated nature. Others say God is the tree and humans are all the individual branches. I like the analogy of a sponge in a warm tub of water, where we can easily differentiate the sponge from the water, yet see how they become one when they are placed in a tub together. The water is in the sponge. The sponge is in the water. The water becomes the sponge. The sponge becomes the water. There is no separation.

> *You are a function of what the whole universe*
> *is doing in the same way that a wave is a function*
> *of what the whole ocean is doing.*
>
> **~ Alan Watts**

Physical pain appeared to be grounding me and pulling me into a whole new experience of physical reality. My fractured bones were bringing my attention completely into my body at times and completely disconnecting from it at others. It was my responsibility to be conscious and aware. I didn't want to fall into an illusion of separation or give such an illusion any energy. Instead, I wanted to invite my soul back into unification and wholeness with my body. However, I was feeling pretty much like a hard, dry sponge stuck in a cupboard somewhere. I longed to throw myself in a warm bath of water. (Oh, how I craved the water. After weeks of sponge baths, I seriously missed warm baths and long hot showers.) And obviously, I was having a difficult time allowing myself to rest in the awareness of my own divine *physical* nature.

Without pain and stress, it is easy to be at One—in peaceful resonance—with the divine, unified field of intelligence. I normally can hold that resonance, that awareness, in an expanded sense of self, quite effortlessly in my normal daily activities. I practice resting in this state during all kinds of situations—healing sessions, group gatherings, one-on-one conversations, alone time, and even during chaotic, stressful events and environments. Often, I am described as a calm presence, even in the midst of the most heated and chaotic storms. Yet, this experience with pain was inviting me to expand my practice.

It was my time to remember I am so much more than my physical body. I am so much more than my sensory awareness. I am Divine Presence incarnated in physical form. We all are. We are spirit and matter, ego and essence, shadow and light, mortal and eternal, human and divine.

Our consciousness is not tethered to our physical bodies. We can be both self-conscious and God-conscious. Like I mentioned, cosmologist Jude Currivan says we don't *have* consciousness; we and the whole world *are* consciousness. We are never separate. The genius of our interconnected universe is marvelous. We coexist with that genius, co-evolving with nature and co-creating with the divine. We are not *this or that*. It's not *either/or*. We are the sacred union of both. This is the divine human—divinely human and humanly divine—resolving duality through unification and unitive Christ Consciousness.

We are whole in all of our separate parts. We are the micro, limited perspective and the macro—with the ability to tap into the All Knowing. We are different from one another and we are fundamentally the same. We are individual wholes as well as an integral part of the greater whole. We are a powerful, multidimensional, co-creative force.

I *knew* this. But at the time, I couldn't feel it or experience it. Pain gripped this higher knowing and violently pulled me back into a temporary jailhouse of separation consciousness. Pain separates and separation causes pain. But there was a *grace* in the reminder to be fully, and even more completely, in my body.

Eventually, I listened with compassion. I honored and accepted this fractured sense of myself, grounded in an awareness of pain and discomfort, as a gift to greater wholeness. I let go of the *pressure to get back to work* and invited an expansive, authentic expression of myself to return. Something shifted. Something significant began happening. I didn't consciously know what it was, and that was okay. I fell into a warm pool of blind faith and soaked up the grace like a sponge.

Shocking, electric goose bumps replaced the spontaneous cathartic moments. My leg became an intensified, yet tolerable, pincushion for the soul. A prickly cascade, dynamic, yet mild, rolled up and down my leg, like waves of healing water. The goose-bump-pin-prick experiences would last anywhere from a few seconds to a few minutes. In a puzzling way, I liked it. Both goose bumps and conscious breathing became a portal—opening a calm, peaceful resonance—bringing me back to myself. I invited more of myself to come back home. I invited more of my soul—more consciousness—to come into my body. I invited the divine human to presence herself more completely.

Conscious breathing. In any situation of pain, stress, anxiety, or whatever may be challenging you in the moment, consciously bringing your awareness to your breath acts as an instantaneous, soothing balm that elicits the relaxation response. This has many health benefits. There are lots of resources online for the practice of conscious breathing and explanation of the role of breath.

Tuning In

Once I remembered that Louise Hay said bones, in general, represent the structure of the universe and bone fractures represent rebelling against authority, hints of my profound cosmic journey began presenting themselves. Was I rebelling against an outdated model of authority that was operating under the illusion of separation? Was I rebelling against a worn-out belief structure and worldview that was limiting my divine expression? Was this experience the breakthrough I needed to leap into my fullest potential? This all brought to mind the woman I met in Chicago a few years before.

One sunny October day, I was sitting in the passenger seat of my daughter's car working on paperwork near the University of Illinois at Chicago, when I saw a young woman searching in the grass nearby, as intensely as if she had lost a diamond ring. She kept getting really close to the ground and feeling around with her hands. Then she moved onto an asphalt parking lot, doing the same thing on her hands and knees. Clearly, she must have been looking for something very small and valuable. When she worked her way back near my car for the second time, I rolled down the window and asked her what she was looking for. Sounding helpless, she said, "MY GLASSES!" The wind was blowing so hard that day that it literally blew them right off her head, and they went flying! And the poor woman could not see well enough to find them.

Well, Chicago is known as the "Windy City." Now, I know Chicago got that nickname as a reference to the boastful antics of their early politicians. Yet on that day, Chicago was living up to its moniker as a literal phenomenon, with the wind blowing more forcefully than any windy politician could. The news reported sustained winds of forty miles per hour. The unusual weather system was producing gusts of up to eighty-one miles per hour, snapping trees and power lines, ripping off roofs, and yanking off a woman's glasses, launching them into the concrete abyss of the city. This strange weather system mesmerized meteorologists because of its size and because its barometric pressure was similar to a Category 3 hurricane. And it had the same effect on both of us, as we joined forces against the gale to look for her glasses.

We looked for nearly twenty minutes along the whole city block, and they were nowhere to be found. She had to leave to go tutor a student in the speech lab, and sadly, knew she couldn't drive home without her glasses. Losing your glasses can be disabling! I decided to keep looking and told her I would put them under her windshield wiper if I found them. I saw an empty cigarette lighter near where she lost the glasses and dropped it shoulder height to see in which direction it would go. It sailed for half a city block before it rolled to a stop. So I headed in that direction. Walking down to the next block, I took a stick to move all the piled-up leaves as I came across them. Surely, the glasses would have taken the same path as the leaves and the empty lighter. Nope.

After a diligent search, up and down the adjacent city blocks, I went back to the car to finish writing the report I was working on. When she returned, she said she had called her boyfriend for a ride since she couldn't see to drive. Resummoning our hope, we decided to look again while she was waiting for her boyfriend. We commented on how scratched up they would probably be if we were able to find them. I headed north, crossed the street, and circled back, stirring the leaves again. She returned to the asphalt parking lot and used her limited vision to search, her hands reaching out to feel her way around.

She found them! They were stuck in a chain link fence half a block away from where they had launched. And they were not scratched! She could see again and could drive home with a funny, true story to tell her family and friends.

I love this story. If that were me losing my glasses downtown in the big "Windy City," I would have been in real trouble. Sometimes when the Spirit moves through our lives, it can be like hurricane-force winds that leave us feeling helpless, disoriented, scared, and unable to clearly *see* our way. Yet, Spirit is always right there to guide and assist—if we have faith and stay present. I had the better vision that day as we searched for the spectacles. However, she was the one led to find them, fortified with the resources of her limited vision, reaching hands, and blind faith.

A dictionary definition of *blind faith* is *belief without true understanding, perception, or discrimination.* Blind faith isn't necessarily blind when we understand how to tune in to our inner spiritual guidance and intuition. I like to say intuition is like seeing with our soul. The ability to trust this *different way of knowing* starts with the practice of mindfulness and present moment awareness. Listen with your heart, with your soul. Breathe. Relax. Stay present. Look within. Be still. Welcome the mystery and learn to live in the questions.

There are as many different expressions of intuition and guidance as there are individuals. And there are as many ways to learn an effective practice. One must find what feels resonant and develop commitment and discipline. There are a few simple practices you can start with. First, tune in to your body sensations, goosebumps, and "gut" reactions. Some people filter their intuitive guidance through physical sensations and the body's responses. When you get a hunch, "Go with your gut." This body language was amplified for me as I listened to all the varying ways my body was communicating with me—cathartic laughing and crying, goose bumps, pin pricks, swelling, pain, and on and on.

You can also tune in to your heart, feelings, and emotions. Some people filter intuitive guidance through emotions and the qualitative experience of feeling. Open, expansive feelings usually mean something different from that of constrictive narrowing. When tuning in to your heart, you tune out the distractions of the rational mind. What do you feel? Follow your heart.

Also tune in to the still small voice. Some discern spiritual guidance by developing and understanding the difference between egoic self-talk and the still small voice. Egoic self-talk usually comes from the place of fear, separation, self-preservation, competition, comparison, and judgment—especially judgment. The still small voice of spirit guides us from the place of unity, love, and the greater good of the whole. The still small voice is simple. It presents in one word or short phrases. It appears to be random, dropping in out of nowhere. It quickly answers questions before the mind kicks in to analyze and judge. It's soft and transient, like a feather floating in the air. You can start with quiet prayer, meditation, and contemplative practices as you learn to tune in. Be still and know.

You can also learn to tune in to signs and symbols. Some develop a sophisticated guidance language based in signs and symbols. When you live in the question, guidance appears on your path in a variety of ways. People, conversations, words, numbers, music, images, and symbols can present literally, and/or intuitively. Pay attention. This is where the wisdom of other people was helpful in my recovery.

I love to tune in to my dreams and visions. Some people develop dependable guidance by harnessing the language of dream symbols and visions. I have had very prophetic, guiding, and illuminating dreams. Access to the subconscious or unconscious mind can occur when the conscious mind is quiet during sleep and meditation. Again, this is another language of signs, symbols, and emotions.

Many people learn to tune in to nature, animals, and the elements. Some develop guidance through communion with nature. Many patterns and possibilities exist in the natural world. If you feel called to nature, ground your practice in connection to the earth and natural world. Tune in to plants, trees, and animals. Connect with your pets and pay attention to wild birds and animals. Commune. Become one with nature. Nature will speak, and it is our privilege to listen. Patterns, cycles, seasons, processes, weather, movements, behavior—almost everything in nature can be used for greater insight. Universal intelligence is in all living things. Connect. Listen. Trust.

We are living in a time of expanded consciousness and amazing global shifts. Guidance is coming fast, and in many cases, instantaneously. We are stepping into the fullness of who we are. We are taking responsibility for our health and quality of life. We are discovering the resources we have within, as we remember and reclaim the interconnectedness with Creator, creation, community; our own divine essence; and the mysteries of other realms we've only imagined. This is not an abstract idea, but a calling for all who are committed to practice unification and break through the illusion of separation. We are divine essence in human form becoming spiritual change agents in the world. Tune in and trust all the different and new ways of seeing, feeling, hearing, knowing, being, and experiencing. Even gale-force winds may be a source of guidance for you. I'm sure my Windy City friend learned a lot that day.

As for me in my healing process, I was called to stay calm and quiet in my chair, create the conditions for healing, trust the unknowing, and open to a greater experience of multidimensional inter-being. Meanwhile, on clock-time, days and weeks and months continued to pass.

CHAPTER REFLECTIONS

We are living in a time of expanded consciousness and amazing global shifts. Guidance is coming fast, almost instantaneously. We are stepping into the fullness of who we are. We are taking responsibility for our health and quality of life. We are discovering the resources we have within as we connect with Creator, creation, community; our own divine essence; and the mysteries of other realms we've only imagined. This is not an abstract idea, but a calling for all who are committed to practice unification and break through the illusion of separation.

- Pain and stress can bring us into our bodies and amplify our experience of separateness. And yet, moments of being fully present in the body can also lead us to experience greater connectedness. Sometimes this is confusing. How do you experience your consciousness? Is it inside your head or outside and separate from your physical body? Is it *what and who you are*? If you have ever had an out-of-body experience, write about it. If not, use your imagination and notice that the *you* that is witnessing or observing you reading these words is different from the you that is holding the book or sitting in the chair. Play with that idea and write about the different aspects of how you experience you and your consciousness.

- Guidance can come in many different forms. We are taught to trust our gut, tune in to our hearts, and listen to that still small voice among other ways. In what ways do you receive guidance? Do you perceive it more as an inner guidance or an external source? It is helpful to learn to listen to your body. What is your body saying in this very moment? What other kinds of inner wisdom do you trust? Some have a stronger connection to an external source of guidance— God, angels, masters, guides—or earth, nature, symbols, and others. There are many ways we experience this. What is your experience with external guidance? Contemplate the difference in experiencing internal and external guidance. What feels clearer? When considering your higher self, in what ways do you trust that you have all you need? Imagine for a moment that your internal and external guidance were coming from the same source, as the same thing. Allow the two to blend, meld, mingle, and coexist. This convergence can strengthen your connectedness and perceptive abilities. Use your imagination or even write a short story about a young child that is just waking up to this world. Imagine the young child turning on all the different senses and sensory perception buttons that connect this little one to ultimate guidance. Play with the idea and really feel into it.

CHAPTER FIVE

Our Interconnected Universe

A human being is a part of the whole called by us universe, a part limited in time and space. He experiences himself, his thoughts and feeling as something separated from the rest, a kind of optical delusion of his consciousness. This delusion is a kind of prison for us, restricting us to our personal desires and to affection for a few persons nearest to us. Our task must be to free ourselves from this prison by widening our circle of compassion to embrace all living creatures and the whole of nature in its beauty.

~ Albert Einstein

I've always been a side-sleeper. I usually curl up into a fetal position before I fall asleep. I went through a stage where I would start the night off sleeping on my stomach with my arms crossed under my torso, but it wouldn't be long until I was curled up on my side for the night. Since sleeping flat on my back was not my natural preference, getting through the night was an interesting experience with my broken leg. My cast had a slight bend in the knee, so it had to be propped up on pillows—just right. If my ankle were placed too low, the cast would cut into the back of my thigh. If my ankle were placed too high, the cast would rub on my knee and create pressure inside my cast. There were a lot of variations in between. Getting comfortable could take several tries of moving and rearranging, and it was different every night. When I would get comfortable, my husband would swing the covers over me, and most of the time, I wouldn't move till morning. It's funny how our mind/body knows how to adapt to the situation and not move during sleep. How does that work?

In the mornings, my body would feel dense, numb, and lifeless, like concrete. As if my body had sunk into the mattress like a hot knife through butter. Although I could go through the night without ever being aware of moving my body, it felt surreal when I would wake up. Intuitively, upon waking, I began rubbing my hands together like a surgeon scrubbing before surgery. Then I would move the scrubbing action up my arms and shoulders, eventually doing this wake-up energy ritual all over my body, including over my cast. I would add some Reiki and Qigong into the practice as well.

Shifts in my energy and physical body became noticeable as I played with this consciously. My physical body was feeling dense and ponderous. But my consciousness was in my light-body, an etheric field, which was a clear, and yet, rather queer, differentiation. I could consciously sense and experience the separation in a way I never had before. Every morning, I began my day by, literally, asking my physical body to wake up and receive my consciousness and asking my consciousness to reintegrate into my dense body. The separation became so visceral and real. I was commanding spirit and matter, and they were responding.

How very similar this seemed to my near-death experience, lying limp like a ragdoll on my parents' bed while my consciousness floated above somewhere. Indeed, it was similar to other out-of-body experiences I've had. I've had many spontaneous transpersonal experiences, many mystical adventures and blissful moments, but never before had I consciously tried to manipulate the mind/body, or energy and consciousness in this way. In fact, I had always felt very little control when those events happened. This new situation, this emerging process was quite different—more like lucid dreaming. Not only was I conscious and awake, I was aware that I was in control of consciousness and matter. I was witnessing energy and consciousness following my thoughts. I began mindfully playing within this curious convergence.

—

The Living Web

I've studied the non-local mind and field consciousness for decades. The "field" is a sea of energy that, as Lynne McTaggart says, reconciles mind with matter. It connects everything. Support for the existence of this cobweb of energy exchange has plenty of research to back up my intuitive knowing. The field has inspired scientists, religious leaders, healers, and spiritual seekers all over the world. Recovering from my fractured leg and this fractured sense of self was the perfect time to dive more deeply into the interconnected universe and the idea of *spontaneous healing*.

Through the web of connection that joins all things (or *is* all things), scientists have shown that the universe is made of a *living* field. Waves and particles of energy respond and conform to the beliefs and expectations we have of our world. This intelligent field of "in-formation" and energy connects everything and affects everything from global healing to personal peace. Miracles are possible when we open to this field of divine intelligence. However, our power to access this intelligence, to change our lives or heal, lies dormant until we wake up and remember.

Awakening usually happens when we spontaneously experience ourselves as a part of everything, rather than separate from everything, "a oneness experience" as some would say. Beyond simply *thinking* of ourselves from this unified view, we literally experience and *feel* ourselves as part of all that exists. Or maybe I should say, lose our separate selves in the oneness experience.

We are in the midst of a great awakening. People are waking and having a spiritual experience of this inherent unity all over the world, in every country, race, religion, and age. As we awaken to our Oneness, we begin to see our integral responsibility for all of life.

Joanna Macy calls this time The Great Turning, a name for the essential adventure of shifting from the industrial growth society to a life-sustaining civilization. She says the most remarkable feature of this historical moment on Earth is that "we are beginning to wake up, as from a millennia-long sleep, to a whole new relationship to our world, to ourselves and each other." She describes the profound shift in our reality as both a cognitive revolution and a spiritual awakening.

With this life-changing shift in perception, we wake to our responsibility and see our interdependent, integral relationship with all that is. Macy says it reminds us that "our world is a sacred whole, worthy of adoration and service." With this connection and unity in mind, we begin to reimagine everything. Our perception shifts. Consciousness shifts. The key to healing and creating a life of peace, abundance, freedom, wholeness, and joy begins with our experiential understanding of how deeply interconnected we are to everything in our reality. This understanding is based in our beliefs. To systemically change our lives, we need to change what we believe about ourselves and our world.

> Your beliefs influence your thoughts, which elicit emotions, which motivate behaviors, which in turn, create your experiences. Learn how to open the aperture of the lens from which you view the world. This will help you shift your fundamental beliefs and conditioned responses. This is a skill you can develop with practice.

A Thin Veil

In the mid 1990s, I had another transformative, non-ordinary experience that helped to further shape my worldview and personal healing journey. I was attending an intensive Mind/Body Medicine Training with Dr. Joan Borysenko in Boulder, Colorado. On this particular day, we went up into the mountains to a Native American lodge. We spent the day learning from an indigenous medicine man from a local tribe. After the morning of teaching and speaking, he intuitively picked two people from the group with whom to do a healing ceremony. I was selected. I had had a hysterectomy years earlier, and I was consciously working to heal some second chakra energetic and emotional patterns of trauma. The other person chosen had a brain tumor. The medicine man knew nothing of our personal lives or health histories before selecting us.

He proceeded to work nonverbally with us standing within the medicine wheel he created. He used many different healing tools, burned a smudge stick, and waved feathers around us while other members of his tribe were drumming and chanting. He danced and chanted to the rhythmic beat, moving purposefully and magically focusing around my second chakra region and my fellow student's head. The healing ceremony intertwined between the two of us simultaneously, focusing on one, moving to the next, and back again. All the other members of our class sat in a circle around the room observing. It was a sacred, deeply moving experience. When he was complete with me, he whispered in my ear, "Everything is going to be alright."

Later that night, I had an optional, individual healing session scheduled with an energy practitioner who was teaching a segment of the intensive. She had developed her own hybrid process of intuitive energy healing. She started by invoking her spiritual guides, Mother Mary and Mary Magdalene. Then, pausing to ask whether I would like to invoke the presence of any deity in prayer, she continued to call in several other masters and guides.

An energy practitioner (one who is engaged in the practice of *energy medicine*), taps into the subtle energies within and the electromagnetic field around your body. This addresses disturbances in your energy flow that may affect your health and well-being. There are many different types and forms of energy medicine and lots of new and exciting research on the topic. From Healing Touch and Reiki to acupuncture and EFT tapping, you are sure to find a method and practitioner that feels right for you.

She began sweeping her hands over my body in broad strokes, specifically over the chakras, to release what she referred to as *energy blockages* and *emotional residue*. She asked me to participate and pay attention to any signs, symbols, feelings, or sensations I might have as she moved across my body. It was her intention to follow the field and my energy as the different cues directed the flow and healing process.

I don't know how many minutes we were into the session when I experienced a profound shift. She was working on the second chakra region, and something was activated. My body began to surge through an unbelievable, extreme metamorphic process of twists and contortions. I couldn't control the movements. My hands curled up like those of my grandmother, who had severe rheumatoid arthritis, and my limbs and torso displayed broad sweeping movements like a person with cerebral palsy. That moment is very clear in my memory—I tried to communicate what I was experiencing to the healer, but I couldn't speak. My mouth and face were captured in the same involuntary, palsied process. She knew. Trying to reassure me that everything was okay, she continued to work with the energy around my body, sweeping and holding the field as I was forced to surrender deeper into the experience. And without a witness, I wouldn't have believed what was happening.

Suddenly the transpersonal realm opened up. The room was transformed—luminous—and I could hear the drums and chanting from the earlier ceremony with the medicine man. The drumming was comforting, like an ancestral lullaby soothing my anxious mind. Yet all the while, I couldn't speak and I couldn't control my body. I was at the mercy of this healer.

Gradually, the room disappeared as the space filled with women. Generations-after-generations of women became visible off to my left, presenting in an inverted triangle. Dressed in drab and modest, pioneer-type clothing, these multitudes of women appeared to span back for miles. Off to my right was what *felt like* an abyss of unmanifested, pure, potential Source energy. I experienced this visitation to be the unborn and future generations of women held by the Divine Feminine. The out-of-time-and-space, altered sense of reality that came with this epic, shamanic-like journey appeared to be a bridge, linking the realms.

A Divine Feminine presence was in the room (of course, the healer had invoked both Mother Mary and Mary Magdalene). I deeply felt the feminine presence extending her gratitude toward me. I also felt the gratitude of all the women who were over in the left corner looking toward me. In a flash, another dimension opened, and I was shown how healing the feminine wound on the planet for the present generation was connected to the healing of the past and future generations. I was shown how we are healing the deep masculine/feminine wound on both a micro and macro level. In that moment, my own personal healing was woven into the integral web of life.

I understood what was being communicated, and I took the healing very seriously. The same Divine Source that connects all things was using this experience to teach me the importance of reconciliation across generations, as the past, present, and future all exist in that infinite flowing presence of now. The sea of connective energy is not only connecting all things present, but reaching across time and space to all things past and future. There is no separation.

When the twisting and contorting stopped, my body slowly unwound itself and softened into a relaxed, but extremely fatigued state. It felt like I had run a marathon or given birth to a baby—I was very weak and tired and shaky. With gentle and supportive assistance, I was able to eventually sit up and talk again. I couldn't stand or walk by myself for quite some time.

Once I sat up, the healer got me a drink of water, and we processed the experience. The first thing out of her mouth was, "Did you hear the drumming?" Those five words were so powerful and redemptive. In that moment, it felt like the universe swaddled me tightly in a warm receiving blanket. She had heard the drumming! She witnessed the multidimensional experience. I wasn't crazy! We had the experience together.

The two separate, healing sessions of the day merged into one profound experience that crossed all boundaries of time and space. Some sort of mysterious connection had happened. Simultaneity between my own personal healing and that of the planet and generations of women had come about. I was asked to receive a deep healing at the same time I was called to assist in the healing of others. I was given new information and instructions, shown new layers of the template.

There was a palpable connection, that day, between my two healers, the field, and myself. With no dialog or medical history, both of them tapped into the mystery of the universal and *knew* exactly what was needed. Their connection to Source/Great Spirit yielded perceptive intuition and guided a radical healing experience. Through this experience, another significant gateway presented. In over thirty years of profound mystical experiences, never before had I intimately shared a multidimensional experience with another credible, witnessing adult. The thin veil between heaven and earth lifted once again, and another person had a simultaneous mystical experience of another realm with me. For the first time, I could openly talk about what had happened with another human being who had shared in the same experience.

None of it could make any sense to a linear, logical mind informed by only five senses. And that was okay. The experience didn't have to make sense. I left with a profound sense of grace.

I want that kind of grace from God that, when it hits,
I won't get off the floor for days. And when I finally do
stagger into a semblance of poise, I will still need a cane
and a shoulder to help me walk, and I will need great
patience from any who try to decipher my slurred speech.

~ Rumi

Being and Becoming

Things are happening simultaneously in the universe all the time— on a microscopic scale within our bodies, and on a macroscopic scale out in the cosmos. As our heart beats, it sends out *and* receives blood at the same time. The blood is pumped to every cell in the body and simultaneously exchanges oxygen for carbon dioxide within each cell. As the lungs breathe, bringing in more fresh oxygen, they simultaneously release the carbon dioxide and the whole process starts over—sending and receiving, expanding, and contracting.

If indeed, we are living in an interconnected, intelligent universe, then what was this new opportunity for healing being presented with my fractured bones? What was this sense of separation I was experiencing, and how could I invite the universal divine intelligence to once again dance with me, commune with me? Why was my body feeling so dense and lifeless?

In prayer and meditation, I asked my guidance whether I could do more intentional energy healing on myself. *No.* I asked if I could call one of my healer friends or go have an energy-healing session. *No.* It wasn't time. I was asked to be in my body, in the denseness, in the pain, in the healing—experience it. I was invited to play with the dense matter along with the light energy. But it was not time for outside healers. Despite my persistent asking, the answer was always, *no.* I would be told when.

With the vigorous wake-up energy sessions in the morning, I continued to consciously play with consciousness. I experienced my body as the clay of the earth, dust, and ashes. I invited God to breathe life into my nostrils so I could be made a living being—a divine human. I would lie there and allow my lungs to expand and contract with the breath of God. God was breathing me. I allowed my heart to beat with the pulse of Creation—touching every cell and infusing more life and light. I brought my awareness into my heart and rode the waves of expansion and contraction, seeing the toroidal field around my body infused with universal life force—the divine substance of Creation. With every rise and fall, I was in the being and the becoming. I was the Divine, being and becoming me, and I was me, being and becoming divine. Everything was being recalibrated. Everything.

CHAPTER REFLECTIONS

With every rise and fall, I was in the being and the becoming. I was the Divine, being and becoming me, and I was me, being and becoming divine. Everything was being recalibrated. Everything.

- There is the saying, "As above, so below." I also like to imagine *as within, so without.* We have a vast and beautiful world inside and outside of ourselves. Simultaneity is always happening within and without, but we're usually not aware of it. Responsibilities of our day-to-day lives can divert our attention to mindless, passive distraction. Yet our soul craves attention and wants to be in full, conscious relationship with all that is. Tune in to the interior design of your life. Know that the external is a reflection of the internal and vice versa. If you are co-creating your life, what needs to be addressed inside? Look for the areas that need TLC, clearing, mending, or adjusting. What one thing can you take responsibility for today that would create the biggest shift on the outside?

- We all have "awakening" experiences and intuitively sense there is so much more than our limited minds can comprehend. Some have huge life-changing events, and others are small moments that are easily integrated in our understanding. Usually, we have a series of experiences over our lifetimes that "waken us" and give us an expanded understanding and awareness. If you have had a oneness experience, write about it in your journal. Describe it in detail, whether it was a huge, life-changing experience, a brief ephemeral moment in time, an out-of-body experience, or a time of non-ordinary consciousness. Next, write your own personal "awakening" story. Focus on the progression of awakening in your life—step by step. Allow yourself to experience awakening as an ongoing experience. Share your story with someone who doesn't know this about you.

- We are all a part of Creation. Creation is always creating though us, in us, and as us. Allow yourself to open and surrender to the impulse of Creation creating through you. This may feel like a shift. It's a process. We are never fully complete or done or "there." Play with the words *being* and *becoming*. Allow yourself to be in the emergence of the being and becoming. Notice how it takes the pressure and constraints off of who you are in this moment.

CHAPTER SIX

Align with the Divine

Whenever you're going through a tough time, generally, you become more compassionate, you become softer, you become more thoughtful, kinder. These are all spiritual qualities that will help you to align yourself with God and God consciousness rather than with a split fear-based consciousness.

~ Wayne Dyer

After six weeks, they took off my full-leg cast and replaced it with one below the knee. The bones had stayed in alignment and showed some signs of healing. The long spiral break in the tibia was supposed to take longer to heal than the fractures in my ankle. The doctor again asked how I did it. He was puzzled by the complexity of the broken bones. It is rare that all the bones would break simultaneously, and he was in disbelief that there was no displacement.

Having spent weeks in the cast, the muscles in my leg had atrophied significantly, and there was still quite a bit of swelling. I was nervous about stretching and bending my knee and didn't want to move my ankle. The X-ray tech, nurse, and doctor all worked with me in a gentle manner. I could feel the instability in my tibia, and my calf muscle continued to have sharp, cramping pains when I moved or twisted even slightly the wrong way. The doctor explained that muscles don't like broken bones. They want strong, solid bones to adhere to. I can understand that. We all want a strong, solid support system when we move into action.

My leg was weak, and my knee experienced sharp, burning pain if bent or moved too much. I had to use my arms to assist in lifting and moving my new cast for all of the next three weeks. Eventually, it felt good to stand and let my leg hang, letting gravity assist in stretching out my leg. But I couldn't stand long. My toes would still turn purple, and my leg would begin to throb. The doctor said I would need to keep it elevated for several more weeks.

My injured bones might have been in alignment, but in dealing with the cast and injury, I found the rest of my body definitely wasn't. My hips and lower back ached from misalignment. My upper torso and shoulders were tight from using the crutches. And I later learned that my ankle had been casted in an incorrect position, crooked, leaving my bones to heal with my foot pointing outward. I had significant "out-toeing" as my foot was locked at a forty-five degree angle. And with the heavy weight of the cast, my left leg naturally rolled out and rested perpendicular to the pillow that propped it up. I sat for months with my left foot pointing out and my right foot pointing up.

Many mind/body resources refer to the left side of the body as representing the feminine and the right side as the masculine. My masculine and feminine were definitely out of balance and out of alignment. But I found it of particular interest that the breaks were on my feminine side. What resulted with the out-toing was that my left leg was pointed the wrong direction; or maybe it was pointing in a new direction? Regardless, to move forward as a whole person, I needed my feet and legs working together, pointing in the same direction. This out-toeing became a significant challenge in my rehabilitation. And it awakened in me a greater courage to look at where my life was out of alignment, or needing realignment.

Have you ever felt as if your life is headed in one direction, but your soul is calling you in another? Have you ever felt like your head wants one thing and your heart, another? *Listen to your gut—* maybe your soul is telling you something very different from your head and your heart.

Our Separate Selves move in a very different manner and direction from our Sacred Selves. Motivation to fit in and compete propels us in ways that are usually limiting and out of alignment from our truest sense of knowing—our highest potential. Harmony and coherence of our head and heart, our Separate and Sacred Selves, our individual and whole selves—all are essential if we want to navigate life's path with ease and joy.

Later, when I began walking, my out-toeing created physical challenges and even further physical complications and injury. When I would walk forward with my knee in alignment but my toe pointing out, I would cause problems in my foot and ankle. When I would turn my foot in, and try to point my toe straight, my knee would turn in and cause problems with the weakened bones and ligaments. It became a vicious circle that eventually brought my entire rehab and physical therapy to a standstill.

Early in my recovery, I mentioned to my doctor that I thought I had injured my knee. My leg still enclosed in the full-leg cast, he assured me it was simply a result of the inactivity. Living with a sharp, stabbing pain going through the center of my knee; a dull, burning pain on the inside of my knee; and a deep, throbbing, bone-pain ache in my tibia and femur at my knee, I wasn't convinced. The inactivity made sense as a cause of the patella tendon/knee cap pain, but the rest was a mystery.

When I went to a half-cast, the sharp pain got sharper and the deep pain got deeper. Every time I would bend or straighten my knee, shock waves shot throughout my entire body. Rolling over on my side in bed was excruciating if I didn't guide and support my leg. Again, when I brought it to his attention, my doctor assured me this was from the inactivity and would eventually get better. It didn't. It continued to get worse. Here began yet another powerful lesson on listening to my body and trusting my inner knowing.

> Your body speaks to you. Your body has its own language to communicate. It will tell you what you need and how to take care of it. Learn to tune in to its subtle cues.

Compassion, Coherence, Resonance

I was doing physical therapy on my ankle, knee, hip, and out-toeing, while learning how to walk again. I progressed from two crutches, to one crutch, to a cane. And yet, my progress stalled with my knee and the excruciating, deep pain. Every checkup, I would report the pain and my doctor would say, "If it isn't better next time, we'll do an MRI." Finally, six months after my accident, I assertively demanded that MRI. My body was telling me something was seriously wrong. I *was* listening, but my doctor wasn't.

Although the quality of the MRI was questionable, it suggested significant injuries that my physician minimized as he read the report. After his suggested treatment plan was a mere cortisone shot, I knew it was time for a second opinion. Clearly, he and I were not in alignment or even on the same page.

I arrived at the new clinic walking funny and using a cane. I noticed how the nurses and medical professionals were all watching my goofy gait, as the nurse escorted me down the long hallway to the examination room. She got me settled in and began asking her initial questions. I couldn't hold back the tears. Six months of pain and frustration rose wildly to the surface, resulting in a display of a rambunctious mix of emotions I hadn't planned on sharing.

I had trusted the care of my first physician. I was patient with my therapy and the lack of progress. Now that I had to report the entire story from the beginning, I felt foolish and incompetent for having waited so long. Guilt and shame overtook me, as if I were tattling on the first physician. Desperate and confused, I sat there crying, like a little girl who was trying to be so brave and strong. I cried through fear and anxiety for the unknown prognosis and for all the treatment, healing, and therapy yet to come.

The nurse was compassionate and sensitive. She gave me a tissue and listened using her keen sense and honed assessment skills. After her interview, she took me down the hall for a new set of X-rays. Again, I felt the compassionate, but curious eyes of many watching and witnessing me walking down the long hall with my impaired gait and severe out-toeing.

My new orthopedic surgeon was amazing. I promised myself I was not going to cry when he came into the examination room. Surely that cathartic release of tears while reporting to the nurse was complete. However, when he entered the room and, with a gentle look and compassionate voice, said, "Hello, I hear you have really been through a lot," again, the unexpected tears welled up. By now, I was feeling an overwhelming sense of *self*-compassion. Yes. That was true. I *had* been through a lot.

This doctor was thorough, thoughtful, and very compassionate. He listened deeply, and tuning in, he worked with me and my inner intuitive knowing. I finally felt coherence and resonance between my healthcare provider, my inner knowing, and my body's own healing capacity. We were aligned, even as my leg, ankle, and foot were grossly misaligned. The significant out-toeing was his first and primary concern. We needed to rule out whether it was set in a crooked position and/or grew back crooked. He was concerned we might need to surgically re-break my tibia.

More X-rays, a specialized CT scan to measure the length of my bones and look at the alignment, and a second MRI of the knee were ordered, stat. The MRI showed significant bone edema (bone bruising) and fractures on my tibia and femur at the knee with significant osteopenia (bone weakness) due to the immobility. It also confirmed a partial tear of the lateral collateral ligament (LCL). The diagnoses confirmed my experience and my intuition. My three separate pains in the knee all had an explanation and finally made sense.

The surgeon recommended a surgical procedure to address the bone edema, strengthen the bones, and heal the fractures. He was concerned about the progression of osteopenia with a prolonged, non-weight-bearing status. However, after lengthy conversation about all the options and side effects, we agreed on a treatment plan. Seven months after the original injury, I was back on two crutches with no weight bearing on my left leg for four more weeks to allow those fractures to heal.

The good news was the out-toeing appeared to have been caused by how my leg was casted crooked, and the subsequent stretching of muscles, ligaments, and tendons. The actual spiral break of the tibia did not appear to be misaligned. I would not need surgery to re-break my tibia at this point. After four weeks, the bones were healing nicely, and I began physical therapy again. It was once again time to learn how to walk.

With my new doctor, I finally felt encouraged. I felt seen and heard. And I felt a deeper, more emotional/spiritual connection with this new team. It was as if the entire experience was elevated somehow. It reminded me of an experience of deep connection I had had months earlier.

> Healing is accelerated when you feel validated, affirmed, seen, and heard. Sharing your journey and story with another brings you more efficiently back into your wholeness. Connection and compassion are proven to be good medicine.

To the Divine in You

I met a Sudanese refugee who had immigrated to the United States. He was an inspiring young man and wanted to become a pastor to serve his church. I'll call him "Steven." Among the many humbling and gracious words he spoke, what stuck out the most was when he spoke about his deep faith in God and enduring love for ALL people. He said he "vehemently" believes in doing things that "bring greatness" to the lives of others as well as himself. With his thick accent, Steven spoke of being thankful to God for granting him many gifts and abilities, and especially for his being able to use them for "doing right things for others." This brave and radiant young man talked about waking up every morning with a smile on his face, knowing that God is always with him.

> Doing things that "bring greatness" to the lives of others is another way of looking at service. There is real value in serving others. Service helps to transcend solitude, loneliness, and isolation. Service moves your awareness and focus outside your body and life situation—moving you away from your pain and suffering. Serving others and the greater whole is more than good for your heart and soul. It's good for your health!

Three powerful themes emerged from my conversation with this migratory, luminous messenger. From his own words, first, we are not restricted by anybody or anything except our own choices. Second, a loving gracious God exists and "resides in us, with us, beside us, around us, and among us," no matter what our race, religion, culture, gender, or life circumstances. And third, serving the one human body of God and individuals in our local communities can bring abundant joy! *That* was his joy, and his effervescent expression of that joy was so catchy. I left the meeting with a new mantra running through my mind, "Align with the Divine." I pondered what that meant to me, as I definitely caught his contagious joy.

After this delightful experience, I drove to our lake house, which is just a few miles from a community that has a significant new population of Sudanese and Hispanic immigrants. I stopped at the local, big-box superstore for a few grocery items. When I arrived, I somehow felt different. As I looked around, I saw "Steven" everywhere. I walked up and down the aisles and couldn't get the smile off my face. I was beaming with the grace-filled lessons of Steven's love, devotion, and contagious joy. My heart was expanded, and with each and every immigrant I saw, it grew even more, filling with love, compassion, and joy. I felt aligned with the Divine and in a strange, sacred connection with everybody. There were no perceived strangers nor a sense of "othering" in that store. And then, something electrifying happened.

As I was gathering my items and looking around, a young Sudanese child locked eyes with mine, smiled, and waved. My heart leaped out of my chest, and I felt the presence of our shared divinity and joy. Such a deeply sacred moment. No words passed between us, just a profound, yet brief, intense connection and recognition. We needed no words. We saw each other. We felt each other. We connected in some mystical alignment of the moment. I walked off, dazed and intoxicated with the lessons of Steven stirring in my heart.

A few minutes later, in the next aisle over, a family passed by. Not paying much attention, I was reveling in the bliss and looking at my list, when a young Hispanic girl pulled her hand away from her mom and shouted loudly to get my attention, "Hi!" I made eye contact with her and was pulled into an eternal gaze, returned a smile, and said, "Hi!" *Seriously? Again?* There was a strange vibe, and we were in a complete state of surreal recognition. It was as if each of these children were reaching out to me to share a soul moment. I was filled with gratitude. There was a familiar knowing between us. Our fervent eye contact felt like an eternity of deeper seeing and remembering. I began to feel a universal oneness with everyone in the superstore as I looked around with curiosity and gentle compassion. What was happening? Was anyone else experiencing this?

When life couldn't get much sweeter, a third young child, a Caucasian, lying on her daddy's shoulder, lifted her head just a few feet from mine, grinned from ear to ear, and with the radiant light of recognition in her eyes, greeted me with an adorable and engaging, "Hi!" I was enchanted, as I stood soaking in the mystery of this unbelievable embodied experience.

I said a silent prayer for Steven in gratitude. His palpable love, joy, and heart for service had created a beautiful resonant field that ignited something in me. He taught me the embodied experience of aligning with the Divine. I believe that the same gracious God and divine spark that resides within Steven, resides within me, and within all people, including the three children I met at the superstore. Maybe the three children simply recognized it sooner than I did, and reached out in remembrance to reconnect in a beautiful, living experience of Namaste. (The meaning of *Namaste* [pronounced 'nä-mə-stä] is both a physical gesture and a spoken spiritual salutation, which is the recognition of the divine spirit [or soul] in another by the divine spirit in you. The word *Namaste* translates simply to *I bow to the divine in you.*) Did I create this experience? Did the Unified Field or Steven's contagious joy attract this to me?

I found the same quality of recognition and alignment with my new doctor. I could feel his exuberant spark of joy in serving others through the practice of medicine. I could feel his recognition of me as an individual. I felt his genuine compassion and experienced the divine spark in him seeing the divine spark in me.

As I pondered this experience, I realized part of that deep connection was missing in my experience with my first doctor. Of course, he had a divine spark, and I think that divine spark looked for the divine spark in me. But he lacked a buoyant joy for the practice of medicine. He was in pre-retirement mode and no longer doing surgery. Any sense of joy or jubilance in his practice seemed to be missing. He wasn't playing in a fertile field of possibility with me. He wasn't living in the moment with *the question*. He didn't trust my intuition or the body's wisdom. From my observation, he was in a mechanical, rote-mode of traditional medical protocol and intellectual probabilities.

I also recognized that my *own* joy was missing. I was looking for my joy. Where did it go? I love summer, being outdoors, and spending time with family and friends. But I was missing my personal joy. Where had it gone?

So Where Is the Grace?

As the one-year anniversary approached, I was frustrated with the slow progress and ongoing issues with pain, swelling, weakness, and out-toeing. I was struggling to keep my signature eternal optimism flowing. I was down, secretly depressed, feeling desperate, and losing hope. I tried to appear strong and cheerful to the outside world. Yet when alone, I was afraid, confused, apprehensive, and cowardly.

The ego-voice of the Separate Self that accompanied my silent, solitary tears was cruel, harsh, and overbearing. It was loud and tormenting: *There must be something seriously wrong with you. You call yourself a healer? A spiritual teacher?* "New Age guilt" ravaged through my years of research, education, and experience, taunting me: *Your beliefs are creating your reality. So, what does that say about you, now? You are weak, lazy, and ignorant. You should be back on your feet by now, Superwoman, running your perfect life.*

In short, *New Age guilt* is a term used to describe the act of using spirituality in order to judge oneself and others. You feel guilt or shame because you are not able to live up to the spiritual standards you set for yourself. For example, if you're a healer and get sick, you may beat yourself up because you, of all people, should know how to stay healthy and whole. Or you may know the laws of manifestation, but fail to manifest something important in your life. I also see New Age guilt as a consequence of spiritual narcissism. Spiritual people think they are beyond the consequences and "should know better."

The mounting desperation and torrential self-abuse was ugly and dark. What would it take to make me whole again? When would I walk normally again? How many more weeks or months of vacillating between good and bad days? Why was I unable to create spontaneous healing? Where was the grace? It was clear I was being asked to walk a new way, or maybe in a new direction, and I literally *could not walk* the old way, or think myself—or meditate myself—into a better mental space. I couldn't do this alone. I felt desperate, like giving up and running away. But I couldn't walk, let alone run.

In one of my lowest moments, I had a conversation with God. I implored the Designing Intelligence of creation to be with me. I begged the healing Life Force to come and heal that which it had created. I was ready to get out of my own way and align with the Divine like never before. After a long, dark pause, I finally heard it: that still small voice. *It is time to ask for more help!* It was time to begin a more rigorous holistic, integral healing process. Besides the periodic energy work I had scheduled with my great friend and thought partner, Teresa Bushnell, I now heard the time had come to find a chiropractor to assist with the alignment issues.

I called my friend, Mitch, in Cape Cod. As he is a deeply perceptive, holistic chiropractor, I trusted his opinion. He suggested a specific technique and gave me some guidance on finding the right doctor. His most important and empowering advice was what NOT to seek. He said to find someone who would tune in intuitively and listen to my body. He discouraged my working with any practitioner who would simply adjust the spine and put me on a several-week standard protocol without reassessing and listening to my body each session.

I felt so empowered by his guidance. It gave me hope and an unfamiliar authority over my care. He helped me to discern what I really wanted—a care team who could assist in co-creating my fullest recovery and health.

After much research and a few phone calls, I had a plan to work with two new healers. I made two appointments. Later I realized that, serendipitously, both were scheduled on the actual anniversary date of my accident. The first healer was my dear friend Sherryl Lin, a medical intuitive and spiritual guide. The second was a local chiropractor, Dr. Sheen.

CHAPTER REFLECTIONS

Harmony and coherence of our head and heart—our Separate and Sacred Selves—our individual and whole selves—are essential if we want to navigate life's path with ease and joy.

- Aligning with the Divine can mean many things: aligning with the divine within you, your Sacred Self, and your soul's purpose; the divine within others, creation, and all of nature; your spiritual practice or faith tradition; or the still small voice, sacred texts, or however you experience the myriad expressions of God. Pause and take a few minutes of contemplation. What does "align with the Divine" mean to you? Write about this as a practice. When do you align? When do you feel out of alignment? What causes misalignment for you? How can you develop this as a practice?

- Seeing the Divine in all things is a powerful healing practice. "Namaste" is a great reminder to look for the Divine not only in others, but also within yourself. When was the last time you gazed deeply into someone's eyes and allowed the Divinity within to pierce your soul? Make a soul-care date with yourself. Go out in a public place—somewhere where you least expect to have a spiritual experience—perhaps a big box store. Wander around with the intention to make eye contact. Really look at people, even when their eyes drop in discomfort. Look into the eyes of those you come in contact with—strangers and loved ones alike. Smile and look with the intention of acknowledging their divinity.

- Harmony and coherence of your Separate and Sacred Selves can be tricky. Our ego has very different needs than does our true essential nature. As we practice to stabilize the essential, Sacred Self, we naturally attract more joy into our lives. Grounding the Sacred is like putting on rose-colored glasses. We see the Sacred everywhere and in everything and can't help but overflow with a contagious, effervescent joy. Reflect on your last week. Describe the times of great joy. How about in the past month? Use this joy-factor as a gauge for what you need to work on. How would you rate yourself? What steps can you take to increase the joy-factor?

CHAPTER SEVEN

Multidimensional Healing

The existence of a living universe tells us that we are part of the world around us, and not separate from it, and that our aliveness is part of a greater aliveness. And as the very goal of life in the universe is to grow, change, and perpetuate itself, these are precisely the qualities that we should strive to embrace throughout the course of our time in this world as human beings.

~ Gregg Braden

A s soon as I made the appointments, my creative juices began to flow at an accelerated pace. I was spontaneously happier and more hopeful. This was a good sign. Profound and hopeful poetry was flowing from me like Niagara Falls. I couldn't stop the creative energy and I didn't want to. The entire twelve months had been an epic creative journey, and this appeared to raise that an octave or two. Anne Lamott wrote, "I do not understand the mystery of grace, only that it meets us where we are but does not leave us where it found us." I was being transported to a new level of creative consciousness and fluidity. Was this manic-like, creative bliss called *grace*?

My little Gollum-like, Merlin-looking man, wearing the lab coat and carrying his scalpel, made a brief reappearance. I suppose it was to remind me to carry the medical model with me into this next phase of healing and energy medicine. My rebellious inner healer was ready to ditch the allopathic route all together. I had gotten caught up in judging my experience and measuring my progress, or the lack thereof. *Seriously, one year of traditional medicine and physical therapy, and I'm not back to 100 percent yet? Am I doing enough? Should I try harder? Is there something wrong? Do I need to push more? When do I push and when do I let up? Can I simply trust my body to tell me what it needs?* Judging and measuring progress took me out of the intimate present moment of experiencing my body, the healing process, and expanded awareness. It dropped me into a finite, self-abusive, Separate-Self mode.

I remembered my commitment to my higher and wiser essential self that had come through in my Gollum-Merlin-pokey-friend dream. It was my longstanding desire to work toward integration. I would stay open and honor both paths moving forward. I wouldn't abandon either. I would listen and look for ways to bridge the two. Or better yet, integrate.

Resolution and Integration

My first session with Sherryl Lin was deeply profound, as well as prophetic. The session not only offered effective energetic shifts and healing, but revealed details about the work I would do with Dr. Sheen. One of the clearings was a limiting belief I was holding. She helped me clear a limiting belief I had about spontaneous healing. Seriously? After decades of study, research, and healing work, I was still carrying some form of doubt in my consciousness. It really didn't matter how much my mind thought I believed in spontaneous healing. I was both tickled and perplexed at the same time.

We talked about how your beliefs turn into thoughts that create your reality. Limiting beliefs keep you caged in a smaller version of who you are—your authentic, magnificent self—and your potential. Limiting beliefs are often subconscious and rooted deep within your psyche. You don't even know they exist. When things aren't going the way you had hoped or intended, find someone skilled in working with the subconscious to help you identify and release your emotional blocks and limiting beliefs.

This brought me back to my Louise Hay lesson: Could there be any connection to my deepest beliefs about myself and what I know about the structure of the universe? Obviously, anything was possible. I always thought I believed in spontaneous healing. Now, with that question presenting, I was open to all possibilities. I was open to entering into a deeper understanding of myself. And I was open to experiencing new layers and levels of healing.

Later that day, I had my first session with Dr. Sheen. We had already met via a nice phone conversation where I explained my case to him and my friend's medical recommendations. He was totally on board and in alignment with my requests. Our mutual friend, Teresa, had previously told him about my work and shared some of our mutual professional interests. He knew I was a healer and talk radio host. He was a fan of many of the guests I've had on my show, so we had plenty to talk about right off the bat.

My first session was remarkable. Dr. Sheen has had extensive training in Quantum Neurology and has a brilliant mind. He is inquisitive, and has developed his own original protocol and assistive devices that aid in his treatment regime. He personalized his time with me and worked quickly with a variety of techniques and assessments. It was as if I got on his table, and in a whirlwind of frenzied, healing activity, he waved a magic wand, lowered the table, and asked me to stand and walk. My left foot was much straighter. It was a miracle.

We continued to work together pretty consistently over the next few months. It was a deep dive into the quantum, multidimensional realms of healing. Peeling back layer after layer, we cleared, aligned, and rebalanced, witnessing dramatic shifts. There were many profound moments.

One of the first was when Dr. Sheen was working around the table, moving quickly, muscle testing as he went along. He stopped and asked whether I had a scar on my left hand. I said, "No." He quickly asked whether I was sure. What a strange question. *Did I have a scar on my left hand?* Then it dawned on me. Yes, I have a scar on my left index finger. I sliced it open on a sharp butcher knife when I was a teenager. I had to get several stitches. He looked at my hand and continued working with the scar tissue, then asked, "Are all of your scars on your left side?"

What? I had to think for a moment. He definitely caught me off guard. *All of them? Are all of my scars on the left side?*

Hmm . . . I began to count. The top of my head, high forehead, above my eyebrow, above my lip, throat, pelvis, and now my fractured bones—all of them were on my left side, with a few in my naval. "I thought so!" he said confidently and continued working. "Feel this," he said as he finished working with the scar on my lip. I touched my scar and paused in disbelief.

I smashed my lip and split it open as a young child, and had to get stitches. When my lip had healed, I told my mom I thought there was a piece of gravel in my lip they didn't remove. The scar tissue was hard and condensed. To a young child, it felt like a pebble was still in there. When Dr. Sheen asked me to feel it, I was amazed. The rock-like, dense scar tissue was gone. The scar was soft and supple.

"What do you think it means that all your scars are on your left side?" he asked. I confidently responded by explaining that it probably had something to do with balancing my masculine and feminine energies. I thought it could be my body asking me to give my feminine energy a bigger role and clearer voice. It was time to integrate the two and honor the feminine more.

He quickly replied, "I could be wrong, but what if it's the opposite? What if you are overusing the feminine? There's no balance. The left side is "breaking down" from overuse? You did have a twin brother. Are you overcompensating for his loss?"

My twin brother . . .

A few weeks prior, Dr. Sheen had been working on a resistant issue and trying to assess the root cause of the symptom. After proficiently muscle testing, he asked if I had ever heard about having had a vanishing twin? "Yes. Adrian," I said. (A vanishing twin is a fetus in a multi-gestation pregnancy that dies in utero, and then is partially or completely reabsorbed.)

Decades had passed since I first learned of Adrian. I was being treated by a chiropractor for a persistent neck issue. Again, through very skilled muscle testing, the doctor said I'd had a twin in gestation. Instantly, a wave of recognition cascaded through my body, and tears rolled down my checks. Yes! That was the chronic, empty feeling and deep grief I carried in my being. Yes! That was the answer to the question I didn't know to ask. Yes! I instantly recognized his name as Adrian. I knew him intimately. He was still with me, but not. He was here, but not really. It was a moment of clarity, remembrance, and recognition. Later, when I got in my car to drive home, a Jewel song came on the radio: "Adrian."

The lyrics were haunting. She was singing my story and my strange feeling of loss and attachment. I wept in gratitude and in grief. It was a profound relief to finally understand this missing piece of my soul—a hole in the fabric of my being that felt ripped and permanent.

In my *knowing*, I understood that Adrian could not be born. It was a cosmic agreement with two primary reasons. First, there was not enough foundational health, nutrition, or energy to sustain a multi-gestation pregnancy. Second, Adrian left to assist me and my soul's purpose from the other side—within the other realms. It was a sacrifice and a gift.

Many intuitive people have picked up on my brother's energy and presence. And my astrology chart indicates a male twin. He comes through in readings all the time.

Speaking of astrology, I have two birthdays.

I was born on my sister's first birthday (so I thought)—December 16th. Every year, I would share my birthday, birthday cake, and birthday presents with my sister. And for the first fifteen years of my life, that was my day—well, *our day*. Then on December 15th when I turned fifteen, my dad called to wish me "Happy Birthday." He told me that my birthday was really December 15th, but my mom had wanted it on the 16th "because it was cute." Hmm. I asked my mom and she continued to profess the 16th. And so it began—the dysfunctional, two-birthday conundrum.

In my early twenties, I needed a passport, so I got a copy of my birth certificate from the state. It said, "December 16." So there— it was settled. I was born on December 16th. For the next several years, I celebrated the 16th, and my dad continued to call me on the 15th. Then one day in my early '30s, my mom gave me the hospital certificate where they put your footprints in ink. It was typed December 16th, but the nurse had signed it in green ink, *December 15*. At this point, I was really confused. I asked my mother again, and she continued to profess the 16th.

Years went by, and the two-birthday chaos continued, until one day my mother called on December 15th. She wanted to bring over a birthday gift. I told her it wasn't my birthday yet. She agreed with that on the phone, then brought the gift to my house. She sat down and quickly said, "Okay, it's time I tell the truth. You really were born on the 15th, but the hospital messed up and put the 16th on your birth certificate, so we just kept it that way."

I have two birthdays. One is my REAL day of BIRTH, and the other is my LEGAL birthday. It's been the 16th on every legal document since I was born. After years of having everyone forget a too-close-to-Christmas birthday, getting combined birthday/Christmas gifts at Christmas, sharing the day with my sister, and years of questions about the date, I decided to claim both days and celebrate life and my birth in an elevated capacity! I discovered I could feel sad about my lack of birthday, resentment for the chaos, grief over my vanishing birthday, confusion for the mystery of it all, or simple joy for the abundance, making the best out of a goofy situation! I chose to celebrate life and all the bountiful blessings in the chaos. And I choose to celebrate *me* and birth a new sense of self-love.

Every year since I found out the truth, I have had my own private, little birthday celebration that lasts for forty-eight hours. (Sometimes it stretches for a week!) I gave birth to a new sense of self and began to love, honor, and cherish all the dysfunctional, crazy, mixed-up ideas about my birthday and who I really am, in spite of it all.

As my twin, Adrian, showed up in the deep healing I was doing with Dr. Sheen, my sense of separation and duality began to emerge and play again within me—cavorting with this twin energy and the double birthdates. Are we separate beings? The same being? What is masculine and feminine balance and integration? What is the meaning of having two birthdays? What is the divine human and this thing about resolving duality through unification? Can the fragmented, Separate Self resolve into a fully-integrated human?

I had some deepening moments. And this led me again to the crossroads of science, spirituality, and consciousness. What really happens with the vanishing twin? Is there a consciousness, spirit, or soul in gestation? What happens with cellular tissue? Is this the ultimate integration? Who is he and who am I? Often, I feel both of us. Organ and tissue transplant recipients often experience noetic phenomena, sensing an energetic presence or having strange personality shifts and preferences that appear to mimic that of the donors. Is all of that possible with the vanishing twin?

I began to feel the early stages of resolution and integration. I knew everything in my life was in transition. Duality was resolving and everything would be transformed.

A few weeks after my work began with Dr. Sheen, I went back to my orthopedic surgeon for a checkup. He told me a month earlier that if I didn't show marked improvement in the out-toeing, we may need to consider surgery. When the nurse did her assessment, I unapologetically reported that I had started seeing a chiropractor for treatment with my alignment. When the doctor came in to examine my gait and measure the out-toeing, he was surprisingly pleased. There was dramatic and marked improvement. He said, "You won't hear very many orthopedic surgeons say this, but keep doing what you're doing. Continue seeing the chiropractor."

A new consciousness was breaking through!

CHAPTER REFLECTIONS

I was being transported to a new level of creative consciousness and fluidity. Was this manic-like creative bliss called grace?

- The same Divine Power that creates our bodies heals our bodies. The same Designing Intelligence, sourced within our being, has wisdom and capacities beyond our imagining. Why would we trust anything less when it comes to our health, healing, and well-being? This is an amazing power, and we are not separate from it. This same intelligence animates life all around us. Understanding how to come into alignment, cooperate, and work with our true nature is the new quantum prescription for our wholeness. How often do you truly tune into this intelligence? Pause and reflect on how you experience your health and wholeness. Do you listen to what you've been taught from others, their beliefs, the media, school, advertisements, pop culture, or a worldview of separation about health, fitness, diet, illness, and healing? Take a good inventory and ask to be shown the truth about your health and wholeness. What beliefs do you hold? If you feel called, explore topics of holistic, complementary, alternative, integrative and energy medicine. Pick up Bruce Lipton's book, **The Biology of Belief.** Read **You Are the Placebo** by Joe Dispenza. Make an effort to peel back your own layers of belief and what you may or may not want to look at. You may *think* you believe in spontaneous healing. But do you really? What would your life look like if you had absolutely no doubt? What would it be like if you didn't believe? Explore your belief in miracles. Do you feel miracles are sourced from within you, from a far off external deity, or something completely different? Create your own definitions of "healing" and "miracle." You are a co-creator of your health.

- It's important for us to embrace all our life experiences—the good, the bad, the ugly, and the strange. So often, when we can't explain things with our rational, logical minds, we jump to the conclusion that it's a fluke or a strange, abnormal happening. Or we disregard it all together. If we can't see it, we don't believe it. Sometimes we make up stories to fill a void in our understanding. Our limited minds usually want to shut down the expansive, sublime power that resides in every moment and every experience. We are not trained to sit in the mystery and welcome the unknowing. We are not taught that we are multidimensional beings. Take a respite from your cognitive experience of life. Take a walk in nature and find a quiet place to sit in silence. Allow yourself to be bathed in the mysteries of life. Use your senses to become one with all that is. What do you see? Become one with that. What do you hear? Merge into the sounds. What do you feel? Loose the sensations of separation and feel into the expansiveness of your environment. What do you smell? Follow the experience to the source of scent. All things in nature are born, grow, reproduce, heal, and die. Become a part of the seasons and cycles. Be one with the pulsing intelligence that is present. Melt into the sun. Fly with the breeze. Ground into the earth. Flow with the waters. Bloom into life.

- The unseen realms of other dimensions—the quantum field (of Love)—is as real as the material world our five senses can relate to. You don't have to have a mystical experience of non-ordinary consciousness to trust the majesty and greatness of our multidimensional beingness. Take a moment and contemplate this text from Genesis: "Then the Lord God formed a man from the dust of the ground and breathed into his nostrils the breath of life, and the man became a living being." Imagine the breath of life—the breath of love. Inhale the breath of life. What does it mean to become a living being? What does the "breath of life" mean to you? In your journal write the phrase, "I am the breath of life." Explore the ways in which the breath of life becomes you and you become the breath of life. Allow yourself to play and interact with the unseen, unmanifested realm. Use the breath of life as the springboard into a more cosmic, expansive exploration.

CHAPTER EIGHT

Waiting for My New Normal

We sense that 'normal' isn't coming back, that we are being born into a new normal: a new kind of society, a new relationship to the earth, a new experience of being human.

~ Charles Eisenstein

One good report from my doctor, and I believed I had turned the corner. It should be smooth sailing from here on out, right? Each layer of healing, every measure of good progress—they were all steps in the right direction. Or not.

It seemed like every time I would take a few steps forward, I would take one huge leap backward. All progress would be interrupted when I tried to get back to my normal life. A brief trip, where I walked, limped, and hobbled all over New York City took days to recover from. Normal ambulation for social, recreational, work, and family activities could be challenging. Some days were great. I would wake up and feel as if I were walking normally. Other days were not so great and I could barely walk. On those days, normal daily activity seemed excessive.

Sitting in my chair with my foot elevated seemed like the new normal. And so was thinking about human anatomy and how it worked. I learned to be mindful and consciously think about every step: *turn-your-foot-in; heel-toe-push-off.* On days when I felt like I was doing great and walking normally, family members would tell me to be mindful of my gait. "Foot in," was a common phrase I heard over and over and over from my husband and other loved ones around me.

I was growing weary.

Over a year ago, I knew this event would change things forever. I could feel it. It was one of those moments that permanently shift your consciousness and uplevel your way of being. I called the accident "my breakthrough." I remember saying that to Dr. Sheen, and his challenging me back, "If this is your breakthrough, what are you breaking away from?"

Wasn't it obvious? Everything in my life appeared to be changing just like everything in our world was. I was breaking down the illusion of separation. I was breaking away from old systems and structures. I was busting through old thought patterns, limiting beliefs, and worldviews. The structure of my universe was collapsing all around me. I began making conscious changes in almost every area of my life. I let go of elements of my private practice when it was obvious that adhering to the medical model was challenging and needed transformation. I was focused on new creative energies emerging—energies focused on the shift occurring on our planet, the evolution of consciousness.

You often hear me speak of both the *evolution of consciousness* and *conscious evolution*. Let me differentiate the two for you. Theories of consciousness come from religion, philosophy, and cognitive science. Many have trouble even accurately defining consciousness. But for the sake of this conversation, let's just say it's the state of being awake and aware. Jude Currivan says consciousness isn't something we *have*, it's something we (and the entire universe) *are*. Therefore, *evolution of consciousness* refers to the continued expansion and evolution of your awareness—or movement through different stages of awareness. *Conscious evolution*, on the other hand, refers to the ability for you, and the rest of humanity, to choose what you (and we) will become in the future—to consciously evolve.

I was speaking about it. I was teaching, coaching, healing, and leading others though the transformation. I was actively working with individuals and organizations that were bringing spirit and consciousness more fully into all aspects of life. I was "giving my gifts to the shift," assisting other individuals, groups, organizations, and audiences to do the same. I was a voice of hope and a calm presence of encouragement. But I couldn't find *my* new normal! I saw the sacred secrets of the universe and knew how to unlock a higher potential, but it was as if I had lost my personal set of keys. Where was the breakthrough? What was I breaking away from? When would I find a new normal?

Things did not work the way they used to, even when I diligently tried. Nothing felt as if it were working. It was way more than just my body that was in total transformation. I had adamantly resisted putting new ideas, templates, and consciousness into old forms and structures. But this was something cosmically bigger than I ever imagined. Old ways of doing business dried up, disappeared.

Old ways of marketing repulsed me. I had a difficult time relating to people and organizations that were operating out of fierce competition and systems of top-down dominance and control. Everywhere I went, I could read people and systems. From apathy to anxiety to anger, the breakdown of systems was wearing on our collective psyche. And there were days it was hard to stay optimistic.

As time went on, how I longed for things to start working again. I was growing weary of the liminal space. Though I could *vision* the light at the end of the tunnel, I could not *see* it. The tunnel was long, dark, sometimes overwhelming and scary. I felt alone—so cut off from others, and the Divine. The proverbial tunnel shifted into an expanding, hellish abyss. This time of being present with my physical body and healing was creating huge gaps between mystical moments of union and cosmic bliss.

I had this chronic *feeling* I was enclosed within a hollow, asteroid-type, spherical shape—a rock, floating way out in space, alone. Visually, I experienced it as a black/brown, dark sphere with a bumpy surface. Kind of a cross between a ripe avocado and a burnt meatball. Deep inside the dark, pitch-black center of the asteroid, I was trapped. And though I was working with many different conscious communities in my professional life, I felt so alone, all by myself, hidden inside that asteroid. Could anyone hear me or see me in there? Disconnected from God, from other people, from myself, and even from my intuitive gifts of vision, hearing, and knowing, I was lost. Returning to any kind of normal wasn't an option—that message was becoming clear. And I had thought I was all about *surrender*, but this surrender involved a cosmic leap I could only conclude I must have been resisting.

I wanted life to stop. I wanted life to go back to the way it was before. I wanted an easy way out of this state—this limited, liminal place of pain and suffering. And then, I remembered feeling this same feeling so many other times in my life.

There was that desperate time when I was eleven years old, not wanting to live on the planet with the humans I didn't understand. I had just wanted life to stop; I was aching to *go home*. And it was like my first experience with childbirth, stuck in the pushing stage, worn out with the pain of labor, the fatigue of pushing, just wanting the process to stop. Witnessing my dad's epic death process, and yearning for it to be over—for him and for me.

Was I in another birth/death canal, feeling stuck? Was I trying to birth myself into the next highest version of who I was meant to be? My egoic, rational mind was aligned with a cultural, New Age myth—a dangerous myth—and told me: *No, you've already done this transformational spiritual work. You've healed on many levels and dimensions. You've done tons of shadow work. You've healed from your experiences of trauma, abuse, and neglect. You've forgiven. You understand your wholeness.* My Separate Self was persistent in deceiving me, allowing New Age guilt and spiritual narcissism to create perennial road blocks.

My soul said, **Relax into this . . .**

◆

An Invitation to Leap Forward

Less than a month after I broke my leg, I had Simran Singh as a guest on my radio talk show. We were talking about her new book, *Conversations with the Universe: How the World Speaks to Us.* She is gifted at reading signs and symbols, revealing how repetitions, coincidences, and synchronicities are part of our personal conversation with the Universe. She encourages the reader to pay attention. Even the smallest of events are intended to provide ease and guidance.

We were visiting about my broken leg before the show. She asked how it happened. I gave her the same explanation I had given so many. I wished I had an exciting story, like I was skydiving and my parachute didn't open. My story is almost so simple and boring that it's unbelievable. "I was consciously and mindfully walking down a hill—a steep, grassy slope—taking careful, small baby steps, when I slipped. That was it. Slip—Twist—Crack, as fast as fast can be! From carefully and mindfully walking down a familiar hill that I had walked down hundreds of times, to multiple broken bones." Then, during a commercial break, Simran caught me off guard:

"Julie, why are you walking down hill in life?"

"Why are you walking down the same familiar path over and over?"

"Why are you being so careful with each step, taking baby steps?"

"Julie, life is inviting you to leap forward with joy and abandon, not caution. You are meant to climb, play, dance, and rise to the top. Find your pinnacle; move up and out into the world. Stop being so mindful and careful. Just do it."

Whoa. I remember the jolt of *something*. But it didn't feel like *my* truth. I processed her words very briefly and rationalized them away in my head as my ego took charge:

I'm not taking baby steps in life. I'm out there following my dream, making things happen, starting new initiatives. I'm not too careful. I'm responsible. I'm waiting for the right people and situations to emerge. She doesn't really know what I'm up to. I need to build the new before letting go of the old—build the new to replace the old. I need to work hard so there's a smooth transition and little risk. I need to have things in place so it's sustainable. I need to make money first, so I can finance my vision. That wasn't the Universe's message to me. The Universe was giving me permission to slow down, sit in my chair, and write my book. That was it.

Dismissed. Or so I thought.

Echoes of Simran's words were manifesting in real life, without me even recognizing it. The first six months following the injury, I'd been forced to take every step mindfully and carefully. I progressed from a full-leg cast and crutches, to a half cast and crutches, to no weight-bearing on my left leg and crutches, to two crutches with some weight-bearing, to one crutch, to a cane. Every step I made was calculated, carefully planned, and executed. I was afraid to fall. I was afraid to slip. I was unsteady on my feet. I was protective of the injury. I was cautious of pain. I was unable to feel solid and stable. I navigated from the place of least resistance and pain.

Over the next six months, I was cautioned by my doctor to be very, very careful when I went back on the crutches, with no weight-bearing on the left leg again. He warned me that with the significant osteopenia and bone edema, my bones could collapse. The risk of subsequent fractures and reinjury was high. I was told to step mindfully. Don't take any risks. Don't participate in any activity where I may slip or fall. Be careful walking up and down stairs. Don't ride a bike. "Move slowly and intentionally, doctor's orders!"

Besides the bones being weak, all my muscles were weak as well. I didn't feel fully supported in my body. I didn't feel strong.

Evidently, this entire script was running in my subconscious. I didn't recognize it, but my husband did. He was constantly challenging me and my new fear-based reality. I was afraid of reinjuring my leg and ankle. Snow scared me. Ice scared me. Water scared me. Wet floors terrified me. Uneven ground scared me. Hills scared me. Curbs scared me. Stepping out of the truck scared me. Trying new things scared me. Walking in the dark scared me. I clearly had not resolved or released the acute stress response related to the trauma.

We create scripts and play them out subconsciously in our lives. We also create stories that we consciously choose. You are the writer and director of your own life. How you view the world and your deepest values influence your scripts and stories. Let me give you an example. When the Prius first came out, I purchased one and drove my new car to a board meeting, assuming my fellow board members would make a comment and ask about the hybrid technology. Instead, they were captivated by another member's wife's new, bright-red Hummer. When I brought it up at work the next day, there were FIVE TOTALLY DIFFERENT responses to the idea of owning a Hummer. The first person, an environmentalist, said, "Hummer. Bummer." The second, an artist, said, "That is one of the ugliest cars out there." The third was a compassionate nurse and counselor. She said, "I don't know how any mother can drive around a military vehicle when we are at war and our children are being killed." The fourth, a practical, down-to-earth person, said, "Those things are so expensive!" And the fifth, a conscious evolutionary, made a comment about the ego's attachment to the expensive novelty and flashy attention-getting quality. Five different people, five different responses. The stories that you live out are uniquely your own.

When he would call me out on it, I would defend my position: "But the doctor said . . . " He asked me what I wanted to *choose* to believe, and what reality I wanted to create. Nonsense. I dismissed him too. I was simply following doctor's orders. I would not be released for full activity until we checked my bone density months from now—at least twenty months after the original accident.

And then, my inner voice would reverberate, *What reality are you creating, Julie? What are you afraid of?*

My egoic, critical Separate Self was ruthless. Were my bones strong or weak? Was I creating this reality? Was I in charge of this process? (Guilt. Shame. Fear.) Was I to heal differently? Was I being too cautious? Was I being a baby? Did I truly, unequivocally believe in spontaneous healing? Was it all in my head? Was it real? Was I open to healing myself and healing myself completely? What was I not seeing?

My life was designed around healing—myself, others, the psyche/soul, the planet. I have healed myself many times—but never from a severe injury like this. This was my only traumatic injury of its kind, but healing is healing, I thought. I have healed my body of serious symptoms and chronic disease. I have healed on many levels with many issues. I have healed from childhood trauma and abuse. I have healed others. I am pretty healthy and whole. I take responsibility for my life, relationships, and actions. I practice self-correction whenever necessary. I'm a pretty conscious individual who values self-actualization, spiritual awakening, and my highest potential.

What was this state of fear and caution that had set in? And what was this illusion and resistance around my own healing process? Irrational fear and anxiety are usually symptoms that come from the illusion of separation. But in my mind, this was justified, rational anxiety and caution resulting from the physical trauma and injury.

Whenever I feel stuck, I try to look at things from a different perspective. If indeed, I was stuck inside of some kind of cosmic birth/death canal, it was time to shift my perspective. So I looked a little deeper and turned the issue around, upside down, and inside out. I came up with a new set of questions:

How am I playing life safe?

How does being cautious and taking baby steps serve me?

How does walking the same path over and over again keep me safe?

What is it that is holding me back from the light at the end of the tunnel; from the vision I have of myself in the world; from my life?

The new set of questions and a different perspective shifted everything.

> Shifting your perspective can literally change everything. If you ever feel stuck, try standing on a chair and thinking about the issue. Get on the floor, look behind you, look in a mirror, go for a walk. There are many ways to help you think outside your proverbial box and shift your perspective.

In the Glow of a Divine Light

I experienced a new kind of "Crack!" in my awareness. I took my questions and my journal to the office with me to muse in between clients. Avoiding my desk and my normal cozy chair, I sat on the sofa where my clients usually sit and began a new stream of consciousness in my journal. In that moment, my awareness broke open like an asteroid breaking apart in space. I was in an altered state of consciousness—back in that hollow, black, asteroid-like sphere out in space, and the walls blew out from the inside. Doors flew open. Not just one door, many doors, in every direction, all the way around me. Abundant light poured in with a familiar magnificence—I'd seen it before. Everything was luminous and visible again. I could see. I was connected. I was never really alone. The answers were right there in plain sight, within me.

Such an astonishing breaking point! Enfolded within an experience of cosmic love, I_transitioned in a flash, accepting the gift of a brilliant breakthrough. Tears of recognition rolled down my cheeks, as I basked in the glow of a divine light and a multidimensional love—one that I so clearly remembered. I was home and I was safe. The Universe had my back. Utterly relaxed, I dropped my boundaries in this infinite moment of bliss and oneness.

I had been hiding. Hiding what some may call the "woo-woo" part of who I am. Hiding my gifts, my passion, my voice, and my service. I could see how I had been limiting myself—obscuring my greatest assets. I was a part-time, cautious, closeted mystic and way-shower, waiting for circumstances, people, and the world around me to change. Waiting to feel safe in order to show myself to anyone. All at once, I was given permission and encouraged to live and fully embody my universal, multidimensional, undivided self.

> As humans, we often retreat, isolate, and hide away without even recognizing we're doing it. Shame makes us feel vulnerable. Fear threatens our perceived safety. Both fear and shame can trigger us to withdraw from life and social settings.

I *am* an evolving, multidimensional human. I am more than I even know. I was called to claim the blessings and responsibilities that go with that.

Julie, are you willing to sit in the mystery of the unfolding, while trusting and being true to what presents in the moment?

That is a big question. I thought I was kind of, sort of, maybe already doing that most of the time.

That's not good enough.

Are you willing to fully embody your multidimensional, universal self and sit in the mystery of the unfolding, while trusting and being true to what presents in EVERY moment?

Mine was a visceral, nonverbal response. I couldn't think to conceptualize the answer. Saying, "Yes" in my head was not enough. Uttering a simple word would have diminished and trivialized the significant honor and gift that was being presented. It was not a yes-kind-of response. It was a pause-and-take-your-breath-away kind of agreement, as my soul begged me to step forward to humbly accept another sacred ordination in a surreal and precious moment of grace.

I humbly stepped forward in reverence and awe.

> We are all multidimensional beings. YOU are a multidimensional being. What does that mean to you?

Fear Not

I had been playing it safe—hiding my visionary gifts, my innate genius, my psychic prowess, my "brilliant, gorgeous, talented, and fabulous (Marianne Williamson)" self. I was hiding my social-change artistry from those around me. I was hiding my light under a basket. After all these years, I was afraid to share who I really was as a planetary healer, midwife of the soul, visionary leader, and conscious evolutionary with my local community. I would struggle to explain to people what I did.

Most people knew me as a respected psychotherapist or counselor. Calculated and circumspect with how I portrayed myself, I developed simple, mainstream language to bridge the gap of understanding and the differing levels of consciousness. But what I learned was that the language, although bridging, remained rather static, confining, and safe. Erring on the side of caution, I was showing only the parts I knew would be readily understood and accepted. I was a mystic in the closet and rarely cracked the door open. I was afraid to be the fullest expression of my authentic, divine, co-creative self.

Fearing criticism, judgment, rejection, and even worse, I leaned into conformity, desperately wanting to fit in and be normal. But like Sherryl Lin reminded me, I'm "not normal." There is no normal. It was time to find my new "natural."

I was lonely, and felt gravely unseen within my own family and community. Ironically, I was shielding myself from view in one world, while becoming highly visible and seen within another.

I live in a very conservative, rural, homogenized area. As a whole, Nebraska is among the most politically conservative states. The population is mostly white (90 percent) and fiscally and socially conservative. Fifty-six percent of Nebraskans report having a religious affiliation. Of those, 98.5 percent are of a Christian tradition. I hold no judgment for my neighbors' race, political views, or religious beliefs. I love, honor, and cherish my pioneering roots and the foundation I have here. However, if I were to embrace my crazy, out-there, woo-woo, brilliant, talented, globally-minded, outside-the-box thinking, cosmic, artsy, mystical self, how was I going to do it here and feel safe and comfortable? After living here most of my life, I knew only a handful of people in the area with whom I could relate, being free and open about my experiences and my authentic self. I did the socially acceptable, people pleasing persona very well. The authentic expression, not so much.

Most of the Christian mystics lived centuries ago, and were protected in monasteries, hidden away from everyday living and the public. In fact, the word *mysticism* is derived from Greek meaning *to conceal*. And yet, mysticism is the consciousness of and direct experience of the transformative presence of God—or union with God.

If it were time to bust those multidimensional doors wide open for good and let the light out as well as let the light in, how might that look? I asked for guidance. And I came to understand then that I need to trust my visionary gifts more completely and calm my fear with a megadose of healing self-compassion. I came to see this array of fears wasn't as indomitable as I was perceiving it to be. Surely, this was irrational fear and some very old, limiting beliefs that were creating more separation.

Within hours of this epiphany, I found myself relaxing and expanding. It was as if I were now free to proficiently harness the fluid flow of cosmic, creative consciousness in my own little corner of the world. I was settling into the full embodiment with far less fear and more optimism.

I had two new phone clients that day, and their sessions were extremely coherent and laser-beam direct. Following my last session, I was given a powerful directive. I heard the call to phone one of my clients who had been suffering and perform a specific energetic treatment. I was shown the how-and-why details of the technique. As soon as I began the session, tears again began spilling down my cheeks. Transformation was happening not only *to* me, but more directly, *through* me. I was, once again, simply a conduit. The light at the end of the tunnel, like that of the *self-birthing-canal,* was shining on my face.

In that moment, being more of who I was becoming, became a beautiful thing.

My little epiphany showed me areas where I was holding duality. Seeing myself as a bridge between worlds for much of my life, I must have poured very deep footings on each side of that bridge. Yes, I could fit in on both sides of the bridge, but I felt called to span the whole of everything. Neither side completely represented who I am. Neither realm was tuned-in to my home frequency. And neither side was really working for me.

I am a scholar and a mystic.
I am science-minded and deeply spiritual.
I am a licensed medical professional and a gifted healer.
I am intelligent and creative.
I am masculine and feminine.
I am conservative and liberal.
I am global and local.

How could I assist others to move toward integration and unity—to experience oneness—when I held this self-imposed limitation on being who I really am in my own local community?

In a moment of doubt, I returned to my head and my egoic, Separate-Self voice began lamenting and judging:

If I can't experience this oneness in my own backyard, how can I facilitate global change? How can I support the vision of a planetary Pentecost and teach others to embody their higher consciousness, if I'm stuck in a lonely, isolated state—feeling sorry for myself and fearing persecution? How am I going to be seen, if I'm hiding in a closet? How much longer can I conceal a local self that fits in a nice, neat package of conformity, and a global self that feels like a heretic, hiding and morphing into a new way of being?

Julie, Stop.

Fear not. You are creating this duality in your mind. This is simply an illusion. You are perpetuating the very experience you teach others to release. Start by resolving this duality and separation within yourself first. You are limiting your potential with limiting beliefs about your situation. You are living the illusion of separation in your own safe, nurturing, and supportive backyard. Sure, you will not be seen and heard by everyone. That's okay. Not everyone will understand and get it. Not yet. And that's okay, too. Not everyone will like you. Will you be okay with that one?

Simply be who you are and love, honor, and cherish yourself with confidence as you love, honor, and cherish ALL those around you. You are loved and cherished. Come home, dear Julie, come home. Bring your magnificent, multidimensional genius and visionary prowess home. Fully embody this consciousness and let your infinite light shine. There's no need to hide or limit who you are. There's no need to apologize or carry shame. I am here. I am with you. I am always with you, within you. Go forward and fear not.

P.S. You're not that special. You're not that "different" from those around you. Stop judging. You've fallen into the spell of the ego in its attempt to perpetuate the illusion. It's okay. Be who you are and walk a new way.

This new normal was more like a "renewed natural." I was invited to simply remember and trust.

CHAPTER REFLECTIONS

I wanted life to stop. I wanted life to go back to the way it was before. I wanted an easy way out of this state—this limited, liminal place.

- We have all experienced hopeless, helpless moments where we can't see in the dark. We are all noticing that things don't work like they used to. Systems and structures built within a worldview of separation, fear, and lack are breaking down. They no longer serve us. As our consciousness evolves with the awakening of our interconnected universe and inherent unity, we desire whole-systems change and structures that better reflect who we are as whole beings. We are co-creating a culture of love and abundance, yet still waiting for our new normal to emerge in the collective. What in your life is no longer working like it used to? Where in your life are you feeling stuck in the dark? What is your new normal? What do you want the new normal of humanity to be? What do you want the new normal of your expression to be—cultural, vocational, political, economic, environmental, etc.? Better yet, what do you need in order to be ready to embrace the change that is *beyond* your imagining?

- Change is difficult. Shifting consciousness can be liberating and expansive, as well as overwhelming and scary. Einstein said, "No problem can be solved from the same level of consciousness that created it." And even though we may begin to see things in a new way, we don't usually rush right out and do life differently. Creating from a new level of consciousness takes practice and conscious commitment. Where are you being too cautious in your life? Where are you playing it safe? Where are you hiding—from yourself and others? Look for the areas in your life where you are trying to solve problems with the same consciousness that created them. Look closely. Be honest with yourself. Allow yourself to explore with *beginner's mind.*

- Liminal space—that point or threshold beyond our knowing and between here and there. It's not easy navigating change within liminal space. Work on your relationship with the unknown and your comfort with not knowing. Embracing this space makes it easier to count on the unseen and trust wisdom and intelligence beyond your limited mind.

CHAPTER NINE

Playing in the Unified Field

Living consciousness somehow is the influence that turns the possibility of something into something real. The most essential ingredient in creating our universe is the consciousness that observes it.

~ Lynne McTaggart

Over Christmas break, our family went on vacation. There were twenty-two of us representing four generations. We tried to schedule a variety of activities that would please everyone. There was recreation, history, entertainment, sports, shopping, art, culture, volunteer service, nature, dining, relaxation, celebration, and play. We did a pretty good job coming together at times and going our separate ways at others.

One day, seven of us went to an art museum. The rest went to a military aircraft museum. For me, this space spontaneously became a playground to practice weaving multidimensional consciousness. An art museum is like a candy shop for my soul. I found myself wandering off alone, taking in the experience of the art—drawn to certain pieces, put off by others. Certain colors, shapes, styles, and images attuned with my body. Others were discordant. I witnessed myself energetically drawn to different works of art like they were a cool spring of water on a hot desert day. I received the refreshing, resonant exchange as good medicine.

When I would meet up with a family member, consciousness would shift, and I would weave in who I was in the moment as aunt, mom, sister, and daughter. We would exchange words, compare experiences, and then wander apart again.

I continued moving into the experience beyond form and structure, beyond thought and ideas to really feel myself in relationship to the art. Bumping into people was a distraction, at first, until I organically began weaving the experience into a blended stream of flowing consciousness: *Think, feel, move, sense. Don't think. Just feel. Don't move. Just sense. Don't think or feel, just move within the sensing.* It was a curious process, this random emergence. I allowed my body to experience the art. At times, when my body was curious, I engaged my mind to read more about the piece. There were times I wanted to feel the artist's intention and explanation. But most of the time, I simply wanted to sense into the artwork and lose all sense of time and space. I was playing in the field and creating a multidimensional experience between two different realms.

Experiencing art through many different lenses and sensory perceptions, I noticed a weaving of higher cosmic consciousness into three-dimensional form, and then back out into the infinite. I played with it. When my mind wanted to think and ask questions, I followed the inquiry but didn't allow it to break the flow. I honored the mind and weaved it into the experience. I stayed in the flowing presence of now, until I wasn't, and then returned again.

I allowed the art to communicate, silencing my analytical mind and judgment. I simply felt into the art and had my experience of accessing a higher intelligence—a field of wisdom that the art and artist were a part of.

Many pieces intrigued my senses. But two, in particular, moved me deeply beyond time and space into a peculiar, ephemeral flow.

First, the artist, Yayoi Kusama, created an incredible, experiential exhibit called *You Who Are Getting Obliterated in the Dancing Swarm of Fireflies* (or *Fireflies*, for short). It's an infinity room—a pitch-black, mirrored room—with hundreds of dangling lights that change colors in a two-and-a-half-minute rotation.

When I walked in, I had to breathe into my anxiety from the disorientation, and consciously transition into the blackness of the artist's altered sense of reality. Once relaxed and re-oriented, I felt weightless, expansive, and cosmic. My fellow museum visitors were gawking, gazing, talking, giggling, and playing inside the exhibit. And they were part of the experience. The noise, the motion of lights, their hidden bodies, the audible voices . . . it all weaved together into the obliteration. There was delight, fear, panic, awe, even a loud bang with an embarrassed, "Ouch," as someone ran into a mirrored wall. It was magnificent. Brilliant. Transcendent.

Relaxing even more into *Fireflies*, I became part of the flowing dance. I experienced myself outside my body as a living, breathing element within the living, flowing sculpture. Waves of energy moved inside the abyss of mirrored light particles. I became expansive and infinite, if not cosmic. I was reflecting the light. I was absorbing the light. I was the light. I was the sculpture and dancing in a field of glowing fireflies. It was heavenly.

Next, there was the sacred sculpture by artist, Cornelia Parker, called *Mass*. I didn't know the name, the artist, or the story of the exhibit at the time. In fact, I didn't read the description card. I simply was present with the large sculpture made of wire, string, and hanging burnt wood. Black charcoal pieces hung eloquently, suspended in space, creating another transcendent form and structure, appearing to be a floating cube in space. The dark pieces against the light surroundings were striking—commanding attention. I stared, walked slowly, and changing perspectives, stared some more as I dissolved into the charred story. I stood in reverent silence, feeling a part of the piece.

There was something magical about this exhibit, something of divine essence. An experience of flowing presence morphed into sacred geometry. Losing track of all time and space, I tapped into a weaving and felt the wood particles speaking to me. There was beauty within random chaos and pain within the collective order. Present to the experience, I was swept into a larger expression of flow, energy, and haunting presence.

I was drawn into a mystery and allowed myself to become the mystery itself. I was the art—creating and building a profound experience by allowing the haunting burned wood to express itself through me. I was the tree. I was the logger. I was the wood. I was the carpenter. I was the fire. There was sadness, a deep grief, and a sense of death. There was also joy and gratitude and an experience of transformation, resurrection, and hope. There was peace.

That was my favorite exhibit of the day. When I shifted back into a mindful space, I took pictures: large pieces, small pieces, individual pieces, the collection as a whole, lines, shapes, and textures. I moved from the deep, reflective *Mass* experience, into the *Fireflies* portal, and then back to *Mass* again.

Leaving the art museum, we quickly transitioned and made our way to an NBA basketball game. Someone asked on the drive over, "What do you do at an art museum?" How was I to answer that question?

The next day, as we all were reflecting on our experiences, the *Mass* exhibit came up in conversation. Among those of us attending the art museum, it was clearly one of our collective favorites. Someone described the exhibit to our family and explained that it was burned wood retrieved from a Baptist church in Texas that had been struck by lightning. Ah, yes! A church. It all made more sense. I had goose bumps and another moment of recognition. The rekindled *Mass* experience hauntingly lasted for days, smoldering in my consciousness.

—

An Invitation to Now

Art is one path that can lead us into the flowing presence of now, somewhere beyond boundaries and beliefs, out beyond thought, time, and space. There are many paths into this creative stream of consciousness. It's been called flow, the zone, bliss, oneness, infinite wisdom, unlimited potentiality, divine intelligence, and an altered state of consciousness. What if "the zone" is really an experiential encounter or union with the unified field of consciousness? Creating and experiencing art, music, poetry, theatre, cinema, sports, intimacy, worship, nature, meditation, and more, can all induce that transcendent state of communion: a moment of grace, an unmerited glimpse of our inter-being with the divine in all things.

> The flowing presence of now . . . I'm going to talk more about the flow state. But for now, I want to pause and remind you of the significant power you have by harnessing the *now*. Your co-creative power isn't in thoughts about the past or dreams about the future. Your power is in the perennial moment of NOW.

This is the realm where consciousness—our awareness—meets the unified field in the flowing presence of now. Therefore, the invitation is to bring our awareness into the present moment, and then transcend the moment into a flowing state of timelessness. In flowing presence, the field beyond boundaries and beliefs beckons to be discovered. Rumi's poetic image encourages us to move beyond the cognitive functions of our small, limited minds, beyond time and space, and open to our spiritual experience beyond the constriction of a three-dimensional, physical world.

What would it be like to truly bring spirit and consciousness into every aspect of life, vocation, and relationship? What would it be like to transcend even mindfulness and present moment awareness? What would it be like to live so fully and completely in a flow state that the unified field is our default, our preferred and normal playground? Is it possible to resolve the limitations and conflict of our dualistic nature and ignite an awakening that would evolve consciousness and create a new paradigm of our wholeness?

During my out-of-body-experience at the age of eleven, I saw humanity moving into this new state of being. My continued dance with a flow state and the unified field has affirmed my sense of faith and hope that this is a real and viable transformation.

People would talk about the second coming of Christ and say they would never see it in their lifetimes. I would grin and hear within, *You might be surprised. It isn't what you "think."* Others would discuss the state of our world, the breakdown of systems, and the direction in which we are headed as a species. I would hold the vision of the earth like a snow globe in my hands and see people *waking* one-by-one and igniting a shift; I would see people harnessing higher levels of Christ Consciousness—in the flow state—affecting all things around them; I would see a grid of pulsing light and love spreading across the planet; I would see the template of woven light creating a palpable field of greater harmonic resonance; I would see consciousness evolve and humanity wake to remember its higher potential. This vision still guides my life. I want others to experience this field and vision.

There are many varying terms and definitions being used in New Age, science, consciousness, and spiritual circles that can be confusing: quantum field, unified field, zero-point field, noosphere, collective unconscious, pure consciousness, the ultimate field of

Being, resonant field, transcendental field, nonlocal consciousness, nonlocal mind, undivided wholeness, prior unity, flowing presence, a unified continuum of energy, the akash, Love, God, Christ Consciousness, and more. Let us not get caught up in definitions or stuck in the "boundaries and beliefs" that Rumi expressed. We are all trying to name and define the mysteries of the universe. Whether we look through the lens of science, spirituality, culture, mysticism, religion, or personal experience, let us rest and relax into the mystery as *it* defines us.

◆

An Invisible Core

We are pointing to an unseen realm of mystery, an invisible core of interconnectedness. Perhaps the different definitions are fragmented pieces of understanding within a unified whole? Perhaps they're all the same thing? Most refer to a wholeness and a reservoir of magnificent intelligence and animating power—a field of all knowing.

Dutch cardiologist, author, and researcher in the field of near-death experiences, Pim van Lommel said, "The mind seems to contain everything at once in a timeless and placeless interconnectedness … The information is not encoded in a medium but is stored nonlocally as wave functions in nonlocal space, which also means that all information is always and everywhere immediately available."

He explains that these wave functions, which store all aspects of consciousness in the form of information, are always present in and around the body. He postulates that the brain and body merely function as a relay station, sending and receiving information in constantly changing electromagnetic fields.

From a scientific perspective, Nikola Tesla agrees. In a famous quote, he said, "My brain is only a receiver, in the Universe there is a core from which we obtain knowledge, strength, and inspiration. I have not penetrated into the secrets of this core, but I know that it exists." Nassim Haramein has often said that looking for consciousness in the brain is like looking inside a radio for the announcer.

Author and researcher, Lynne McTaggart, explains in her book, *The Field*: "Some scientists went as far as to suggest that all of our higher cognitive processes result from an interaction with the field. This kind of constant interaction might account for intuition or creativity—and how ideas come to us in bursts of insight, sometimes in fragments but often as a miraculous whole. An intuitive leap might simply be a sudden coalescence of coherence in the Field."

Spiritual leader and developer of Transcendental Meditation, Maharishi Mahesh Yogi, saw this unified field as having the dual characteristics of existence and intelligence. He explained, "The unified field is fundamentally a field of consciousness. The field is known as atman, meaning 'pure consciousness,' or 'self,' since the unified field constitutes the deepest reality and hence the true identity of everything in nature."

I love the idea that everything exists at once in a timeless and placeless interconnectedness in and around our body, and that unified field is pure consciousness—our deepest reality—our true nature. Being present to this realm means losing ourselves and our individual identities outside of time and space, and bringing our awareness fully into the timeless, placeless, flowing presence. This presence—the Field—is an active participant of our co-creative experience.

Creation takes place amidst a background sea of energy, which metaphysics might call the Force, and scientists call the "Field." (Officially the Zero-Point Field) There is no empty space, even the darkest empty space is actually a cauldron of energies. Matter is simply concentrations of this energy (particles are just little knots of energy.) All life is energy (light) interacting. The universe is self-regenerating and eternal, constantly refreshing itself and in touch with every other part of itself instantaneously. Everything in it is giving, exchanging and interacting with energy, coming in and out of existence at every level. The self has a field of influence on the world and vice versa based on this energy.

~ Lynne McTaggart

Finding Flow—States of Consciousness

Many access and have a relationship with this unified field in myriad ways and experiences. There are just as many different altered and non-ordinary states of consciousness, as there are the definitions of the unified field—awakening and oneness experiences, mystical experience, out-of-body experience, near-death experience, nonlocal states, and bilocation are a few.

States of consciousness can come and go like waves in the ocean. Different states of consciousness are experienced throughout life and are often induced through spiritual practices like meditation and prayer, physical practices like yoga and exercise, communion with nature, the arts, relationships, intimacy, spontaneous random events, religious experience, trauma, and drug-induced experiences.

Stanislav "Stan" Grof, psychiatrist, researcher, and one of the founders of the field of transpersonal psychology, is a leading authority in the field of non-ordinary states of consciousness (NOSC). In an interview with Walter Mead, he explained:

> NOSC are characterized by dramatic perceptual changes, intense, and often unusual, emotions, profound alterations in the thought processes and behavior, and by a variety of psychosomatic manifestations. The emotions can range from profound terror to ecstatic rapture, and the content of these experiences is often spiritual or mystical. It involves sequences of psychological death and rebirth and a broad spectrum of transpersonal phenomena, including feelings of oneness with other people, nature, the universe, and God, past life experiences, and visions of archetypal beings and mythological landscapes as described by C.G. Jung. There exist many different forms of NOSC; they can be induced by a variety of different techniques or occur spontaneously, in the middle of everyday life. (http://www.stanislavgrof.com/wpcontent/uploads/2015/02/Healing-Potential-of-NOS_Grof.pdf)

Flowing presence or a "flow state" is one expression. It is a bit different than present moment awareness and mindfulness. Mindfulness is a mental state achieved by focusing one's awareness on the present moment, while calmly acknowledging and accepting one's feelings, thoughts, and bodily sensations. It is often used as a therapeutic technique and meditation practice that brings inner peace.

Mindfulness brings us fully into the present moment through our five senses and the body, while training the mind to let go of judgment, analysis, projections, and comparisons. The goal is to "be here now," without worrying or projecting into the future or lamenting and reliving the past. Here, we get in touch with the awareness behind the thoughts that arise. This is the initial stage of conscious living—being at one with the present, rather than being controlled by the ego and trapped in time. This present moment awareness creates a sense of peace and aliveness.

A flow state, also known as "the zone," is the mental state of functioning in which a person is fully immersed in a feeling or experience of energized focus, full emergence, or active involvement. The person can get lost in the enjoyment of the process or experience of the activity. The flow state, or being in the zone, marks a complete and often spontaneous absorption in a process with little, if any, thinking or awareness of self. There is a deep focus on nothing but the experience itself, often triggering a pure state of joy, bliss, and heightened sense of unity with all things. This experience moves people to feel like they are in a realm outside of time and space— outside their finite body and their five senses—and in a flowing stream of life force as it moves and flows.

New technologies, consciousness exercises, and spiritual practices are assisting not only those exploring consciousness, but also athletes to access the flow state on command. No longer do we believe that getting in the zone is a serendipitous, spontaneous moment of epiphany in sports or a rare mystical experience in life. Scientists, psychologist, athletes, and coaches are learning how to harness the benefits of the flow state and train the mind/body to stabilize it. Being in the zone is another way to play in the unified field.

Back in the art museum, I was practicing mindful, present moment awareness and getting lost in a flow state. Moving back and forth between these states created a playful joy that was intoxicating.

I often experience the flow when in nature and through the arts. The first experience I remember of the flow state in sports was when I was seventeen years old. I began running the summer between my junior and senior year in high school. I remember the moment I switched out of my five-sensory awareness and all the physical sensations within my body, and entered the flow/zone. One moment I was hot, tired, breathless, sweaty, hurting, and in my head, complaining and wondering why I was running in the first place, and the next I was in a weightless state of bliss, feeling powerful and invincible. My body became one with the road, and I felt as if I could run forever and never stop. This "runner's high" was magical. I was no longer "thinking" about running, the gravel road, the time of day, my tired body, or my breath. It was like the physical process of running joined my breathing, heartbeat, and digestive processes, and became part of my autonomic nervous system on autopilot.

It's exciting to know that athletic coaches and trainers are learning how to coach athletes to enter this magical zone. *The Sports, Energy, and Consciousness Group* is leading the way in those efforts. They are an integrated collective of doctors, psychologists, scientists, world-class athletes, and leading-edge coaches with a mission to do more than just explore the flow state. Their mission is to accelerate the global evolution of human consciousness by providing transformational practices that translate the wisdom of sport's Ideal Performance State (IPS) into practical training methods that include energetics, awakened states of consciousness, and the unification of body, mind, and spirit.

Other scientists, researchers, and groups are exploring the accessing of the unified field as a collective experience. From group prayer and intention experiments to circle technologies and group resonance projects, groundbreaking research, technology, and social systems are demonstrating the dynamics of our interconnected, interrelationship with all things and our capacity to move into harmonious, coherent relationships with one another, nature, the earth and the universe as a whole. This body of knowledge, emerging technology, and social forms based on a holistic worldview are assisting to find evolutionary solutions for the critical and systemic challenges we are facing on our planet.

More than just a religious or spiritual experience, playing in the unified field is garnering new levels of collective genius and powerful forms of co-creation. Creating a resonant field in community opens the experience to transcend individual identity, agenda, and ego, and moves the group to an ascended realm where universal, collective wisdom can emerge. Work groups, organizations, businesses, and communities are developing the practices of *group resonance* and *field consciousness*. This union is creating a new understanding of consciousness in the world.

The Global Coherence Initiative (GCI), a part of HeartMath Institute is one such organization. They are helping people not only create deep resonance, but nurture a coherent, heart-based connection with others and the earth. The Global Coherence Initiative seeks to "activate the heart of humanity and promote peace, harmony, and a shift in global consciousness"; they seek to demonstrate that "increasing heart connections will lead to intuitive solutions for global challenges and the transformation of our world and consciousness."

States of consciousness are transient. But stages, levels, or structures of consciousness are more fixed or permanent, more like developmental milestones we reach. They represent a measure of growth and maturity. Arrival at one stage signals a new kind of awareness of self and the world. States of consciousness are interpreted within these developmental stages, therefore, contributing to the plethora of differing reports and descriptions of non-ordinary states of consciousness.

The leading edge of human evolution is occurring in the space between us. Mutual awakening is powerful, effortless, and multidimensionally transformative. From this shared consciousness, new possibilities for humanity arise.

~ Patricia Albere

The beautiful thing, in my opinion, is that we don't have to figure it all out. Personal experience is personal experience. There is no *one* right way or wrong way to be in the world; no right or wrong way of awakening or playing in the unified field; no right or wrong spiritual path or practice; no better or worse level of consciousness. Understanding states and stages of consciousness as developmental and different aspects of the same thing can move us into a place of compassion and tolerance. Let us not judge, strive, or create more boundaries and beliefs. Let us relax into a full honoring of this evolutionary path of development, as creation continues to create through us.

There is a lot to be hopeful for in this fast-paced world of dramatic change. But we mustn't get stuck in our "ideas of wrongdoing and rightdoing." And we mustn't rely solely on our individual selves, independent and alone, to "be the change we wish to see in the world" (Gandhi). We have the field to play in—an infinite source of potentiality and universal intelligence—within and around us—at our disposal in any given moment. And we have others. Look around. People are gathering, connecting, and co-creating everywhere. In fact, conscious communities are organizing on every continent of the earth—in person, in community, and virtually. Technology is supporting the emergence via the Internet. Relax. Witness how like-minded individuals attract one another. Trust. This divine intelligence is flowing. We are waking and we are growing. Creation is creating through us, in us, and as us. We *are* the unified field playing within itself.

*People without faith walk around with their eyes technically
open, yet remain blind to the helping hands of God and the
universe trying to reach out to them.*

~ Anthony William

CHAPTER REFLECTIONS

*There is no one right way or wrong way to be in the world;
no right or wrong way of awakening or playing in the unified
field; no right or wrong spiritual path or practice; no better or
worse level of consciousness. Understanding states and stages
of consciousness as developmental and different aspects of
the same thing can move us into a place of compassion and
tolerance. Let us not judge, strive, or create more boundaries and
beliefs. Let us relax into a full honoring of this evolutionary path
of development, as creation continues to create through us.*

- Non-ordinary states of consciousness are different than developmental stages of consciousness. We all have moments of non-ordinary states—from simple daydreaming and dreaming during sleep to blissful moments in meditation. There's shamanic healing, mysticism, Kundalini yoga, usage of hallucinatory plants, and ecstatic religious experiences. You don't have to have a near-death experience or out-of-body experience to feel the unity and communion with all that is. We all have this potential as whole-beings within creative consciousness. Once again, revisit the idea of experienced non-ordinary states of consciousness. Write about it in as much detail as you can remember. Tune into the experience and focus on grace and benevolence. What gift did the experience leave with you?

- When we learn how to relax into the mystery of life, the mystery, itself, opens and reveals more to us. Learn to treasure the unknown zone. Develop a welcoming relationship with the mystery. Moments of flowing presence come when we surrender to that which we cannot understand with our rational minds. We must get out of our heads. Think back on artistic and/or athletic performances. Describe a time you have been in the zone. Now, in what other ways have you experienced the zone or moments of flowing presence? Describe a moment of flowing presence. Describe a time when you relaxed into the mystery of life. How did you feel? What did you learn? Are there words to describe it? Play with this idea. Take a moment in nature, sports, or the arts and intentionally play with the unified field and different states of consciousness.

- Co-creative groups are emerging everywhere. People are gathering in communities to intentionally share the "we space" of the field and co-create together. New techniques and technologies are being used to harness the art and power of co-creation. If you are a part of a co-creative group with practices and tools to presence the unified field, write about your experience. Different tools and techniques work differently for different people, and resonance with the others in the group is essential. Notice what works well for you and what doesn't. Notice how you relax when you're in resonance with others. Notice what dissonance in the group feels like. What are your personal favorites and what are your stumbling blocks. There are many resources for more information on co-creative groups and how to start one of your own.

CHAPTER TEN

Authentic Connection

We often forget our human connectedness . . . This connection is a powerful thing, with the ability to transform lives, and ultimately transform human experience.

~ Kristi Bowman

When I first discovered social media, I began networking and connecting with powerful women from across America and Europe. I could see how the Internet and social media were potential replicas of the template I saw in my vision. Energy naturally began to pulse into this greater field of opportunity, and I was in awe at how connected one could feel. I wondered what would manifest with this new kind of relationship and where we were going with this technology.

I teamed up with my friend, Sherryl Lin (whom I met online), and we completed a cross-country tour called the Let It Shine Road Trip, in conjunction with a five-city, Awesome Women Hub live event. I was meeting incredible women, face-to-face, after connecting virtually. I naturally began expanding my interests, developing my voice, and reaching out more. My vocational career began accelerating in new directions. Who would have imagined social media would afford me such opportunities? Not me. Yet, I could see social media in a multidimensional way. It became a readily available, user-friendly tool to connect with others and express.

Organically, I developed a platform that others could relate to, without even knowing what I was doing. I began teaching online and holding space for individuals and groups to explore consciousness, spirituality, and healing. As my online community grew, virtual clients emerged. My traditional psychotherapy, healing, and spiritual-direction practice was spontaneously evolving and morphing into a higher form all by itself.

At the same time, my new conscious tribe was growing with all the people I was meeting. It was comforting to stay connected in shared purpose and vision. We all felt called to give our gifts to this shift on the planet. It was profound. We had so much in common and needed to tell a new story.

Without me realizing it, a larger, more connected, personal world began to weave and converge. Connections of light and heart were being made. Creation was creating through me. I learned quickly to follow the resonance as ideas, opportunities, and guidance continued to present.

One of those opportunities was radio. Several emails showed up inviting me to have my own radio show. My rational mind thought it was absurd. I never conceived of myself as a radio talk show host. I was often a guest on other people's shows, and I saw myself doing television, along with speaking to live audiences. But talk radio?

I ignored the emails for months. And then one day, I went into my office to find a message on the answering machine. It was a producer from New York City. He wanted to talk to me about being the guest expert on a reality television series he was producing for the Oprah Winfrey Network. Oprah Winfrey Network? Reality TV? That rattled my awareness into submission. I felt like I was being asked to wake up and pay attention. What were these media invitations about? Was it time to take a leap of faith and do something new? I said yes, and the next day, I got another call about hosting my own radio program and *The Dr. Julie Show: All Things Connected* was born.

I knew I was to tell the story of those on the leading edge of personal, social, and global transformation. Our world desperately needed to hear good news of humanity's social and spiritual potential. I saw the show making connections that would inspire and accelerate individual and collective awakening. I began inviting visionary leaders and change makers from around the world to address a myriad of subjects related to my theme of interconnection. I wanted to explore social change, the generative power of conscious, co-creative practice, and what is emergent with health, science, spirituality, and the evolution of consciousness. I wanted to, literally, break through the illusion of separation with each show and explore the infinite field of possibilities with my guests.

Pre-show production began. I was scared to death. I had no idea what I was doing. Nonetheless, I had two great coaches in the early days: Dr. Pat, the owner of the first network I was with, and David, a friend and former radio personality. So I began booking guests—calling people I knew and reaching out to others I didn't. And in less than a year, everything came full circle for me when Dr. Joan Borysenko's publicist contacted me asking if I would host Joan to talk about her new book on my show. For decades, Joan had been my mentor, teacher, and mind/body medicine idol. It was in her intensive training where I had one of the most powerful, prophetic visions and healing. *All Things Connected* was reconnecting something within me.

I have had the honor and joy of hosting many incredible guests as varied as the number of books on my bookshelf. The show has afforded me greater connection. Most of my guests share a deep purpose and mission to assist in this great awakening, this remembering, this global transformation. I love the varied responses I get when I ask, "What does *all things connected* mean to you?"

Besides all the incredible discoveries being made by science and all the sacred teachings of spirituality that speak to the same, *All Things Connected* is also about relationship—our relationship with all things. This is an important conversation on the planet right now. Relationship is everything, and it's time to teach conscious choice, conscious love, and conscious reconnection. We affect change, and it's imperative that we take responsibility for our actions and choices, or lack thereof. Our mindless actions affect everything around us the same as our conscious choices do.

Spiritual Community as a Conscious Choice

Recovering from the multiple bone fractures was a wake-up call—an invitation to look at my own relationships—my relationship to myself, my body, those around me, and Earth. In my work, I encourage others to develop intentional, co-creative lives, to align with spirit, attune to their hearts, live in harmony with nature, and maintain resonance with others. The time I had spent in my chair gave me endless opportunities to reflect on this. And months into my recovery process, I had a huge realization. Not only was I afraid to be fully who I was—the visionary mystic—but also, where was my *local spiritual community* in this time of need?

When I broke my leg, my sister and my husband were amazing. All my basic needs were cared for. It was eye-opening to be in witness of the care I received. Other family members brought in a few meals, a few friends came to visit right away, and I got phone calls and cards from other friends. I continued to get on weekly calls with my global tribe, so I felt very connected, loved, and cared for there. In fact, my global friends were absolutely incredible at expressing love, care, healing, and concern. From them, I received a plethora of healing gifts.

Yet, I wasn't feeling the *presence* of my local spiritual community. They didn't reach out or show up. A few individuals asked my husband and sister how I was doing, and some sent Facebook well wishes if I posted some sort of update. But other than that, there was a huge void.

At first, I felt sad. Then my sadness moved to a deep grief as I realized the absence of authentic, meaningful connection and relationship within my lifelong community of faith. My grief evolved into a serious inquiry of my faith, the meaning of authentic connection, and a closer look at myself in relationship to the community: What kind of friend and community member was I? How do I respond when friends and congregational members are in need? How do I connect and stay connected with spiritual community?

For decades, as an adult, I had attended and served my community of faith in myriad ways. I was a devout and faithful servant, attended worship and activities, read lessons, and assisted with Communion. I taught classes and sponsored the youth for over twenty cumulative years. I also served the larger church body for decades in a couple of different leadership and service roles.

But when someone was on the local prayer list, did I send a card, make a call and go visit, or take a meal? Sometimes. Depended on how well I knew them. After gathering for weekly services, did I reach out to connect with individuals? Not really. While attending services and events, did I make a deep heart-to-heart connection with others? Well? Rarely. Things pretty much stayed social and on the surface. I take full responsibility for this. I failed to live for the good of the whole church.

Living for the *'good of the whole'* pertains to families, groups, organizations, and communities of all types and sizes. If you belong and are a member of a group, pause and reflect on how you affect the good of the whole. Do your thoughts, words and deeds align with and reflect your highest service in relationship to the whole? Your experience with any organization is dependent on how you see your role. Are you serving yourself or in a healthy, reciprocal relationship serving the whole?

I desired deeper spiritual intimacy. I craved a soul-to-soul connection within this community. I wanted to engage in conscious conversation about real, authentic God moments, spiritual topics, and real life. I wanted to come out of the "mystical closet" and share my reality and experiences. But never had I felt a safe, resonant, conducive, or fertile environment for such depth of communication and literal communion within my local faith community.

Thinking back on all the individual encounters over the years when I had tried to engage at this level, I realized that all the conversations, all the attempts to make authentic connection, after just a few minutes of sharing, had fallen flat. I remember one interim pastor warning me to stay true to the teachings of the church, another pastor cautioning me to stay away from New Age thinking, and another's glazed-over, blank stare when I began talking about my near-death experience. I wanted to be more of who I was within that setting and explore the deep mysteries in communion with others, but the container was always too small and squeezed me out as I tried to fit in. I wanted to talk about how Jesus loved and lived and healed. How he created miracles. It seemed like I would attempt to open the mystic's closet door, and others, made uncomfortable, would stuff me back in and shut the door. Obviously, my authentic, expanded self didn't fit in, and I quit trying.

Ironically, my global tribe is a spiritual community. My long-distance friends and I have self-organized practices, calls, and structures to stay deeply connected and in heart resonance. We prioritize and practice creating high levels of resonance and maintaining a loving, heart connection. We speak truth with love and trust so that any discordant energy will be smoothed out and resolved quickly. We share from a deep place of trust and vulnerability. We are authentic and transparent. We ask for what we need and respond to the needs of others. We have agreements and mutual intentions. We have shared purpose and values. We are an interfaith, interspiritual tribe, very respectful of one another's paths and supportive of exploring and understanding our unique differences and beliefs.

I asked myself, *How can this be? How can one feel so connected and close to friends rarely seen face-to-face? How can one feel so disconnected and invisible within a face-to-face community of faith?* My answer: intentional heart connection and deep resonance.

Creating Heart Resonance

In physics and in music, *resonance* is the reinforcement or prolongation of sound by reflection from a surface or by the synchronous vibration of a neighboring object. Resonance *attunes* and makes harmonious. In relationships, creating resonance is essential. It helps to move us out of our head and our thoughts and into our hearts where we can feel one another.

Several years ago, I was at a retreat with many of my global friends. I was sitting in a restaurant with three other people having a nice conversation. A friend from Germany arrived and came to find us. In his overwhelming excitement, he arrived at the table and began talking and talking and talking—very fast and with passion and purpose, trying to connect. A friend from the UK sitting next to me went into a trancelike stare. Her eyes glazed over, and she looked like she was going to fall asleep. All of sudden, the friend from Germany noticed.

He stopped talking and asked her whether she was okay. She gently and compassionately responded, "I can't feel you." Immediately, the energy shifted as they looked into each other's eyes and established a deep, heart connection. The rest of our time together was precious.

Resonance and heart coherence is being taught by many organizations. One of the leading authorities on the subject is the HeartMath Institute out of Boulder Creek, California, which I mentioned earlier. They are a research- and education-based organization that helps people of all ages to reconnect with their hearts, rebalance and rejuvenate by reducing stress, and learn to self-regulate emotions. HeartMath has made important scientific contributions related to stress, the power of positive emotions, and heart-brain interactions, as well as the emerging fields of intuition and human energetics. They are exploring the intelligence and capabilities of the human heart, and how we are interconnected. Overall, heart coherence is found to decrease stress and increase energy, creativity, intuition, flow, and cognitive functioning. It has dramatically improved health, mood, and sleep for many.

> The Global Coherence Initiative, an initiative of HeartMath Institute, is measuring changes in the earth's magnetic field, and hypothesizes that people's individual coherence can affect the earth's energy field, ultimately advancing world peace.

Establishing a heart connection between people is a valuable practice that has potential to change the world. And like HeartMath says, it "connects us with the heart of 'who we truly are,' helping us to live healthier, happier, and more fulfilling lives while building a brighter future."

My relationship to my local spiritual community was missing the heart connection—missing heart resonance. Was that just my story and my personal experience? I'm not sure. It was an important question for me to explore. But what I *did* know is that authentic heart connection is important, and essential to me. Thus, I began to question all my relationships and take a deeper look at the quality of connection.

Authentic connection is vital in a community. It also creates resilience and sustainability.

Resilience

As a young psychotherapist, I was on the board of a local agency that reached out to at-risk youth. As part of the commitment, we did some extensive training on resilience. What do we know about resilience? Even decades later, the research still says the same thing: the foundation of resilience for at-risk children rests in relationships—positive, affirming connection with others. Youth who have strong relational connections in their homes, schools, and communities have higher overall achievement. We know that just one, single, authentic connection can make a world of difference to a child. But the more connections, the better the outcomes. Simply put, human connection is essential to our functioning—to our survival.

In this age of technology and the Internet, we are more connected now than ever before. Nonetheless, we are not yet proficient at making those authentic heart connections through technology and social media, or in person. We are figuring it out, though. Incredible technologies, practices and techniques are emerging on the planet that assist in creating sacred space, connecting in shared intention, engaging in prayer and meditation, and joining our passion and genius with others in co-creative play and work. Beautiful platforms and apps are popping up every day. There is a lot of good happening in our world. You can find an extensive list of resources on www.GOODoftheWHOLE.com.

But let us not forget the face-to-face authentic connection. Learning to love the ones we're with and love our neighbors is crucial. These times call for us to demonstrate kindness. Show compassion. Get interested and take the time to make an authentic connection and have a conversation. If the key to at-risk kids' health, well-being, and success is connection and relationships, then I would advocate the same for our world at large.

Authentic Connection with Soul and Purpose

All this connectivity and creativity is for nothing, if we're not connected with our own divine essence. I like to call this our "soul-esteem," rather than our self-esteem. We all have a higher calling that will lead us into awakened action and enlightened service. We enter the call through the heart and land it in the body. The how and why of what we are here to do rarely emerges from thought or thinking about what we want. It naturally flows when we are aligned with our heart, soul, and unique gifts.

As a young professional, I had many aspirations. In my pursuit to be the best at everything I did, I was going for it! My first professional job landed a quick promotion into management. And that promotion led to a job offer with a bigger organization. I was on my way somewhere, though not considering my soul's desire or calling. I was simply advancing my career. That's what a young twenty-something is supposed to do, right? Within the first year,

I was recruited into a position I had never imagined for myself. I was good at what I did. Actually, I was really good at what I did. And that led to the organization creating a new, more prestigious department and function, asking me to run it.

My masculine drive was activated. My ego was on board. I was on a fast track to success, climbing the corporate ladder. Within a few years of entering the professional work force, I was making great pay, wielding power within a large organization, and exercising significant influence with high-level professionals. While I was not doing anything for which I had trained, I was respected for my professional integrity and unique skill set.

At this level, I was part of a strategic team that influenced many lives and businesses within our region. And sadly, I saw the shadow side of ego and corporate greed rear its ugly head. Decisions weren't always easy, and once made, definitely not always popular. I was into pleasing people and had a unique way of helping in any situation. You could count on me to be a calming presence in the storm, whether I was engaged in a heated boardroom discussion, or a tense, negotiations meeting with political powerhouses. I surprised myself and didn't realize how caught up in the corporate culture I was.

My boss was horribly abusive. He used inappropriate, vulgar language, kicked doors, and threw temper tantrums. I remained calm and tried to ignore the uproar. I was good at tuning out negative emotions and behavior.

Of interest, my body began talking to me. But I still hadn't learned how to listen. I began spotting between menstrual cycles. I thought little of it, but reported it to my gynecologist. After months of this, he became concerned. It wasn't normal. Test after test showed something wasn't quite right, but no clear diagnosis was formulated.

No big deal. I ignored it. I was also good at tuning out my body and ignoring symptoms after my early childhood near-death experience. Besides, I was a young working mom with two small children, as well as an ambitious professional with a full-time career and a part-time private practice. I was too busy to tune in and listen. Actually, I had no idea I was even supposed to. My inner work ethic said, "Work hard and keep going."

After a year of receiving doctoring with these strange, ongoing gynecological symptoms and increasing regular pain, a surprise pregnancy occurred. I experienced significant early complications and was ordered bed rest. Predictions of a premature birth and need for medications kept me cautious. I was forced to slow down. I was compliant, as the Fierce-Feminine-Momma-Bear in me waged a fight for the pregnancy. The health of my baby came first. I carried him to term, and we had an overdue, healthy, *big* baby boy.

During the pregnancy though, something more woke in me. My fierce, feminine warrior, my urge toward a sense of maternal fight continued stirring beyond the pregnancy. The world began to feel different. The job began to feel different. My boss was the same, but my working relationships began to feel different. And my uterus continued to weep, even after the pregnancy . . . month-by-month . . . spotting . . . day-by-day. My soul began to speak, and I began to listen.

Julie, why would you allow anyone to treat you like that? To speak to you like that? You wouldn't allow anyone to treat your children like that, would you? You would protect them with your life. Wake up. You don't deserve this. This is an old script running from your childhood. It's time to heal this old pattern. You can no longer fall silent in your ragdoll mode and allow abuse of any kind. Wake up. What are you going to do? It is time to transcend these old patterns and align with your higher purpose.

Higher purpose? Oh, yeah. My childhood out-of-body experiences laid out a clear vocational path for me. How did I stray so far away from this calling?

Recommended surgery and a six-week medical leave gave me time to heal physically, emotionally, and spiritually. I began visioning and dreaming into my higher purpose, into my values and future potential—my divine blueprint. I learned to be still and listen to my body as well as that still small voice again. There was a deep honoring for all my body had endured and all the wisdom my body held. There was grief over how I'd neglected and abandoned myself. The grief lasted quite a bit longer. This situation showed me how *self-abusive* I had become. I had ignored my own truth and got caught up in an ugly, unhealthy miasma of masculine drive. I had climbed the corporate ladder, and it was leaning on the wrong wall!

When we tune into our life purpose, and pay attention to what calls us, we are tuning into the impulse of Creation. I said yes to the impulse within me. Within a year, I left that job, began working on my doctorate, and was guided deep into the study of mind/body medicine. I embraced my feminine and began a new healing relationship with my body.

> Life purpose—living with purpose—has become a hot topic. There are many Life Coaches, Spiritual Directors, spiritual teachers and mentors available to help you discern purpose and how to tune into the soul's calling. Find a guide that you feel resonant with and enjoy the exploration.

In fact, I shifted to the opposite extreme along the masculine/feminine spectrum. I rebelled against masculine energy and masculine-type systems and structures. I turned 180 degrees and began an extreme feminine recovery process, reclaiming my feminine with my body and soul. There was much to heal and overcome, as I had little experience with self-love, self-compassion, and self-nurturing. I had compromised my connection with my higher self.

Saying, "Yes!" to the impulse of Creation within me activated something deeper and greater. Seeds were sown and the field was cultivated. Change changed me. And an intimate, authentic relationship with myself began. I had much to learn, much to heal, and much to remember.

I discovered how developing an intimate, authentic relationship with myself was essential before I could develop intimate, authentic relationships with others. In my study of human development and relations, we focused primarily on infant and child development, the aging adult (mostly gerontology), and parent and family-life education. What about the in-between stages? Where were integral theory, eco-spirituality, the stages of psycho-spiritual development, levels of consciousness, and all the yummy holistic models? There is a span of four to five decades during which a rich and adventurous unfolding begins for most adults, and I had to begin my own self-exploration into psychospiritual development and the evolution of consciousness.

We are pioneers of our own conscious lives and relationships. Developing the ego and then transcending and including ego into a higher consciousness is crucial. Spiritual development and our relationships to Source are paramount. Returning home to connect with the earth and all the bountiful gifts of our interdependence is basic. Understanding mindful, present moment awareness, transformative practices, our creative potential, and the evolution of consciousness is key. This all is part of our adult spiritual development. Growing up, waking up, cleaning up, and showing up (Ken Wilber) as a species are essential in creating sustainable peace and functional justice in our world.

Authentic connection with *all that is* appears to be a most poignant prescription. *All Things Connected* is more than a catchy phrase for a radio show. It is a powerful meme that has the potential to move us into remembering our wholeness, our inherent unity, and our authentic true nature.

Back in my chair and the healing of my leg, I was invited to look deeper into the sympathetic threads that weave us together and walk a new way in relationship to all those around me. Moving deeper into a conscious, authentic relationship with my body and soul, I could take direct responsibility for my creative actions and experiences in a way that appeared so prescriptive and nourishing. Nurturing conscious relationship, with all that is, became a healing balm that stirred a profound, *living presence* within me. I began paying attention to human connection everywhere I went and in all my interactions, both local and global.

Inspiring Human Connection

My husband and I enjoyed a company trip to a beautiful Cancun resort. Upon arriving, we received bright-green wristbands in our welcome packet. We were told to wear the wristbands at all times, especially to meals and group events to help identify ourselves as "part of the group." I was on crutches and pushed in a wheelchair to get around the gorgeous resort. That in itself, draws lots of attention. But I watched as something else unfolded.

Early the next morning, we went down for breakfast. As we proceeded along the long corridor to our ocean-side breakfast destination, I noticed a peculiar trend. People wearing green wristbands were smiling and greeting each other with a friendly recognition and a confident cheerful, "Good Morning!" When there was no wristband, there was no greeting. The bearers of the band would literally walk by naked wrists, turning their heads the opposite direction, not even making eye contact.

Throughout the day, I watched as complete strangers began conversations initiated by a green-wristband association, while others wandered around in silence and avoidance. In the busy, populated beachfront area, community was born with a color—a rubber bracelet—labeling and defining our connection. We were a group, a green-band-induced community. The public tag of association turned previous strangers into friends. Our trademark gave us an assurance that we had something in common and invited us to strike up a conversation. Courage from the rubber bracelet gave us a power to connect, share, converse, and exchange contact information.

On the other hand, complete strangers riding the elevator or lounging at the pool would not be spoken to when there wasn't the signal or invitation provided by the green wristband marking our newly formed conglomerate of familiarity. It was a sad sight. I watched as those with green bands initiated conversations in elevators but excluded those with no wristbands. The bearers of this green assembly walked past those without wristbands, in the name of networking, community, and common purpose. The emerald bangle created an instant classification system garnering safety, comfort, recognition, and community for those with the opportunity to adorn the cheap trinket. But those without, were not included. The friendly green-banded posse became an exclusive club.

The green wristbands inspired my own campaign. I decided that I would initiate conversation with all those around me—green band or, mostly, not. The children made it easy. Talking to, smiling at, and playing with toddlers splashing at the pool was sure to lead to a newfound friendship with their parents. We exchanged words, laughter, recommendations, ideas, and beautiful companionship. We talked about our lives, our homes, family, vocation, and the joys of our day.

In every moment, regardless of location, skin color, nationality, language, or green wristband, I made connections: the family from Mexico City on vacation with their friends and small children; the family from Brooklyn, where the relocated wife from Vietnam was missing her family back home; the family from Atlanta who shared their immigration story, having come from Nigeria, and exchanged entrepreneurial inspiration. For someone uncomfortable initiating small talk, I easily made some meaningful connections.

What were the lessons? What is the invitation? Connect with others! **People want to connect.** We crave connection and relationship. We are wired for it. We want and need to belong. We are an interconnected, interdependent species that thrives in community. We tend to look for safe and familiar ways to create that connection. However, for many, that is not easy. Without the traditional markers of community association (green bands!), we shy away from talking to strangers. In our fast-paced, high-tech, digital world, high-touch is a powerful prescription. Slow down, bring yourself into the present moment, and give it a try. Connect with those around you—in person. They likely long for personal connection as much as you do.

We can always find something in common. You may look at others as strangers or simply people you just don't know personally yet. Finding commonality is as simple as saying, "Hello." To begin, just be who you are: reach out, shine your light, and smile. Make eye contact and speak with a simple greeting. Better yet, share an authentic expression of your experience. Look beneath the surface of things and connect with your essence—your heart. You are sure to find something you have in common. Maybe you overhear them using a beautiful name that you have an affinity for. Maybe you appreciate their conscious, gentle parenting style. Maybe you make eye contact by playing peek-a-boo with a toddler. Maybe you offer assistance, your service in opening a door, helping a stranger in need, or gifting something unique to the moment. It is likely that, because you are in the same place at the same time, you will find something in common to build an association around, even if only transient in nature.

And don't stop with strangers. This is a great practice with your not-so-familiar friends and neighbors: the checker at your local grocery store, the waiter at your favorite restaurant, and the co-traveler on public transportation. And yes, my spiritual community back home! Put down your excuses and artificial barriers—and engage.

> Connection contributes to health, longevity, and a meaningful quality of life. Reaching outside your comfort zone and entering the space of others builds your psycho-social-spiritual muscles. It's a practice that develops confidence, courage, compassion, and most importantly, unity.

Finding the common humanity behind our differences is good for our individual and collective soul. Begin connecting with others as a routine spiritual practice. Your world will blossom with possibility, potential, and greater well-being. The energy of creating new connections will attract more, and life will begin flowing with ease and grace. Try it. Research shows that quality relationships and being in community increase your overall health, happiness, productivity, longevity, and well-being. It's a win-win.

When I returned home from Cancun, I had a dream I started a green wristband campaign where I purchased thousands of wristbands and began giving them away to anyone who expressed an interest and the shared value of authentic connection. I called it "Green Between Hearts: A Conscious Connection Campaign." Strangers all over the world organically began talking to each other, making heart connections, sharing life, and building community. It was a beautiful dream.

CHAPTER REFLECTIONS

But let us not forget the face-to-face authentic connection. Learning to love the ones we're with and love our neighbors is crucial. Demonstrate kindness. Show compassion. Get interested and take the time to make an authentic connection and have a conversation. If the key to at-risk kids' health, well-being, and success is connection and relationships, then I would advocate the same for our world at large.

- Humanity is starved for human connection. We all want to be seen, heard, felt, loved, affirmed, and acknowledged. We want to feel and *know* we are a valuable part of the whole. Take an honest look at your relationships and the authentic, intimate connection you have with others. Where are your strongest connections? Where are your weakest connections? How would you rate yourself in the neighbor department? How about strangers? Write about twelve (12) relationships where you have an authentic, meaningful connection. How do you steward and tend to these relationships? Include your relationship with your partner or significant other. You are responsible for and accountable to your connections. Where are you strong and what needs more attention? Where do you hold back? What do you hide from others? In what ways do you connect through the heart and allow yourself to be completely vulnerable? In what ways do you play it safe?

- Our relationship with ourselves is the most important relationship we will ever have. Explore your relationship with yourself and your higher being. What kind of relationship do you have to your life, your body, mind, spirit, soul? Your soul's purpose? Your creativity and passions? Give consideration to how you love, honor, and cherish yourself. In what ways do you neglect or abuse any aspect of yourself? How do you tend to your authentic connection with yourself? This relationship is so much more than time for health practices, meditation, and fitness. This is self-reflection and self-nurturing—getting to know yourself intimately. This is also intimate connection with your shadow as well as your light. Dig into this process. Start a special journal for the exploration of who you really are. Pick up some art supplies and play. This is priming the pump for all of your other relationships.

- Pause and reflect. Look deeper into your relationship with all things: the earth, nature, spirit, animals, plants, food, art, beauty, God/Creator/Source. So often, our exterior landscape mirrors that of our interior landscape. Our relationship with the outer world can reflect our relationship with our inner world. Create the same exploration in your special journal. In what ways do you relate to the material and nonmaterial worlds? How do you treat other objects, animals, the earth? Do you hold all things sacred? If not, what prevents you from seeing the divinity in all things? This practice will move you from perceiving what exists around you through the habitual, ego-based Separate Self into seeing the world through the lens of your connected, Sacred Self.

CHAPTER ELEVEN

Co-Creating Greater Works Than These

My confidence comes from knowing there is a force,
a power greater than myself, that I am a part
of and it's also a part of me.

~ Oprah Winfrey

I was a child heretic, a precocious and curious child heretic. I was always afraid of that word *heretic,* and yet didn't know what to do with my contradictory thoughts, conflicting feelings, and contrary beliefs that had resulted from my early childhood experiences. Raised in an ELCA Lutheran church (Evangelical Lutheran Church in America), I was baptized as a baby, attended confirmation classes for two years, was confirmed, and attended worship services during religious holidays and occasionally in between. During Confirmation, we had to take "sermon notes" and were expected to be there every week.

Growing up, I loved attending church with my grandparents. There was something beautiful about witnessing their faith—the prayers, tight-knit community, religious objects, and the esteemed picture that hung on the wall in their small dining room.

Grace, a much-loved, world-famous photograph taken by Eric Enstrom, looked exactly like my grandpa. His white hair, kind face, full beard, and posture of prayer at the table were reminiscent of many times I watched my grandpa sit at that table. In fact, when I was quite young, I thought it was a photograph of my grandpa. My family seemed so pleased and proud of that print hanging there. There was a Polaroid picture of my grandpa in the same pose tucked in the lower corner of the frame.

I wanted to believe in the same God my grandparents did. I wanted to profess the same faith, and I loved the Jesus I knew. I wanted so badly to belong and fit in with their community of believers.

One day in fourth or fifth grade, I was out riding my bicycle alone. I rode through the alley by our church and stopped in to use the restroom. The pastor greeted me. We had a short conversation, and wearing a friendly, ear-to-ear grin, he handed me a youth bible. I felt so proud and honored. I took the gift and rode swiftly home to begin exploring. I loved reading the explanations in the margins and examining all the black and white photos. I could take or leave much of the Old Testament, but most of the New Testament resonated so deeply.

Over time, I began noticing the incongruence in liturgy, sermons, and people's conversational reflections. From my limited, youthful perspective, I loved when Jesus said, "I am in the Father and the Father is in me." And "You will know that I am in my Father, and you in me, and I in you."

Like I mentioned in the Preface, I studied these verses for hours. Why did we take the sacrament of Holy Communion to be the "union" between Christ and man, the joining/communing with God, and the real presence of Christ, if we still collectively believed in some separate God-man who lived so far away that we can only get to this being when we die—if we are good enough to earn our way?

Many things like that bothered me. I remember asking my pastor once, "If I am in God and God is in me, then why do we say God is in Heaven and not right here? Wouldn't heaven be right here and everywhere?" My inquiry was quickly dismissed with a silly chuckle and big placating smile. The omnipresent God that I knew didn't have a separate address. The ever-present God that I experienced was a creative power greater than myself, but yet very much a part of me. Evidently, my pastor must have thought I wasn't ready, or too young for that big conversation.

Formal religious teaching paled in comparison to my living, dynamic understanding. The words, doctrine, and theology were just heavy head-stuff. Memorizing the Creed and The Lord's Prayer without a dive into the juicy context bored me. I didn't want to "think about" a God that was separate from me. I didn't want rules and structure that lacked meaning and substance. I wanted to be seduced by the beauty and wisdom of a living Christ. I wanted to sit *presencing* my Sacred Self and feeling the presence of God, and then compare notes with others. I simply wanted to live in the Oneness and embody the consciousness of what Jesus was teaching.

Embodying this presence—this higher power and creative force—is what communion and co-creation is all about. No one ever taught me to embody the impulse of creation as it moved through me. Besides worship, prayer, and Communion, we didn't learn practices that unite us with a power greater than ourselves—Divine Wisdom, Christ Consciousness, Creative Source, the Designing Intelligence of the universe, or however you want to see it. This omnipresent God Source that is right here, right now, always, wasn't taught in my religious education. However, I knew that God was as available and accessible as the very thing we all do constantly: breathe.

—

Waking to Divine Presence

Divine union is our birthright. Sacred union is life. It is the design of creation—divine essence in physical form—embodied presence. Just as we constantly commune with the 75 trillion cells of our body, God communes with us. Like Oprah said, we are a part of God and God is a part of us. This benevolent, harmonious (Omni)presence enhances healing, sustains peace, inspires creativity, and resonates with joy.

Humanity is waking to this presence—this level of unitive consciousness—and learning to harness the co-creative power we have always possessed. As we bring spirit and consciousness more fully into every realm of life, we are evolving into a co-creative culture and stabilizing this new consciousness.

Co-creation is so much more than cooperation or collaboration with others. Barbara Marx Hubbard defines a *co-creator* as "one who is experiencing the creative intention of the universe incarnating as their own intention, expressing that intention as an essential self in creative work, and joining with others doing the same; one who co-creates with spirit, with others, and with nature."

In *The Co-Creator's Handbook*, Carolyn Anderson and Katharine Roske say a co-creator is "one who surrenders and aligns his will with the intention of Creation, the universal mind, the designing intelligence, Spirit; one who shares his gifts and actualizes his dreams in synergistic play with other co-creators to bring forth a new world."

Throughout my life, co-creating with God has been a gift I am so grateful to have discovered. As an artist and writer, I definitely could tell the difference between creating with my small mind vs. co-creating with the impulse of Creation. As a psychotherapist and healer, I counted on the benevolent Creative Source to assist, opening myself to be used as an instrument of God's peace—a channel. Co-creating is so much easier and more meaningful. It compels me to be an open, loving presence and conduit.

If I'm feeling no divine inspiration, and no joy or resonance in the field and with others, I'm likely stuck in my head. If I'm with a client and I feel stuck during the session, I recognize I'm thinking too much. One deep breath, a little prayer, and I'm plugged back into co-creator mode, channeling the benevolent consciousness and holding a peaceful field of love and resonance. I like to tune into the subtle energy vibration of *joy* and allow this frequency to express through me. If I'm not in joy, I feel out of alignment. Without that co-creative relationship, life is laborious, boring, and difficult to navigate or complete things.

Turning to art or journaling is something I often do as a tool to get out of my headspace and the pallid limitations of simple thought or the chaos of wrestling negative emotion and the hidden demons lurking in shadow. I purge what's on my mind and empty out completely, so God, the Creative Source, can fill me up again. Or maybe it's simply getting outside my mind so I can *feel* the pure Presence and guidance again—knowing it is always right here, right now. I call this process *conscious composting*. I lead an experiential journey called Conscious Composting, utilizing the creative arts, and I've taught it to clients for years. It's a powerful process leading to greater inspiration, insight, creativity, and transformation.

Purge journaling is a technique I use to release and let go—to mentally and emotionally purge. It's the first step of conscious composting. When the digestive system has been invaded by something toxic or harmful, the body purges by vomiting, diarrhea, or both. Purge journaling is like mental vomiting or emotional diarrhea. It's our conscious choice to release when something toxic has invaded our mind and heart. Sometimes the toxin is simply getting stuck in our own ruminating thoughts.

What is purge journaling?

Sit down in a quiet place where you won't be disturbed. Have something to write with and let your thoughts and feelings flow out onto the surface of what you are writing on. The only rule is that there are no rules. Pay no attention to content, sentence structure, spelling, grammar, or penmanship—nothing! Write until you absolutely cannot write anymore.

You will go through a cathartic release, ups and downs, a variety of emotions and moods. At times, your pen may slow and barely kiss the page as you discover a tender place where tears meet the ink, leaving small puddles of grief and sadness. Your hand may go crazy, moving around the page in broad strokes, talking faster than your mouth ever could keep up. And then, you may release toxic anger and rage with a hand so heavy it feels as if you're piercing right through the surface of the page with a cathartic vengeance. All is well. Release the plethora of emotions and thoughts. Let go. Purge until there's nothing more to come up and out.

Then, once you are empty, you allow God, your higher self, or however you want to see that greater power, to fill you—to rush into the energetic void created by the purge. Receive. That is generally when all the good stuff comes. In this state, it's easier to sense the presence of God. It's easier to feel the divine union. It's easy to hear the still small voice and get divine guidance. In this stage, I write down the flashes of insight and sparks of creativity. I call them pearls of wisdom.

The process is pretty universal. When walking a labyrinth (a walking meditation or path of prayer), there are three main stages: release, receive, and return. Walking in toward the center of the labyrinth, we release what's on our hearts and minds. Being at center, we receive—guidance, insight, answers, and often comfort. And walking back out into the world is the return. All meditative practices are similar. We learn how to let the "monkey mind" become quiet and be still as we return to wholeness—journey to our center. Once we've emptied out or quieted the mind, we are a clear vessel again.

In Conscious Composting, I teach a more detailed, transformative technique that allows one to utilize the purge process and transmute the inner landscape of discordant thoughts, emotions and beliefs into a higher, more coherent order that leads to deep healing. It's a beautiful spiritual practice and one path where people can learn how to commune with God. Anything that moves us out of our head, and more fully into our heart, activates the abundant flow of higher order consciousness. We learn to attune and bring ourselves into resonance. Then we learn how to move within the resonance and flow through the field.

The genius of Creation is within us. The designing intelligence of nature is always accessible. A power greater than ourselves—to heal and create—is infinitely present. Like Oprah said, it gives her confidence. If we truly were to understand the full capacity of this creative force and our ability to access it from within, our world would be a different place. How can we teach our young people to be in a more intimate relationship with the Divine? How can we inspire each other to commune and co-create with one another and allow this field of grace to take care of our collective needs?

—◆—

Where Two or Three Are Gathered

We are called to create this harmonious resonance with one another. The power of co-creating in a group is stunning. In Matthew 18:20, Jesus said, "For where two or three are gathered in my name, I am there among them." This is another one of those verses I was obsessed with as a young person. It's as if Jesus were teaching us how to co-create, before *we* named the process *co-creation*. Like I mentioned in the introduction, Jesus also said that the one who believes will do the works that he does and even greater works. How cool.

When we come together as a group in the presence of this higher power, allowing the Creative Force to create through us, we can do great things. We can heal the sick. We can feed the hungry. We can create Heaven on Earth. We can perform miracles. But we must come together as one body, believe, and remember our wholeness. We must acknowledge our individual spiritual gifts and come together in service of the whole, the common good. We are designed to work together. We are created as one collective body. We are born of one human race.

This is our time to remember—to "re-member"—ourselves as whole. And put that remembering into action.

> When every cell within the living organism does its individual part, contributing to and in service of the whole, the whole is healthy and gives back to each cell. When the whole is healthy and gives back to each individual cell, the cells are stronger and healthier individually. Cells in the heart do what they do best by serving the whole body, pumping blood to every cell. In turn, every cell is nourished and sustained. Heart cells don't serve the heart alone. They are the full expression of unique, individual cells, fulfilling their unique function in service of the whole body.

When individual cells break down, other healthy cells within the organism send out mutual aid, energy and resources to repair, restore, and rejuvenate until the whole system creates balance and homeostasis again. They work together. When too many individual cells break down, the whole system becomes compromised, and at risk for complete failure. When individual cells serve only themselves, and not the collective whole, then cells, tissues, systems, and organs malfunction and create malignant growth. Cancer may grow and rob the entire body of health and wholeness.

Harmony and balance within the system, as a whole, is health. Synchronicity and resonance within the individual separate parts creates greater health. And working together collectively in coherence jumps the system to even greater heights. We are like cells within one collective body. Infused with a power greater than ourselves, and working collectively in service of the whole, we co-create even greater works.

Seeing our God Source as "out there," separate from us, has created chronic fear and anxiety. Seeing others as separate from ourselves has created colossal competition and generations of conflict. Embodying this co-creative force and being conscious of this powerful union is good medicine. Working together—literally co-creating our present moment—we remember who we truly are and create an epic love story of conscious evolution and healing for the good of the whole.

CHAPTER REFLECTIONS

Divine union is our birthright. Sacred union is life. It is the design of creation—divine essence in physical form—embodied presence. Just as we constantly commune with the 75 trillion cells of our body, God communes with us.

- We are called to co-create "greater works than these." We are called to step into the grandest version of our highest expression and serve the good of the whole. Regardless of your faith or religion, the process of communing with the Divine and co-creating with the Designing Intelligence— the animating life force—is universal. Take a moment and really contemplated the verse John 14:12. *"What I'm about to tell you is true. Anyone who believes in me will do the works I have been doing. In fact, they will do even greater things."* Spend some quiet time and invite the verse to come alive and inform you. Really engage with the words. Imagine Jesus saying this to you. Putting all religion aside, tune into the *idea* that Jesus said YOU will do the work he has done and even greater things—that greater things are even possible. What does that mean to you? What does "even greater things" bring up in your imagination? Pause and reflect on dreams you have had. What would you like to co-create in this world? What is on your personal greater-things bucket list? How does this empower you? In what ways are you co-creating greater things in your life right now?

- You are a divine human—a gifted, unique individual—created as a valuable member of the whole. You are uniquely designed to serve and live for the good of the whole. Co-creating with this potential opens us to even greater things. Take a moment and pause. Reflect on your highest potential. Look for any questions, topics or stuck points that are not sitting well with your capacity for greater works. Sense into any discordant energy or emotion. Try purge journaling. Practice the technique mentioned. Allow yourself to emotionally flow with the purge. Write and write and write until you cannot write any longer. Don't pay attention to spelling, grammar, content, penmanship, or sentence structure. Simply purge and let go. This is a great therapeutic practice to develop. When you feel complete, look for the pearls of wisdom and insights. Record them somewhere for you to keep, and discard the purge. Let it go! Then allow that freed-up, open space to be filled with Source consciousness.

CHAPTER TWELVE

Expanding into Our Fullest Potential

If we do not balance our pessimism about human nature with optimism about divine nature, we will overlook the cure of grace.

~ Martin Luther King, Jr.

I woke up with the answer. The night before, I was driving home from a meeting in Omaha. I had a conversation with God and asked for the deeper meaning to my question: "If I am being asked to '*walk a new way,*' what does that really mean?"

I had ideas about that in my head—thoughts, intuitions, and generalizations. Quite literally, I was walking a new way—learning to bring my toe in, learning to bend my ankle, working to strengthen my muscles, working to come back into optimal alignment, and trusting my body to walk down stairs. I *was* walking a new way. Metaphorically speaking, I was walking a new way through life as my consciousness, energy, and body was rapidly shifting and evolving. But there was a nagging sense inside—a burgeoning irritation— that wouldn't let me rest. I was being encouraged to 'walk a new way,' and I knew my healing would not be complete until I really embodied this guidance. So, what did that really mean?

That night I had a dream. My children and I were at home in our backyard, playing. There was a beautiful patio and garden area. And we had two pets in small, black wrought iron cages: a miniature giraffe and a miniature panda—both were no larger than twelve to eighteen inches tall. They were adorable, and we loved them so much. We had fun playing with them. We kept them in their cages all the time, petting, feeding, and playing with them through the iron bars. We were all happy.

The dream shifted quickly into a lucid moment. When I became "awake" in my dream, I began assessing the situation. First, why did I have these very small, miniature animals in a cage? They were gentle, tame, loving, and playful. In fact, they were adorable. They wouldn't hurt anyone if we let them out of the cage. And second, they were so small that they really didn't need to be caged. Our back area was fenced in with a beautifully landscaped stone wall. They couldn't escape, run away, or get lost. *What was the function of the cage*, I wondered?

So I decided to let them out. As I opened the cages, they both casually stepped out onto the stone patio. The panda sat down. The giraffe stood. The children were happy. And I knew it was an important moment in the dream as my lucid awareness watched the unfolding.

Within seconds of dreamtime, the giraffe and panda began growing and expanding. We watched as they instantaneously morphed before our eyes. When the giraffe reached about ten feet tall, he stopped growing. He appeared to be a young juvenile in stature. The panda continued to grow into her fullest potential—her mature, adult size. I paused to ponder the inconsistency, thinking that was strange. I knew the giraffe was supposed to be twice that tall. Why did he stop growing? Yet, the panda grew into a full expression of a real-life, adult panda. Her presence felt whole and complete. But the giraffe was stunted. His growth was interrupted. Why did he stop maturing at half his normal size? Why did she grow into her fullest potential?

As I lost myself in the mystery and wonder of what was unfolding, my awareness focused with compassion on the giraffe. And then I looked up.

There was a cage around my house and yard!

When I looked up toward the roof of the patio area, I observed a nice, neat, clean, and shiny, black wrought iron cage around the entire house, a replica of the animal cages. I was in a cage just like the animals! We were all in a cage—larger than the animal cages, but a cage nonetheless. Unknowingly cooped in, I'd been living contently within the boundaries of a wrought iron enclosure. My home, my life, everything existed within this open-air crate. My first reaction was, *Wow—what a big surprise*, followed by an almost instantaneous, eye-opening *knowing, Aha . . . Of course!*

In that moment, I knew that when I removed that cage, not only would the giraffe grow into his fullest potential, but so would I. I was shown the self-imposed restrictions I had placed on my life. And I was encouraged to remove the iron cell. In my lucid state, I knew the only thing I needed to do to remove the cage was to acknowledge it was there. There was no need to struggle or fight to get out. I didn't have to work hard to escape or try to find a key to unlock it. I simply had to acknowledge *I* put it there. Once I "got it," the cage disappeared with ease.

A deeper message was clear—our fullest potential *already* exists within. When the bars were lifted, the giraffe and the panda automatically began to grow into a higher expression. The only thing that halted the giraffe's full expansion was the larger cage of limitation. Once that was removed, it could continue its growth effortlessly.

So, what was my cage?

I knew instantly.

Thirty-six hours before I had this dream, I was on a conference call. My friends, Bob and Noel, host a call the third Thursday of every month. Due to scheduling conflicts, I am not always able to get on. However, this past Thursday, I had an intuitive urge to join the call. I had planned to go to bed early that night, since I needed to get up at 4:00 the next morning and drive three hours to a meeting. Yet, without any plan to join in or even having the call time marked in my calendar, I found myself on the call, listening.

The conference call included a guest who does angel readings. She was informative and talked about her life and career, how she began doing readings, and what she experiences. She then opened the call to do individual readings for anyone who wanted one. She asked if anyone had any questions. I didn't have a specific question to ask the angels, but I kept listening to the conversation as others asked their questions and received feedback.

And then I heard: ***The angels have a message for you.***

Participants continued to jump in, receiving personal readings, one after the other. As they asked their questions, I kept hearing: ***The angels have a message for you.*** However, I didn't engage because I didn't have a question. *If the angels have a message for me, they are going to have to find a way to deliver it,* I thought. Well, when angels have a message, sure enough they find a way.

Out of nowhere, one of the hosts, Noel, singled me out and asked, "Julie, do you have a question?"

Why did she ask me that? She hadn't called on anyone prior to this. In fact, her husband, Bob, was moderating this entire part of the call up till now. He was simply opening the call for the next person who wanted to speak up and ask a question. The process was very self-organizing and self-directed. No one was being called on or asked to engage.

I thanked Noel for the invitation and told her I didn't have a question, but that I was continuing to hear that the angels had a message for me. Sure enough, the woman giving the angel readings began with a message. *Yes, the angels have a message.*

She delivered a message encouraging me to bring out the inner-child within me and let go of any expectations and attachments as to how things should come about. She said that part of me wants to have things manifest in all kinds of ways, but there also is a fearful part that recognizes if things do manifest in the manner I envision, I will be "publicly recognized and feel larger than life." With that exposure comes more responsibilities and accountability; regardless, she said that I was to let go of these expectations and fears, and step into this much more public and wider platform. I was to let go of fear and "expand into my fullest potential." But I was to do so by allowing my inner-child to come out and play.

She illustrated a way of being more childlike by using an example of an art museum, "If a child had the choice of sitting and listening to a lecture on the comparison of fourteenth-century art with modernism, or go into a room with clay, pastels, markers, and paints, which room would the child go into?"

I giggled as I thought of my recent trip to the art museum. My inner-child was literally playing with energy and consciousness, colors, vibration, shapes, and textures. I had a blast playing that day. When I shared the story, she laughed with me and was in a playful state herself. "Yes! Yes! I'm not surprised. Take that feeling and then translate that into all other areas that give you absolute joy and bliss, and really nurture your soul."

She said this play is creative, and it is gifted in my soul.

Then she abruptly stopped, shifted, and asked with exclamation, "Have you written a book?"

I responded I was almost finished with my first book. She was thrilled, "Yes, yes, the angels are pointing to the book and saying the book is part of being more public and having a wider platform. You have to let go of any expectations, attachments, and fear." She encouraged me to open myself up and not restrict myself with how I *think* things will manifest.

The second point in her reading was that my marriage would become more "enhanced" and advance to a deeper level as I step into the fullness of who I am, because I would be opening myself and not restricting myself so much.

The third point was that every time I ask for something in prayer, or visualization, or intention, I am to watch what I ask for and how quickly it manifests. Things were going to unfold now. "This is quite the year," she said. She advised, I would have physical, tangible results for my desires as long as I let go of the expectation of and attachment to how they are to come in.

This was a delightful experience. The call ended shortly after, and I went to bed, not giving it much further thought. I had to get some sleep so I could be fresh for my drive into Omaha for that 8:00 a.m. meeting. I fell right to sleep, but was woken by another dream around 2:30 a.m. I got up, went to the bathroom. and then laid my head on the pillow, expecting to go right back to sleep. But no, there was no more sleep. Finally, I got up and prepared for my day.

My Omaha meeting was a continuation of this emerging theme. Though, I didn't recognize it at the time. Only after I had my "caged-in" dream did all these strands become coherent, and start to make more sense.

During this all-day meeting, the Bishop of the ELCA Nebraska Synod joined us for our regular check-in and updates. He said he would like to invite a few guests in for lunch, if we didn't mind. They were the "President Pastor" and Bishop of the ELCA companion church in Argentina and Uruguay, and an English professor who taught at an ecumenical seminary. They were in Nebraska and making other stops in Minnesota and Chicago because their seminary was closing after forty-four years.

It was a fascinating conversation. They explained that the established seminary—the Upper Evangelical Institute of the Institution of Theological Studies—was founded ecumenically in 1972 and supported by nine historically Christian denominations. When asked why the school was closing, they acknowledged there were issues of both money and student enrollment. They knew they would create something new, but before they made any plans or decisions they wanted to honor the closing and "give this corpse (the seminary) a proper burial."

One issue, they explained, was that as an ecumenical institution, they "could never fully be what they wanted or desired to be." They could not expand into their fullest potential. Each denomination honored and respected the others, yet none of the denominations could express their fullest, authentic theological identity. Instead, in working together to prepare their students to be future church leaders, they ended up creating a more general, ecumenical curriculum and broad educational experience for their students.

> Sometimes in our attempt to create greater unity and harmony, we create generic expressions of ourself in order to fit in and blend. Yet, what is being called for is a symphony of strong and full-bodied diversity. Be who you are and allow yourself to evolve into an even greater expression. There's room for everyone and we can co-create unity in diversity.

There it was again.

The night before this conversation, the angel reading told me I was to release my expectations and restrictions and expand into my fullest potential. In my conversation with the guests from Argentina, they spoke of the restrictions they felt and how they couldn't expand into their fullest potential. And then, that night in my sleep, I had the lucid dream of the black wrought iron cages with the message to release the restrictions and expand into my fullest potential. It doesn't get any clearer than that.

Release the Restrictions?

No question—I had fears that created a restriction around my life and career. When I imagined the "expansion" of my vocational expression, I had many negative expectations and judgments about traveling more—being away from home and away from my family and husband.

I love my home. Home and family are of the utmost importance and priority for me. After a turbulent childhood, I intentionally created a very grounded and stable home life and beautiful, creative environment. I made important choices where home was center and family came first. I had always put my children and their well-being, health, and developmental needs before my own. My kids and being their mom always came before my career. I also valued a strong marriage and selfishly loved the life we had created together. Time together was precious. Time at our lake house was blissful. Planned and spontaneous time spent with our now-adult kids was priceless.

I love to travel. And I love to travel with my husband. Thinking about increased travel without him leaves an empty, disorienting spot inside of me. The potential to travel more gets me excited and sad about leaving, all at the same time.

Over the past several years, I had begun to travel more without him, and it just wasn't the same relaxing, expansive, rejuvenating experience. I always felt like I was missing something. In fact, I began a pattern of minimizing my calls home. If I had to be away, it was easier on me to be completely away, fully engaged in my work.

But it was harder on him when he didn't hear from me. Clearly, I needed to adjust my expectations and limiting beliefs about travel, career, and time away from home and family.

What would the experience of life be like if I were to expand into my fullest potential?

My giraffe-and-panda dream showed me that the growth and expansion could be a natural, spontaneous, effortless, and healthy process. Yes, if I were to step into my fullest potential, my life would look very different. I knew that. But the "different" might not be the different that I thought or expected. That way of thinking was creating a self-induced limitation. As an acorn naturally grows into an oak tree, so too, I was called to grow into my soul's higher expression. Who was I to stop the progress and potential? Who was I to fear my greatness? Why would I think I knew better than God— the Designing Intelligence of the universe?

꜒

Our Deepest Fear

A beautiful piece of calligraphy hangs in my office. I commissioned this work to be created by a talented local artist/calligrapher. It's the famous quote by Marianne Williamson: "Our deepest fear is not that we are inadequate. Our deepest fear is that we are powerful beyond measure."

I have loved these words for decades, and here they were challenging me to step into my greatness. The angel reader was right. I was afraid (more than I thought) and created restrictions. Yes, I was attached to my sense of safety, home, and family, but there was also a deeper fear hidden inside that wanted to be recognized and resolved. It was the part about being more public and larger than life. Marianne's quote goes on to say:

It is our light, not our darkness that most frightens us. We ask ourselves, Who am I to be brilliant, gorgeous, talented, fabulous? Actually, who are you *not* to be? You are a child of God. Your playing small does not serve the world. There is nothing enlightened about shrinking so that other people won't feel insecure around you. We are all meant to shine, as children do. We were born to make manifest the glory of God that is within us. It's not just in some of us; it's in everyone. And as we let our own light shine, we unconsciously give other people permission to do the same. As we are liberated from our own fear, our presence automatically liberates others.

Here was the pattern once again! I have encouraged clients for decades to shine. I traveled around the country on the Let it Shine Road Trip. I have written and spoken about how "playing small" doesn't serve the world and about how we are called to be the divine expression of God. And yet, I was playing small. I was playing safe. I was living caged.

The words of Simran Singh came echoing back again: "Julie, why were you walking carefully downhill and taking baby steps?"

I was afraid. I didn't want the life I had created to change. I loved my life. I didn't want to step outside of my comfort zone and into the twilight zone of unknown, cosmic proportions. Every new step was calculated and safe. Every new creation kept me tied somehow to the life, home, career, and relationships I cherished. Every baby step I thought I'd been taking in a new direction was possibly an illusion. I wasn't opening myself to radical change. I was open to safe, miniscule change, and this was keeping me stuck!

I remembered a poignant comment in passing from a dear friend. As a young mom and ambitious professional, I was shining and shining bright! Remember that job where I was climbing that corporate ladder, the one leaning on the wrong wall? Well, I projected the outward appearance of success. I wore nice clothes with all the "perfect" accessories—my shoes and jewelry paired ambitiously with my expensive business suits. Then one day, my friend said almost incidentally, "Julie, if I didn't know you, I would hate you." I was appalled. Time stood still. I didn't get it. Stunned, I asked her, "Why?" She said, "You are perfect. You are beautiful and successful. You have the perfect life. If I didn't know you, I would hate you."

I was crushed and in disbelief. A voice in my head mirrored the words of Marianne Williamson's quote, "Who am I to be brilliant, gorgeous, talented, fabulous?"

That self-sabotaging voice stayed with me. I didn't want to be hated. I wanted to be loved. I wanted to be respected. I wanted to be seen. But I didn't want to be hated.

Instantly, I began hiding, and dimming my light. Did people really think and feel like that? I didn't hate successful or beautiful people, did I? It's strange. People are so funny sometimes. An acorn doesn't say, "I don't want to grow into a huge oak tree because others will hate me." A baby giraffe doesn't say, "I don't want to grow into my full magnificence. I can't show my long awkward legs and beautiful tall neck. What if others will hate me?"

My cage dream planted other seeds of potentiality in my consciousness. If I were to expand into my fullest potential, what might that look like? If I could dream and dream big, how might I express myself? Not only was I guided to remove the self-imposed cages I created, but also encouraged to grow into my fullest potential. So, what did the giraffe and panda have to teach me about that?

~

Dreaming Big

The symbolic meaning of *giraffes* in dreams is fascinating. A giraffe's most obvious feature is the neck. Symbolically, this asks us about "sticking our necks out" in terms of family, community, business, creative endeavors, etc. In this way, the giraffe is a messenger, supporting us to stretch ourselves, claim our visionary skills, and reach as far as we can. The giraffe often makes an appearance when we need a little reminder that we are incredible beings with a remarkable potential to *rise above* challenges. The giraffe also demonstrates grace and ease in reaching and striving for things.

The giraffe reminds us of a *higher vision*—a big picture, cosmic, otherworldly, future-oriented, and psychic vision. With its head lifted above the treetops, the giraffe's vision is focused on the horizon and the great frontier. This makes us think of visionary leaders and a pioneering spirit. When the giraffe shows up, not only do we have a gift of higher perception, but also we're very sensitive about *what* we vision. Giraffes have three horns called *ossicones*. One is situated right between, and just above, its eyes in the "third-eye" area, which represents intuition, and heightened sensory perception.

With my history of chronic neck and throat issues, and needing to find my authentic voice, I'm surprised I hadn't remembered giraffes appearing in my dreams before. It was time to fully reclaim my strength, my vision, and my voice. I decided to listen to giraffe's message and apply it to my own ability to be strong with my voice and be effective in my words—and in this way, with giraffe's help, allow myself to elevate my message and make a greater difference in the world.

One of my greatest fears has been "sticking my neck out." Geez! This one was difficult. My perceived fear of rejection created so much distress in my mind. I saw the world differently than many people around me, but didn't want others to think I was strange. That whole social pressure to conform and fit in dictated much of my life. Ironically, I was always uncomfortably taller than my classmates, friends, cousins, and sisters. I wanted to literally shrink to fit in. It was easy to claim my visionary gifts and intuitive abilities privately. But was I truly ready to stick my neck out? I heard:

Julie, you're not going to be able to walk a new way until you learn how to stand proud and stick your neck out. It's your gift and your strength. You are fully supported. Grow into your giraffe essence.

Witnessing a panda in your dream is a reminder of the spiritual strength, power, and growth of the unconscious mind. This dream symbol means that sometimes you need to remind yourself of your childhood and childlike happiness. It was interesting how my angel reading just thirty-six hours earlier talked about being more childlike and having fun.

The panda also represents stamina, in that you will undertake situations requiring mental and psychological strength. I could relate to that. The past several months felt like I'd been running a marathon barefooted on the hot desert sands. I had little physical strength and endurance, but I could almost always count on my mental and psychological strength and toughness. Was it time to let go of that and surrender into the childlike wonder and playfulness? Was it time to shift out of the mental and psychological strength to allow the unconscious mind and spiritual power to blossom even more? I could roll with that.

Panda also brings the gifts of abundance, prosperity, and pleasure. It shares the symbols of carefree spirit and conservation. The panda is one of the most loved and adored animals in the world. It is most recognized for gentleness and compassion. If I were to grow and expand into my fullest panda expression, I would be so happy and free. I could feel the gentle compassion expanding in all directions. I desired a greater carefree spirit. And heaven knows I was poised and ready to receive greater abundance, prosperity, and pleasure. Panda was good medicine. Panda and Giraffe together were so intriguing. I decided to work with both in my journal and on a vision board. This felt powerful and significant. And then, there was the issue of removing the cage.

There are many dream dictionaries online. Google it and find one that resonates with you. There are also many resources for interpreting different animal totems that show up in your life. Have fun with it.

Simple awareness of the cage seemed like the magic key to liberation. It felt like a huge revelation in my dream when I looked up and saw the cage I was in. I remember thinking simultaneously, *Seriously?* and *Oh yeah, of course!* It was an instant recognition leading to greater joy and freedom. I didn't need the cage. It was just there. I didn't need to climb out and escape, work hard to remove it, or spend time and energy searching for a key. I needed simply to shift my awareness. I said a little prayer, thanking the cage for serving me and keeping me safe all these years, and let it go. Poof. Gone.

The cage transmuted into a vague, translucent grid. And now, it was activated to serve a higher evolutionary purpose. It was supporting my highest expression. It was connecting the planet and our beautiful, cosmic potential.

A piece of artwork I created in high school had been on my mind for months. It was a rather cosmic piece inspired by a plastic strawberry basket. Back then, strawberries came in a square, light green, grid-like basket. The painting was huge, and had been executed on three separate canvases. It was a study in perspective, and the grid moved your consciousness from the present foreground out into deep space. Behind the grid was a single, large, spherical shape, floating in space—our Earth, perhaps? Creation? Unity consciousness? The entire cosmos?

Wondering where that painting ended up, I asked my mother whether she had it or remembered where it went. She said it was not stored in her possession. I didn't have it either, and not locating it made me kind of sad. It was speaking to me and asking me to listen more deeply to a message. I consciously felt the presence of a cosmic grid or matrix. But I sensed there was more meaning in the painting for me to discover. How I wanted to see it and feel it again—to remember the creative consciousness I'd been immersed in back then.

The cage dream invited me deeper into releasing all the cages that had ever held me back from speaking my truth and sharing my vision. So much of my art back then was prophetic and visionary. Adults would validate the "old soul" in me and affirm the creative genius demonstrated in both my artwork and creative writing. Now, on the precipice of something new, it was time to reclaim that prophetic voice and creative vision.

The experience was asking me to remember my creative power and artistic gifts. Childlike play with art and writing was my medicine. No thought. No analysis. No figuring things out. It was time for a childlike abandon into the abyss and bliss of artistic, creative self-expression. Trusting what had always come through in those flowing moments of presence.

As I step out of the cage, I can expand beyond my current state of being—be who I was born to be.

Indeed, I was ready to step out of the cage and expand into my fullest creative potential. And like any root-bound plant being repotted in a larger container, there was sure to be stress in the change, a brief disorientation, and a time of pause to adapt and adjust. But I was ready.

CHAPTER REFLECTIONS

Every baby step I thought I'd been taking in a new direction was possibly an illusion. I wasn't opening myself to radical change. I was open to safe, miniscule change, and this was keeping me stuck!

- We are playing small as a humanity. We have put ourselves in cultural boxes, political cages, religious containers, gender cartons, and sexual packages to name just a few. The cages perpetuate the illusion of separation. They also contribute to the illusion of a limited potential. Make a list of all the cages and boxes you have put yourself in. Make a list of all the cages others try to put you in. Imagine you are in one of those cages and write about your thoughts and feelings. What does it feel like to live within the boundaries? Now, recognize the cage. Greet it. Talk to it. Acknowledge it for serving you and imagine yourself stepping out of the cage. What does it feel like? Know you will begin to expand and grow in ways beyond your imagining. And remember, you don't have to do a thing or think or plan or anything. Your fullest potential is coded within you. Removing the cage is all it requires for your expansion. What does that feel like to know you can be liberated from your perceived limitations? Be honest with yourself. Are you living your highest and fullest potential? After thinking about your cages, what is it that prevents you from naturally being and expressing who you really are?

- Many of us are conditioned to play small. Marianne Williamson says we're afraid of our light. Identify areas where you are playing small. Look deeper and sense into the fear attached? Really sit with the question, "How am I playing small?" Live with the question. Allow the question

to percolate in your consciousness for as long as it takes—
hours, or maybe days—until you can get to the deepest
roots of the fear. It will be there. Once you've identified
the fear, write yourself a love letter. Encourage yourself
with compassion and love. Recognize and affirm the fear
and let it go. Love up on the place of fear until it dissolves.
Next, identify one area where you might choose to stretch
yourself today. Pick a goal, large or small, and commit
yourself in a love letter to yourself. Encourage yourself.
Create a plan of how you may take one step into your fuller
potential right here, right now.

- Being childlike is good medicine! When and in what ways
do you allow yourself to play and explore? Contemplate
developing a practice or routine to allow your healthy child
to express itself and schedule some time to play this week.
Make a list of all the ways you enjoy playing and maybe
even some new ways you want to explore. How can you
allow your inner-child to express more?

CHAPTER THIRTEEN

Walk in Perfect Love

The True Self—where you and God are one—
does not choose to love as much as it is love itself already.

~ Richard Rohr

I have been contemplating how to best teach the stabilization of our "True Self," that Richard Rohr speaks of, since before breaking my leg. How do we activate and sustain this truth—this reality, this mystery—"where you and God are one" as our new way of being? How do we live day to day *being* love itself? We have been conditioned to UN-LOVE ourselves. And in fact, many of us are downright self-abusive, hateful, and our own biggest bullies. If we are already "love itself," and if that is expressed as our "True Self"—the place where we are one with God—then do we realize what we are doing to our relationship with God? Every word of self-criticism whispered in our heads chips away at that place where we meet God. That harsh voice is simply the false, fear-based sense of an illusion of separation. There is a gentler, more loving, soft voice within.

We are not separate, dear one. We never have been. Let us love that false sense into remembering.

I haven't been very good at loving myself, more specifically, my body. In fact, the dream with the wrought iron cage opened an old wound that had been scabbed over and ignored. Just before I broke my leg, I had been feeling really good in my body. Besides waterskiing and being active in the summer, I was walking regularly, riding my bike, and running some.

I had a huge epiphany a couple weeks before I broke my leg. My husband and I went to a three-day meeting in Kansas, and he wanted to go for a walk. I told him I forgot to pack my walking shoes, so we went to a sporting goods store. At the store, I began trying on clothes from the sales rack—running shorts, running shirts, an athletic jacket. I was really comfortable in my body and loving the feeling of that. Later that night, we went for a run. He pushed me, and we ran through a park around a couple miles, over a steep overpass and back the distance to our hotel. I felt on top of the world. I was falling in love with my body.

That summer, I noticed how I would look at my body and feel authentic love and appreciation for it. I looked at my legs when I was sitting in the boat, and without any hesitation, I basked in an unfamiliar feeling of acceptance and appreciation. The body love continued to grow. Feeling great in my body, I enjoyed getting dressed in the morning. My self-talk and thoughts were overwhelmingly positive, loving, and kind. This was new. I didn't remember ever feeling like this before.

When I mentioned to my friends how "at home" I was feeling in my body, a healing wave of grace washed over me. Sensual and sexual and beautiful. Confident and courageous. I was strong and enjoyed being active. I loved my body, which was fit and trim. For the first time in my life, my physical body matched my mental body image. All my life, I vacillated back and forth between feeling like my body was bigger than it actually was and feeling like my body was smaller than it actually was. I was discovering a new sense of liberation and self-compassion. I loved my body. The love was young, tender, and maybe, still conditional. But I loved my body.

And then I broke my leg.

Suddenly, I was at the mercy of my husband for help with everything. He was amazing. One of his first concerns was how to cook for me. I have been gluten- and sugar-free for years. I minimize dairy and rarely eat processed carbs. When I cook for us, I always create options and variety or will simply prepare two different entrées. He is a good cook and a healthy meat-and-potatoes kind-of guy. He loves my cooking but will happily cook. We often prepare meals together.

With my broken leg, I told him not to stress or worry about cooking anything special for me. He had way too much on his plate. I would simply eat and appreciate what was prepared and served. He was so kind and compassionate. He started every morning with my ritual coffee and a green smoothie. He tried and did his best with lunch and dinner. Yet, specialty cooking was not his forte.

Weeks went by. Not only was I eating things I normally didn't, but I was sitting around unable to move much. But somehow my broken leg temporarily calmed my fear and self-criticism. I had compassion for myself—for being immobile and immersed in an acute healing time. The self-love lingered far into my recovery time. It was as if I were eating the love and gratitude of my husband's compassion and service. I had no guilt. No fear. My mind rationalized and approved of the temporary shift. I could tell I'd gained a little weight, but held that awareness within the affirming space of my own self-love and compassion during this transitional time of recovery.

Once I began moving around more from two crutches, to one crutch, and then a cane, I noticed the ego-induced, self-defeating, abusive thoughts sneaking back into my head, escorting the familiar fear, worry, and eventual disgust. An obsessive barrage of toxic shame returned with a vengeance:

I am going to gain weight. I shouldn't be eating this. I was feeling so good in my body and now I'm going to be right back where I started. This is only temporary, but . . . I wonder how much weight I have gained? I can't help that I broke my leg. I need to be grateful for what is served. Kevin is working so hard. I can't ask him to do any more. I never should have allowed myself to eat all those carbs! I'm going into the winter. This isn't going to be good. This is really going to be bad. What if I blow up like a balloon? Will I ever feel good in my body again?

The barrage of worry, stress and fear was deafening. I couldn't stop the loud, negative voice.

Guilt means you feel bad because of something you do. For example, you knock a lamp over and break it. You feel guilty. But shame is feeling bad for who you are. For example, because you broke the lamp, you are a bad person.

Embody Great Love

In 2003, I could barely walk a block without severe pain in my hips and pelvis. I had lived with pain in my knees, but this was different. In fact, I had pain everywhere! I thought it was normal because it came on so gradually and was chronic. My husband would reach over and give my leg a loving, gentle squeeze of affection, and it would send me into orbit. "Ouch," I would exclaim! He would look at me in disbelief and say, "What?" I told him how much it hurt, and he thought I was crazy. I never gave it a second thought. It was my now normal. I was so out of touch with my body!

At my annual checkup, I told my doctor about my pain. She ran several tests and told me my bad cholesterol was high, my blood pressure was high, my blood sugar was high, and my inflammation was high. I had fatigue, chronic muscle aches, joint pain, and a myriad of other symptoms. She offered to refer me to a rheumatologist to rule out fibromyalgia, lupus, and other autoimmune diseases (my mother, father, and two sisters all have or had multiple autoimmune disorders). And she wanted to prescribe medications for my blood sugar, blood pressure, inflammation, and cholesterol. And then she suggested, "Maybe we should try LAP-BAND surgery."

What?

She hadn't asked me about my life, relationships, work, stress level, recreational activity, creative pursuits, spiritual practice, diet, or anything about my social-emotional status. Seriously? I was floored. She suggested an invasive surgery for weight loss without digging any deeper into the *whole* of the situation? I was shocked. I intuitively told her to give me some time to process all of this. She told me if things weren't improved within six months, I would *have to* get on the medications.

I left the clinic and drove back to my office. When I walked in, my friend Teresa and one of her friends were sitting in my office. I burst into tears. In my disbelief, I explained that the doctor had suggested, "LAP-BAND surgery!?"

Teresa's friend was intuitive and said, "Teresa, do you remember that book? There's something in there for Julie. I don't think she needs the whole book, but something in there will lead her to what she needs. Can you share it with her?"

She was right. I threw myself into the path of research and discovery. I was reading everything I could about inflammatory foods, food as medicine, autoimmune diseases, the latest research, and what was new in mind-body, energy, and integrative medicines.

I studied different cleanses and detox approaches. I found the book *Clean* by Dr. Alejandro Junger. And I began a different relationship with food and my body.

First, I did a month-long restrictive detox and cleanse with extreme clean eating, where only organic fruits, vegetables, and lean proteins went in my body, and only organic hair and skin-care products touched my body. This was four weeks of 100 percent organic, clean everything going in and on my body. As suggested, I began walking. I walked through the pain. Within a month, I was walking four miles every day. I felt so much better, and the pain and inflammation had subsided.

Next, I went on the *Clean* program for another month. I felt so good. Eliminating sugar and gluten was huge. Intuitively, I knew sugar was part of my inflammation issues and gluten was part of my digestive issues. (Ironically, a few months later, my daughter was referred to a doctor for food allergies. She was diagnosed with gluten sensitivity and cautioned to avoid sugar, dairy, and corn. Somehow, this felt like validation.) Increasingly, I was feeling better and moving my body. I could touch any muscle and give it a squeeze without excruciating pain. I was healing my body and feeling good.

Every year since, I have done routine cleansing, detoxing, and periodic fasting. I learned to listen to my body, and it became easy for me to have routine structure and live within those boundaries.

This was one of my biggest wounds of separation—my relationship with my body. Body image was at the root of my personal shadow work. I didn't know how to comfortably be in my body. I didn't know how to love, honor, or cherish myself in my body. I didn't know how to truly nourish myself and receive it. I denied myself pleasure. I was so disconnected from my body.

How do we learn to authentically love ourselves and bring our divine essence all the way into our physical bodies? A wake-up call was manifest in the quote by Richard Rohr when he said, "The True

Self—where you and God are one—does not choose to love as much as it is love itself already."

Remembering my brief time of authentic self/body love before I broke my leg, I resigned myself to the idea that I am "LOVE itself already." My True Self that is ONE with God is my essential self; my expansive self; my Sacred Self. I was learning to tune in and listen to the gentle, healing voice of self-compassion. The innate intelligence of my True Self was calling me to really, really BE the love that I am. There was nothing to do, nothing to prove, nothing to search for outside of myself. God and I were already ONE in that sweet space of TRUE, authentic beingness and love.

The voice of criticism was my familiar, limited Separate Self/ego sabotaging my experience of life and love, tricking me into believing a false, culturally conditioned idea of beauty and body image. The louder the voice, the more stress. The greater the stress, the more fear and anxiety. It was a torturous spiral into the depths of a fiery hell, but I was finally getting a glimpse of light around this wound. The entire journey with my fractured bones dropped my awareness down into my body and the throes of my intimate relationship with it. Stirring up my old, dysfunctional body image issues moved me farther and farther away from my expansive, peaceful state of divine inter-being.

One more round of healing the subconscious—clearing the shadow—began. I began to visualize the creative impulse of love pulsing through my veins, washing through every cell, lighting, lightening up, and enlightening my body and mind with great healing compassion. I was guided and shown a new energy technique to clear my field of the negative, toxic waste I had been carrying for most of my life. A new daily practice of self/body love began.

Replacing negative self-talk with loving compassion took persistence and constant vigilance. I was to rediscover my undivided wholeness and accept what is. I shifted my focus to how I felt in my body, not how I looked or my need for acceptance. I wanted to feel radiant and I could do that by simply breathing in radiance and allowing it to be. When I felt it, I lived it into being in a whole new way. I would mindfully be the self-love that I desired. Feeling at home in my body was as easy as breathing in love, light, radiance, and beauty. My experience followed my mindset.

I remembered the new, loving, body conversation I had had before that dreaded "snap!" Now I was ready to snap out of the self-defeating barrage of criticism and into the love that was innately me. I saw that love as an embodied presence, not as something I had to think, say, or do. To embrace my divinity, I was to embody great love.

—

Voice of the Soul

I kept hearing: *Walk in love with yourself. Walk in love with your body. Walk in perfect love.* It became my new mantra. *Walk in love.* It meant so many things. Playing with punctuation, I made it an engaging puzzle:

Walk in love with yourself. Walk in love with your body. Walk in perfect love.

Walk, in love with your Self. Walk, in love with your body. Walk, in perfect love.

Walk in love, with yourself. Walk in love, with your body. Walk in perfect love!

Walk in love with your True Self, for you are love. Walk where you and God are one within your body. Walk in love, for you are love itself already. Walk in love with the Beloved. Walk, in love with the Beloved. Walk as the embodiment of Love. You can't walk in love without your body. Love your body so you can walk as Self. Love your body as your Self. Walk with God—in your body. Walk, with God in your body. Walk with you and God as one—with God as your body. Walk. Love. Be yourself. Be love.

The play with this new mantra grew into a healthier and deeper understanding of my relationship with my authentic True Self and my body—my True Self, as embodied. There was a haunting, feminine call to come home to myself and my body, an invitation to fully receive and embody the sacred in the imperfect, mortal flesh of my human experience. I began my own personal "Occupy Body" movement. The dissolution of separation between self and Self—ego and essence, divine and human—began grounding and stabilizing. I was shifting gears from fear to love and from temporary thoughts of separation to the perennial awareness of my inherent unity. It began with the conscious awareness of my inner voices—both the egoic, Separate Self and essence of Sacred Self.

The voice of the ego is usually harsh, critical, and judgmental. It analyzes, compares and measures. It condemns and creates inner chaos and conflict. The voice of the soul—our True Self or guidance from the Sacred Self—is usually short, brief, nonemotional, and nonjudgmental. It's simple. It's random and comes out of nowhere—usually out of context. It speaks in symbols, feelings, images, words, emotions, hunches, and gut reactions. Sometimes it speaks as one small piece of the puzzle, but other times it comes as the complete picture.

For me, the intuitive language of my soul has been auditory, visual, and visceral. Sometimes I would hear, sometimes I would see, and sometimes I would know. I never really thought to tune in to guidance for small, benign issues and seemingly insignificant moments. However, experiencing the impact of Rohr's quote made me rethink everything. When I heard self-criticism, I experienced a false self and deeply felt the separation.

Every time I caught myself in thoughts of self-criticism or fear, my higher True Self came in with a healing dose of love and compassion. Negative thoughts about food quickly morphed into nourishing experiences of self-love. Negative body judgments transformed into deep gratitude for the embodiment of love. The shift was simply my expanded awareness and a trust. It was time, once and for all, to stop battling with the delusion that kept me separate from my sacred body—the human sanctuary for my soul. To heal my unhealthy body relationship, I shifted to an awareness of fully *embodying* the God within.

My higher True Self wasn't separate. God/Creator/Source/ pure divine consciousness wasn't separate, disconnected, or unreachable. I was making my True Self at home IN my body, welcoming the divinity within.

I always used to tell my kids, "Practice makes permanent, not perfect." I was practicing this embodiment into a permanent state of being. Stabilizing this divine union, I began listening for only the voice of my authentic True Self, succeeding and failing, playing and having fun, following the threads to greater awareness. The practice was discernment, trust, grace, and self-compassion. I listened for the subtle differences and began moving at the speed of higher guidance. The *Voice of Knowing* was not a faint whisper outside myself. I was experiencing it within, and I aligned with it. Guidance wasn't something outside myself, transmitting from a distant celestial realm. It was *within*.

Listening to this guidance was not always easy or clear.

One day, I was sitting at a beautiful outdoor lunch on an ocean beach in Costa Rica. My husband and I were on a business trip with others in a group. It was a lovely lunch under the shade of trees and in the company of a dozen or so iguanas. With a gentle ocean breeze offering relief from the intense heat and humidity, we went through a beautiful buffet line. I filled my plate with greens and vegetables from the salad bar, fresh guacamole, one chicken skewer, and two vegetable skewers.

Back at the table, I pulled the veggies off the skewers and began eating my lunch, while enjoying our conversation. After most of the food on my plate was gone, I picked up a lone, small, button mushroom with my fingers. In a strange, suspended non-ordinary moment of time, I lifted the mushroom to my mouth, looked at it, and had a sensory response. In a peculiar flash, that still small voice lovingly spoke to me, **Don't eat this mushroom.**

From a place of higher awareness, I observed my small Separate Self questioning the *Voice of Knowing* in disbelief and rationalizing and arguing with it: *This mushroom is good for me. Vegetables are a good, healthy choice. If there's anything wrong with the mushroom, it's probably too late. I've already eaten all the other vegetables off the skewers. Why wouldn't I eat this mushroom? It doesn't make sense. I made healthy choices, and in this social situation, it would be polite to eat what's on my plate. Of course, it's okay to eat the mushroom.*

Don't eat the mushroom.

Seriously? Not once, was I thinking this was the voice of my higher self—my wisdom, intuition, guidance. Though, I have heard that random voice of truth so many times. Was I blinded by the menial focus on a mere bite of food? Why wouldn't my higher guidance step in and warn me? The suspended moment ended as I placed the mushroom in my mouth and cleaned my plate. We sat there socializing, laughing, telling stories, and having great conversation for another hour or so. We watched the iguanas, taking pictures and videos as the professional kitchen staff cleaned up the lunch buffet.

Later that evening, when we sat down to dinner in a luxurious open-air restaurant with a gorgeous sunset view of the ocean and marina, I wasn't real hungry, and nothing sounded good. My elegant entree of Mediterranean sea bass and vegetables came, but it wasn't looking too appetizing. I noticed I wasn't experiencing an inviting aroma, nor was I aware of much taste. After a few bites, I felt full and unable to complete the meal. It was becoming evident that something wasn't quite right. Severe stomach cramping spoiled our evening walk by the ocean-side shops and marina. Later, in the middle of the night, I was up with a violent food poisoning.

I didn't listen to the voice. I didn't heed the warning or guidance, ***Don't eat this mushroom.*** My Higher Self was certainly testing me, or else playing a cosmic joke with my disbelief.

It was a great lesson. I missed one full day of my vacation in Costa Rica, because I didn't trust or listen to the still small voice— that compassionate, loving voice of wisdom that was present to assist me no matter what the issue—big or small. I left Costa Rica poised and ready to tune into the ever-so-subtle guidance with a keen ear and magnified attention. This voice was stabilizing itself as a constant and friendly companion focused on self-love, not just occasional flashes of revelatory insight, guidance for work and clients, or ground-shaking, intuitive hits. I could now count on the voice for real, moment-to-moment guidance to heal the separation with my body.

It quickly became clearer than ever before. As I shifted my awareness to the abundant wisdom within, I felt no separation between the flowing Divine Presence and myself. The egoic, terrorizing voice of the small self began to disappear. My authentic True Self was once again grounded in love and compassion. I was walking in perfect love with God and I as one.

Higher wisdom is infinitely and abundantly right here whether we tune in or not. Divine guidance is always accessible. This guidance is here to help us heal. Even the smallest issues are not too small in that place where we and God are one. I learned to love my body—my *whole* self—by practicing and actualizing this divine union, by walking a new way. An amplified abundance of this deep wisdom and boundless love thrives within each of us. All we need to do is focus our awareness on it—and trust.

CHAPTER REFLECTIONS

In the past, when I've been in a state of whole beingness, I experience an infinite peace that transcends my body. However, when I slip into a state of limited awareness and separation, the chronic issue that has challenged me is my body image.

- Love thyself? We are conditioned to be self-centered or selfless, yet many of us (especially women) are disrespectful and dishonoring of ourselves. It is time for us to embody the shift into whole-being and divine partnership. Self-love is easier to practice and realize when you experience yourself in your divinity. You are LOVE itself. Rohr says your True Self is where you and God are one. Spend a few minutes in contemplative silence with this idea. Allow the message to really deepen into your being. When you recognize it as true, how does it feel? What is your experience of living as one with God inside? How might this understanding shift your perception and relationship with God? With yourself?

- Divine union between God and your True Self is magical. The world is transformed and everything becomes sacred. This is a foundational part of your whole-being. Consider planning a private, sacred ceremony of divine union. Join, as one, your True Self with God. How might you recognize and celebrate this sacrament as you consciously live into it more deeply in this present moment? Next, practice listening to the voice of your authentic, True Self. Ask more questions of the True Self throughout your day. Don't act or move until you hear the answer. Be in an affirming state of grace with this authentic True Self throughout your normal daily routine.

- As we explore our divine union—our divine humanity— often the "humanity" part gets in our way. It's easier to consider our divinity as something we achieve after death. Our human flaws, faults, weaknesses, mistakes, and imperfections occupy our minds, making it difficult to buy into or experience our divinity. Hiding our shadow becomes a game that keeps us from fully embodying the light. Yet, those imperfections are a part of our being and becoming divine. We are divine. We are human. We are perfect and whole as we are! As we embody more and more light— Christ Consciousness—we clear, transmute, clarify, purify, and grow into more light. Write about your relationship with your human self and divine self. Write about your light. Briefly reflect on your history with shadow and your humanness. What does it feel like to be growing into your divinity—your light?

CHAPTER FOURTEEN

The Wound of Separation

In truth everything and everyone
Is a shadow of the Beloved,
And our seeking is His seeking
And our words are His words ...
We search for Him here and there,
While looking right at Him.
Sitting by His side, we ask:
'O Beloved, where is the Beloved?'

~ Rumi

I was being challenged to really ground and stabilize this *whole* new way of being the love that I am. Practice makes permanent. It was as if I were in a continuous laboratory upgrading my operating system. I was downloading layer by layer by layer. The invitation was to practice and stabilize the next highest version of this evolution. But you can't download the new without cleaning up the old! In computer terms, it felt like one download would almost be complete, and then old unnecessary garbage taking up space on my hard drive would interfere with the transmission. I would have to stop, do the clearing and cleaning up, and then start over from the beginning. But each "restart" was easier. I'd have a faster recovery, more quickly bouncing back. Extensive shadow work and debris were clearing; fragments were reconnecting; light was weaving; and wholeness was being restored. Yet, I was being tested again and again and again, over and over and over. Could I trust and love even more completely?

Are you going to get it this time, Julie? Will you put your best foot forward and step completely out of this illusion? Will you trust me to guide you—every step of the way? Will you learn to walk in perfect love and heed the call to wholeness? Will you leap and trust that I have always been here to catch you wherever you land?

A few months after working through this body-image, shadow, self-hatred crap, I attended a gathering with visionary leaders in Colorado. I saw one of my friends there who I hadn't seen for six months. When we were alone together, the first thing she said, in a disappointed tone, was, "Jules, you gained all your weight back."

I was stunned, embarrassed, and speechless. It shook through my newly formed, tender self-love and confident relationship with my True Self. Here was my shadow, my shame, my body issue re-emerging, once again, for one more round. I found myself stumbling over a barrage of words and puking up an explanation of the weight gain, like a little girl pleading her case in front of a big, scary judge: how I did a cleanse and had eaten 100 percent organic and vegan for a month and gained most of the weight during that one month; how I had been doing things differently and was working on loving myself more completely; how I was changing my relationship with my body and learning to trust it and love it more; how my focus was to feel beautiful and radiant and allow my body to follow; how I had been riding my Peloton bike three to five days a week, working hard, sweating, burning calories; how I was working out for forty-five minutes and riding twelve miles at a time; how I was sitting in my dry sauna religiously; how I was mindful of all the shifts and changes occurring as a natural part of evolution; how I was not putting energy or focus on my weight or body size as a measure of my value or self-worth . . .

I sounded ridiculous!

A lack of confidence knocked me over as I tried to ease the sting of her blunt and piercing observation. Such shame I felt while I rationalized my weight gain and what I perceived was her disappointment, as if I were a young child needing approval for my weight, my body, and my appearance. I witnessed myself explaining things in my own disbelief, resisting and wanting that moment (and my body) to be different than it was. The encounter triggered that old dark, destructive, terrorizing self-talk and activated my ego as I crumbled into a full-blown relapse of my deep wounding. The tender new growth and the progress I thought I had made slipped instantly into an abyss of ugly, self-conscious, ego-induced despair. Yuck!

My awareness shifted from a universal prowess and the flowing presence of Sacred Self, back to a superficial, finite, ego-bruised focus on my appearance and need for self-acceptance. Once again, I was challenged to break through the powerful spell of ego's seduction and its influence over my vanity—with all the cultural dysfunction and shallow definitions of beauty, value, and self-worth. And I failed. The seeds of doubt had already begun to sprout in the fertile soil of my insecurities. I was tripped up and fell hard, back into a barrage of abusive, hateful self-talk. The war with my body resumed with a vengeance, as I entered a vicious, new battle with shame. I felt like a complete failure, and things spiraled downhill very quickly.

Immediately, I was uncomfortable in my body. I couldn't sit in a chair or walk by a mirror or be in the group with ease or joy. I was obsessed as I tried to resist the battle with shadow. Naively, once again, I thought I had healed the pathological, love/hate relationship my ego had with my body. I thought I was past this familiar place of warring—terrorizing myself with criticism. I thought my daily practice of self-love had stabilized my True Self and essential nature. I believed I had healed these old wounds and laid to rest the battle scars of dysfunctional vanity and ego. I fought that demon in endless battles, over years of wasted time and energy, and yet, it was back with little reprieve. Surely, I could switch into my essential self, or failing that, stuff it all down and make it go away? *We are making this whole story up anyway, right? We have collectively created this wound as a result of faulty thinking, an illusion and cultural myth, no?*

Again, I was invited to go even deeper and clear yet another layer. Making note of my weakness, I journaled a bit, and shifted my awareness back to the gathering of people I was meeting from around the world, the social synergy, the shared purpose, and the incredible conversations we were having.

Where Focus Goes, Energy Flows

Later in the gathering, remnants of conflicting worldviews and layers of separation consciousness were presenting within the collective. Threads of spiritual narcissism, shadow, and collective ego were begging to be cleaned up, cleared, and integrated as well. I noticed how our collective process was so relevant to the greater evolution of consciousness on the planet. I was a microcosm of this macrocosm, and we were a microcosm of the greater macrocosm.

My small but mighty battle with a compromised body image seemed so silly and insignificant compared to humanity's escalating conflicts and severely wounded sense of self and identity. I suggest that humanity is struggling with a similar, catastrophic, collective body image. We certainly are judging and hating parts of ourselves, terrorizing and killing other parts, and creating an escalating campaign trying to resolve separation, while racial, religious, and gender tensions grow, plummeting our collective psyche into even greater breadths and depths of pain and suffering. My pain and torment became humanity's pain and torment. As my issues came to the surface to be loved, I could see how our collective human body is suffering and battling with itself. We, as humanity, have a significant issue with body-image, with self-image—a broken, dysfunctional worldview—that keeps the voice of our Separate Self active and busy.

A collective discordance has emerged in our world with a vengeance. And I also noticed it emerging in this gathering with visionary leaders. It was fascinating. Although I was confronted with my individual issues, I had enough proficiency in my expanded awareness to witness the collective process. My gifts of higher vision and synthesis are well integrated and always turned on. I could see something curious unfolding.

We were talking about processing and translating levels of consciousness from multiple, different levels of consciousness. Unknowingly, as a group, we talked about "integral and non-dual consciousness" from a *pluralistic* perspective. We strategized about "creating unity" by *dividing* the population into fractions and percentages of *us and them*. We practiced "social synergy" while protecting *individual platforms*, within *different sectors of society*. And the most interesting observation for me was that we sought to anchor a "global purpose" and "unify a movement" while two distinct worldviews were coexisting, simultaneously running, within the group's collective consciousness, begging for attention.

Ken Wilber Skyped in and gave us a talk about consciousness. He taught that there are three kinds of self: the False Self (the broken or illusory self-image), the Actual Self (the authentic or healthy, integrated self at any particular stage of development), and the Real Self (the timeless Self behind and beyond all manifestation). He also talked about the two different vectors of growth, which he calls *transformation* (the vertical ascent through different stages of consciousness) versus *translation* (making sense of the world from whatever stage you happen to be at, in the healthiest way possible).

He simplified this into "grow up" and "wake up." This is a critical distinction, especially for those who consider the goal of a global movement to "raise consciousness" and transform the world. Wilber said that forcing individual or cultural transformation is not only impossible, it's really not very compassionate. Conscious, visionary leaders should be focusing not on transforming the world, but rather on helping people better translate the world from wherever they might be. He suggested the work of "clean up (shadow work)" and "show up" are even more critical. The best way to foster and support people's growth in the long run is to make them as healthy as possible in the short run.

I don't know how many were aware of these subtle dynamics playing out in our group. We heard Wilber speak of the 5 percent of population that was at the integral stage of consciousness, and each of us took personally the imperative plea to grow it to 10 percent. I shared into the group, and presenced the collective shadow that had been moving among us. I named our spiritual narcissism: "We are the ones. We must raise consciousness on the planet!" I also named the two simultaneous worldviews we were holding.

The first distinct worldview is a *whole* worldview with a belief and confidence that the same impulse of evolution that has been moving through Creation for 13.8 billion years (http://bit.ly/yearsearth), as an integral part of the whole, is moving through us, as us, and that we are becoming conscious of it, and are in the midst of another great turn. My body wants to relax into this *whole* worldview and trust the impulse to guide all of our next best steps through the great transition and change. I want to align with that impulse, allow it to "in-form" me, and harmonize with the natural order of things as they unfold in the flowing presence of now. I want to experience myself in relationship with all that has come before me, and all that will follow. I want to actualize my unique purpose in this unfolding. With this *whole* worldview, I am motivated by love and a deep call to serve and live for the good of the whole. I feel passionate about assisting others to develop intentional, co-creative lives—aligned with the impulse of Creation, attuned to the heart frequency, in harmony with nature, and in resonance with others in community. With this *whole* worldview, I feel empowered, inspired, and *enough*. The answers and solutions lie within and are accessible.

As with the healing of my leg, the Designing Intelligence that created the world can and will heal the world. It's a matter of whether we humans can get out of the way, stop causing more damage, and allow the healing to come forward. It is time for us to align with the design of nature and act as instruments of the healing process.

The second distinct worldview is of separation, grounded in fear, alarm, and urgency. It holds a belief that our planet and all of humanity are in dire straits because of the chaos and mess we have created as a species. We have to do something **now[!]** to save ourselves! If we don't evolve and change—and do it quickly—our survival is in question. We may destroy ourselves completely. We must come together to **make change happen**, develop unity and social synergy, find solutions, create greater connectivity, and jump the system to a higher order. Threads of truth seduce us into the spell and pressure of this materialistic view of the world, anchored in reductionism and our separation.

With this worldview, there's an urgency and sense of impending doom. Fear doesn't motivate me to want to work harder, smarter, or faster. It feels helpless and hopeless, as if I am not enough and it is already too late. Looking at the whole of humanity through this lens, with our social structures and broken systems, I want to throw in the towel and give up. There's too much to do. The crisis and chaos in the world is overwhelming, painful, and hard to assimilate. Finally, my system gets overpowered by the gravity of the situation. The stress response narrows my vision and focus, constricts my sense of purpose, and I freeze, believing there are no easy, or even doable, next best steps. I feel alone, separate, and inadequate.

Two worldviews and two different feeling experiences were creating two polarizing responses. And yes, they coexisted. One was a startling wake-up call—a litmus test for our human resolve, higher potential, resilience, and co-creative prowess. The other was a measure of our faith, compassion, acceptance, and willingness to show up and do our own personal work—to participate in our individual and collective healing—to contribute to and serve the greater good.

Beautiful. Messy. Brilliant. Scary. Comforting. Strange.

It became so clear to me in that moment. Healing our worldview is foundational to healing our planet and our relationships with one another. Evolving our worldview will evolve our collective consciousness. Seeing the world through the lens of fear and separation is causing more fear and separation. Experiencing the world with love and wholeness creates more love and wholeness. What we put our attention on grows. Where our focus goes, our energy flows.

The impulse of Creation began moving through my experience, challenging me to stretch, grow, expand, and once again, find my voice. I put my attention on the call to wholeness and lost that nagging, egoic False Self in the expansive flow of conversation and activity. I became intoxicated sitting in a palpable field of resonance and heart connection. We joined our innate genius, and powerful new connections were created. On my drive home, I reflected on the patterns that emerged and the possibilities that presented. I left with a renewed sense of hope. Not necessarily from a result or outcome of what was accomplished in the four days, but for the coherence that was felt, the seeds that were planted, and the patterns that emerged in full view.

———

Uniting Science and Spiritual Wisdom

Humanity and mass consciousness has been steeped in a story of separation for centuries. This belief and worldview of separation has assisted in our human development and technological advancements thus far. Yet a new whole worldview is emerging. Shifts of consciousness are occurring. Humanity is waking up, and that old story no longer serves our highest good. We have believed ourselves to be disconnected from others, God, Creation, and the Universe, and now we know otherwise. The worldview of materialistic reductionism is breaking down, and with the help of science, a whole worldview is in-forming our path forward toward health, wholeness, and reconnection.

> We're wired for connection. A growing body of research shows that our need to connect is as fundamental as our need for food, water, and shelter. Connection is essential to our survival. We are profoundly shaped by our social environment, and we suffer when our bonds are threatened or ended. At this time of unprecedented complexity and chaos, escalating violence, and systems breakdown, new discoveries in science are providing an opportunity to upgrade our fragmented worldview and understand our true interconnected nature.

Indigenous cultures and spiritual traditions have taught this for thousands of years. You may have heard the Web of Life, Indra's Net, and the Akash. Now science is teaching us about the Quantum Field or the Unified Field of Consciousness. We are all connected. We are valuable parts of a unified, whole living-system. Whether you see it through a spiritual lens as the Creative Source, or the scientific lens of the Unified Field, the scientific evidence is mounting.

A *whole* worldview unites scientific research with universal spiritual experiences—all the non-ordinary states of consciousness and multidimensional realms. Jude Currivan writes about this in *The Cosmic Hologram*. This cosmology—this global perspective— changes everything. We are not separate. We never have been. We just "think" or "believe" we are. From believing the world is flat to understanding the world is round, it is now time for an evolutionary leap into our interconnected, multidimensional reality.

New discoveries have evolved and elevated years of scientific thinking. We understand, without a doubt, that we are a magnificent part of an interconnected, interdependent web of life. It is time to transcend the crisis we are in. We will do that with a new story, combining the best of scientific discoveries with the best of spiritual wisdom, as we come to understand who we really are. We are not what we have been taught, and we are more than what we have imagined.

> If we are, indeed, that place where we and God are one, in embracing who we really are, we will become better people and create an extraordinary world.

When I returned home from the gathering in Colorado, I picked myself up and got right back on my path, practicing healthy self-love and self-care, stabilizing the multidimensional awareness, listening to the voice of wisdom within, and healing my leg. With the reminder of Wilber's "wake up, grow up, clean up, and show up," I was inspired to look more closely at our collective shadow alongside my own persistent, perceived human weaknesses. The invitation was to efficiently take responsibility, do my personal clearing, and with ease, move it out to the transpersonal realm. I was looking to consciously transcend any worldview and belief structure that no longer served my highest good, or our collective good. I saw these issues placed into the transpersonal dimension and blessed and loved into greater wholeness. Humanity needs a taste of the higher order of interconnectivity—the unified field of consciousness—that is operating behind the scenes of our everyday lives.

Where the Light Enters

I looked again at what was mine to heal and clean up. Where were the remnants of fractured ego yearning to be illuminated? Where was my shadow work incomplete? How was I holding spiritual narcissism and the two separate worldviews? Who was I to think I was so special as to help heal the world and raise consciousness? Who was I to think I was so separate as to be unworthy and insignificant? It's the same narcissism—the same separation and fractured sense of self. I navigated through the remnants of opposing worldviews, faulty thinking, and old beliefs. What other ways was I needing to evolve the False Self? What was mine to do?

There are so many ways to heal. Arrogance may have a place in technology, but not in healing. I need to get out of my own way if I am to heal.

~ Anne Wilson Schaef

I would serve this fractured sense of self best by not getting stuck in pain or suffering, and once again, tease out my own capacity for self-love, self-compassion, and self-care. Holding it in a gentle, trans-egoic frame of reference, I could bring more light and healing potential to the broken pieces. I was challenged to push through this dichotomy—both personal and collective; break through the personal, singular experience and love the universal, wounded ego of humanity more. My healing is our healing. Our healing is my healing. Personal healing can come through our collective experience, and collective healing can come through one's personal experience. My embodied presence becomes humanity's embodied presence.

Rumi said, "The wound is the place where the light enters you." I was open to allowing all the healing light in that I could absorb and filter.

One sunny afternoon shortly after my return home, I went downstairs to ride my Peloton bike, geared up with my towel and water bottle, clipped into the pedals, and began a live class. It was a productive day, and I was feeling great. I was full of energy and looking forward to my ride. Within a few minutes, the instructor asked, "What is that heavy weight you've been carrying around? What is the burden you need to put down? We are going to ride it out today. Release it. Put it down and ride it out!"

Immediately, a tidal wave of desperation hit me. Imagine getting knocked off a boat going full speed and losing your orientation under water. It was like that. I didn't know what hit me and I didn't know which way was up or down. A dark ugly shadow swirled into the raging waters and consumed my entire being in a swift shift of energy. It was heavy, extremely heavy. (My heavy weight?) I couldn't breathe. Rolled under the fierce torrent of moving water and emotion, I was suffocating. Violent, tumultuous, and overwhelming emotions were rushing in, launching me into instantaneous, uncontrollable sobbing. A piercing voice emerged from the shadow: *You are worthless. You have absolutely no value. You are such a failure, a worthless pile of shit. You are nothing.*

An unceasing barrage of darkness overtook me. Uncontrollable grief, shame, and sadness came up and out with brute force. Where did it all come from? I felt so hopeless and helpless. I knew I was feeling down and self-conscious about my weight, body image, and prolonged healing journey, but seriously? This was a way bigger and heavier load than I thought I was carrying. I must have primed the pump of eternal shame, suffering, and damnation. Was this coming from the ultimate wound of separation from God? Was this mine or ours? As the storm continued to rage and swell, I sobbed and convulsed and "rode it out" as the instructor suggested.

I kept moving until the waves began to calm. Each pedal stroke moved me farther away from the horrid, tyrannical voice that had terrorized my once peaceful day. Every new breath and bead of sweat brought seeds of grace. Composure traded places with the grief, as a fragile sense of strength sent the barrage of insecurity back to hell, from where it came. I finished my ride in wonderment and awe of the huge, unexpected, cathartic release of toxic waste.

Unclipping from the pedals, I removed my shoes and socks and stepped into the preheated sauna with a full bottle of water and my partly dry hand towel. I usually sit in quiet meditation for thirty minutes following a bike ride. A stack of soft bath towels eased the transition from the hard, narrow bike seat to the stiff wooden bench. I sat in contemplative, sacred space as my 128-degree sanctuary continued to rise in temperature. Trusting in the continued purge of all that no longer served my highest good, I breathed into the release with gratitude. And I heard:

I am nothing without Source. I am no-thing but Source. I am only Source.

The wound is where the light entered.

CHAPTER REFLECTIONS

Unknowingly, as a group, we talked about "integral and non-dual consciousness" from a pluralistic perspective. We strategized about "creating unity" by dividing the population into fractions and percentages of us and them. We practiced "social synergy" while protecting individual platforms, within different sectors of society. And the most interesting observation for me was that we sought to anchor a "global purpose" and "unify a movement" while two distinct worldviews were coexisting, simultaneously, within the group's collective consciousness, begging for attention.

- Shadow. We are called to do our own inner shadow work. Alchemy comes from within. We are being asked to claim our shadow, not be afraid of it, and do the alchemical work of transmutation. We are also challenged to not separate ourselves from the collective. The "us vs. them" mentality keeps us polarized and in conflict. Look at your life and see where you may be projecting on to others ("If only they would . . . "). There are often times we get stuck in a judging mode. Ask yourself how you are projecting your own issues onto others. Take responsibility. Where might you feel inferior or superior? Where might you create separation? Where might you protect your selfish interests? Where are you stubbornly attached to faulty thinking? Make a list of these places and do some purge journaling. What can you learn? What is yours to own, heal, purify, and clean up? Relax and trust the process. The same Designing Intelligence that created the earth can heal us all. Healing is a natural part of our being and becoming. Tune into your own connection with this alchemical, healing power.

- Our level of consciousness, with our thoughts and beliefs, create our worldview. If you believe the world is flat, you might be fearful to set sail toward the horizon. As we expand our consciousness, we evolve our worldview. Explore the idea of worldviews and how they affect our behavior and choices. Do you see the world as *out there* or *in here*? Do you see the world as safe or threatening? Do you see the world in dire straits or divine evolution? Do you see the world with fear or love? Play with the two different worldviews—one born in separation and fear, and the other born in wholeness and love. Do they coexist within you or are you firmly planted in one or the other? Are you willing to evolve your understanding beyond where it is today?

- Meditate on the phrase: ***I am nothing without Source. I am no-thing but Source. I am only Source.*** Play with this idea in your journal. How are you doing differentiating the voice of ego vs. the voice of your Sacred Self? Are you ready to see yourself as nothing but Source? The "I AM Presence" of Source is a different relationship than a connection with Source. Sense into your readiness to evolve and experience this truth. What remnants of shadow continue to block your ability to see clearly?

CHAPTER FIFTEEN

Trusting the Impulse of Creation

Healing may not be so much about getting better, as about letting go of everything that isn't you—all of the expectations, all of the beliefs—and becoming who you are.

~ Rachel Naomi Remen

Birthing happens in the dark, and healing happens in the unseen realms of mystery. The time comes when the dark womb is crowded and no longer supports life. We outgrow the womb. At some point, we must leave our safe, warm cocoon-like environment. It becomes too constrictive, like the cage in my dream. We push against the cage that constricts us until we transcend the limitations. Butterflies push and struggle against the cocoon until it breaks open, and they emerge with their wings.

We are creative beings and we are birthing ourselves through a more co-creative, universal consciousness. We can create anything. We are creating and recreating our lives every day. We create stories and beliefs. We create boxes and safe containers. We have made incredible technological advances. We create according to our level of consciousness and perception of the world, seen through the lens of our beliefs and what we've been taught by our culture, schools, religions, media, and our families.

But do we truly understand how powerful we are?

It's always good to remember that "we don't know what we don't know until we know it." That's how consciousness works. We expand into a bigger picture—a fuller sense of awareness. We apprehend our wholeness. We grow into higher levels of our creative potential, evolving, understanding, experiencing, and "getting it" more and more along our path. We go through many stages of development, looking outside ourselves and within. When we fully awaken to a new stage of development, we think we get it—the whole picture. But we don't. Not completely, because we can't. Again, that's how the ever-evolving development of consciousness works.

We seek spiritual enlightenment. We yearn for greater liberation. We strive for self-actualization. We want to follow a path of awakening. But for millennia, we haven't been able to flip a light switch and have everyone wake up and grow up at the same time—together. We are all on individual paths with trajectories unique to each of us. Continued enlightenment happens naturally as we birth, and rebirth ourselves out of the dark.

Yet, we *are* evolving as a species and we are evolving consciously. We are becoming more and more aware of our higher potential and the limitations we have created for ourselves. We can create life and we can destroy it. We can build cages and consciously choose to stay in them. Or we can look beyond our current situation and onto the next frontier. We are pioneers. And just like birth happens in the dark, we have come to a place in our collective consciousness where we recognize we have been living in a dark womb of limited consciousness, embedded in the illusion of separation—asleep.

An acorn may not be aware that it is a mighty oak tree waiting to grow, and a fetus in utero may not be conscious that it is a baby human about to be born. Yet, humanity is becoming aware that a greater potential exists outside of the current container of limited perception. We are evolving, and we are conscious of our evolution. We are a species waking up inside a great awakening, seeing through the illusion of separation. We are recognizing that our thoughts are creative, beginning to believe our beliefs are prescriptive. We feel like nothing is real and everything is real. And we're tuning into other realms, dimensions, and alternative realities as they exist in the here and now. The veil is thinning, or might I suggest *disintegrating*, as we shift our consciousness and relax into our divine union with Source.

I am nothing without Source.
I am no-thing but Source. I am only Source.

Remember We Are Home

We are not separate physical bodies. We are no-thing. We are the pure consciousness—awareness, source energy—that resides within all "things." Experiencing this divine union—or communion—with Source changes everything. As we dissolve the boundaries of our perceived separation, we shift our reality. As we rest in our being and becoming, the dominant, material worldview of separation that used to contain and sustain us, doesn't make sense anymore. It doesn't work. It's breaking down.

Like a gentle tear in the amniotic sac, our dark womb has been pierced with the light of consciousness. The light has entered, and there's no turning back. Yet we have choice and free will. We get to co-create this new world, this new life, together with the impulse of Creation. We get to choose how we birth ourselves. We can move into our being and becoming with purpose and be love, being and becoming more love. (I'll say that again.) We can *be* love, being and becoming more love. Or not. We can choose to be tender and compassionate in our birth and invite more love and consciousness into the process.

We are also becoming conscious of Creation co-creating through us. As we receive more love and light, we birth a deep, limitless creative love more reflective of our divine nature. It's a beautiful emergence. And here, we surrender to all that is, allowing and trusting as we live in the mystery of unknowing. This is new terrain. We let go of all we thought we knew and surrender to a perfect higher order.

This creative potential assists us to see beauty in a broken world. When we open ourselves to the flowing Presence of creative impulse, we also experience the harmony, resonance, and unity that are inherent in Creation or Nature. In search of the Sacred, we seek unity with the transcendent and we find it within our embodied presence. In putting the broken pieces back together, we discover a benevolent universe, a benevolent grace, moving through our human experience.

We remember we are home, and always have been—*home* in the Beloved. We are remembering our divine humanity. We are calling our soul home and inviting ourselves to incarnate more completely—to bring spirit and consciousness more fully into every aspect of our lives. Here in this yet new stage of our development, we bear great fruit. This IS it. THIS is what we have been dreaming of. This is what we have been waiting and yearning for. We are it and this *is* it. There is no separation.

> *I am the vine. You are the branches.*
> *If you remain joined to me, and I to you,*
> *you will bear a lot of fruit.*
>
> **~ John 15:5**

—

Nothing to Find, No Need to Search

Now, at this pivotal moment in history, we can choose to see the universe through the eyes of our limited, fragmented, disconnected selves or flip that view and see ourselves through the eyes of the Divine. The first option feels constrictive and limiting and is founded in separation. The second feels expansive and creative, grounded in our undivided wholeness. Let us release our attachments to how we *think* life should be and release our expectations of what is yet to come. Let us welcome the unknown, the unknowing, and the unknowable. Welcome change. When we stop trying to figure it all out, we receive more.

The heart simultaneously sends and receives blood, not wondering or worrying if the blood will come back, and not trying to figure out how the blood serves the body. The lungs simultaneously receive oxygen and release carbon dioxide, not holding onto either process until the other does its thing. We are designed to live in simultaneity with this creative force, trusting the Divine Intelligence that is at work in the universe. We are called to trust the process of giving and taking, sending and receiving, birthing and dying, with the universal intelligence directing the flow.

> We are continuously being in-formed by the Unified Field of Consciousness. At the same time, *we* are in-forming the field. Science is beginning to demonstrate how this reciprocal relationship works. We are living in exciting times! Notice how science is discovering what different spiritual traditions and wisdom has been teaching us for centuries.

Artist Arthur Hopkins created a well-known painting of a young girl reaching up to knock on a door. It's called *The Visitor*. I have loved this painting for decades. I have a print hanging in my home. One day, my friend Shelley pointed me to the print for further inquiry. I noticed the young girl in the painting was standing on her tiptoes and even then, she could not reach the doorknocker. For years, I had admired this image and never noticed that she couldn't reach it. The symbolism really touched me. How often have I felt like this young girl—in a state of separation? How many times have I reached for something and fallen short? How has my life been shaped by believing a door or barrier separated me from what I knew was possible?

With this new awareness, I altered the print. I literally took the beautiful frame, ornate mat, and print apart and altered it by inscribing the scripture Matthew 7:7–8, "Ask, and it will be given you; search, and you will find; knock, and the door will be opened for you." It continues, "For everyone who asks receives, and everyone who searches finds, and for everyone who knocks, the door will be opened."

The idea in this scripture is powerful. For everyone? Yeah.

To me, this represented the simplicity and wisdom of Divine Union and our higher co-creative potential. Trying to manufacture something from a limited perspective of separation always leaves me feeling like the young girl in the painting. I have to work really hard and I can't reach the door. However, calling on divine, infinite wisdom, I can achieve so much more.

I was attached to the print emotionally. I loved the image, the colors, the frame and mat. I loved the blue door, the little girl, her apron, and the sweet basket in her arms, the greens growing over the door, the bench, and the welcoming plant. I loved her little brown boots standing on tiptoe. I resonated with it so much. In altering my print, an even more dramatic appreciation occurred.

"Ask, and it will be given you; search, and you will find; knock, and the door will be opened for you." I felt the verse morph and shift into a peculiar simultaneity: it is given as you ask; it is found the moment you seek; it is opened as you knock. To carry this even further: there is no question that hasn't already been answered. Our limited minds, perceiving from a perspective of separation, creates the question. Our expansive minds, interconnected with all that is and sourced in the unified field, rests in the awareness of wisdom and truth. There is nothing to find, no need to search. The only door to open is the door of illusion.

I was not that little girl any more, believing I was on the outside of a door asking, searching, and knocking. The experience of being fully in my body and through this epic healing journey had shifted yet another layer of consciousness. I was embodying a unitive consciousness that was unlike the previous stages. A subtle birth occurred in the dark and shifted my relationship with all that is. Without trying, I moved from touching those moments of grace, to living in the flow of grace and embodying it.

In this state, I feel alive, nourished, healed, connected, and full. I have everything I need in the moment. "I am no-thing but Source." I am whole and complete. The Divine is as close as my breath. The door had never been closed. I had never been shut out, separate, or removed. Like consciousness, you don't know what you don't know until you know it.

Imagine the result if this divine union became expressed fully in our lives and on the planet. I am not separate. We are not separate. I am no longer waiting for a door to open or the veil to lift or the cage to be removed. I remove myself from the teaching and limiting belief that I have to connect with a God outside of myself. I can see through that door of illusion. I had been separating myself from the mystical spiritual realms, in my head. Yet, there is the light of pure divine grace deep within my embodied consciousness.

In remembering my wholeness, I was "re-member-ing" the God of love that resides within.

—

In This Holy Moment of Now

During my injury and recovery, it seemed like all the old fractured parts of myself from previous stages of consciousness re-emerged to be cleared and healed completely. As they did, I was invited to claim the pieces and parts, take responsibility for how I created the fractured sense of myself, and lovingly tend to the old ways with humility, vulnerability, and great compassion.

Now it was time to stabilize, fully embody, and express Christ Consciousness in ways I could never understand or conceive. Somehow, without me working at it, I released the belief that the two worlds were separate, and moved into the simultaneity. There was no more moving back and forth, as if on a bridge between them: "On earth **as it is** in heaven." I am one whole organism. I am one whole system, and one with all that is. I have never been separate. I am the manifestation of heaven on earth—as heaven and as earth—a divine human.

In dissolving duality at an even deeper level, I was understanding how to embody my bifurcated nature in service to the divine blueprint. I was living in the blessings of synchronicity. That perceived door is an extraordinary open doorway, a magnificent portal of an entirely new and different way of being that is unimaginable. The need to direct and control is reprogramed as Creation is creating as me and through me.

With the reminder, I am open to ancient wisdom and cosmic guidance, I welcome the creative impulse and universal truth. I am in joyful receivership of Christ Consciousness and the "Christification" of Julie. I am receptive to the incarnation of a higher magnificence, abundance, wholeness, and greater, unimaginable love.

Like the example of the heart and lungs, our sacred, divine nature is right here, right now. We are vessels for an infinite flow of Creative Source consciousness and universal intelligence. Only our thoughts and beliefs can create a perceived separation and block that flow. And we are really good at creating those blocks. Our minds create the story of the door, and the little girl who can't reach the knocker, as well as the actual need to knock.

Our False Self has the capacity to step outside of the flowing presence of now and get stuck in thoughts of past and future. The moment we step a nanosecond into the past or future, we lose our co-creative power. We don't tell the healthy heart to stop and back up a few seconds. We don't ask our vibrant lungs to breath into tomorrow. We simply trust our cardiovascular system is doing what it is doing in this Holy moment of now in service of a greater whole.

Tap into the flowing presence of Source. The great Presence within us is in the present moment of now. When our minds receive a spark of insight, we tend to attach to a specific outcome, and project the idea into the future and/or the past. If we think it's a great idea, our minds want to leap forward, engaging the brain to try to figure things out: *How do I get from point A to point B in the quickest way?* If our minds go to the past, we begin comparing and contrasting the new idea with past experiences. We leave the creative power and flow of Presence and try to rationalize and make sense out of the new information. Our awareness must stay engaged with the flowing presence *in the moment.*

This life-giving force is the same creative impulse that is healing my bones and creating new forms and structures on the planet. The impulse of Creation is in-forming us and creating more life all the time. Expanding. Growing. Outgrowing. Leaping. Evolving. Cycles of life, death, rebirth, healing, and evolution are found everywhere in nature. This impulse of Creation moves through us like the winds riffle through tree branches and the waters flow downstream. It is endless, absolute, and infinite.

Ask, and you shall receive. Don't wait for an answer and let your mind create stories, doubt, or analysis. Simply receive the perpetual wisdom and guidance as you live into the question. Open yourself with childlike faith that everything is already done. Allow the unending grace of God's presence to be yours. Align your potential with this Creative Source and turn your will over to Divine Will. Create a beautiful dance of co-creative simultaneity and immeasurable abundance.

Childlike faith is essential. As a child, I would get lost in the zone of flowing presence and surrender to the innate unity of our interconnected universe. I experienced a power beyond what I understood or what people could teach me. We all have the light of divine intelligence within and the capacity to access it in any moment. My ongoing conversations with God yielded instant guidance and benevolent results. However, when my rational mind filled with doubt and limiting beliefs, and analysis interrupted the flow, I limited my own field of possibilities.

Trusting a Higher Power

My husband and I went to California's #1 Luxury Resort and Hotel for a company trip. The resort had impeccable, unrivaled "Five-Diamond Service." They had a Five-Star Spa and exquisite dining options. It was an incredible experience from the moment we stepped our reverent feet on the property. The elegance and comfort invited an epic sense of wonder and awe as the senses were continually delighted with the aesthetic attention to detail.

We had a free day and were talking about our options for the evening's meal. A staff member suggested dining at Addison, their "signature" restaurant. A local was there visiting and agreed—bragging of their world-acclaimed chef. His artisanal approach to cooking combines local, seasonal ingredients with a contemporary French influence. The dining was by reservation only and had two select options: the Four-Course Menu or the Chef's Tasting Menu, which we fondly called, "Chef's Choice." The experience was touted as "an unforgettable, multicourse evening of surprise and culinary creativity."

My husband was more than curious. As the locals continued to talk about the unique dining experience, the intrigue got the best of him. He got up and said he was going to go check with the concierge and ask more questions. When he returned, he had made a reservation for that evening. He saw it as an adventure, entertainment, and an educational experience. We both love fine dining. We both love trying new things. He saw it as a once-in-a-lifetime opportunity and vacation experience.

Arriving at the restaurant was like entering another world. They greeted us by name and ushered us to our table amidst an ambiance of elegance and mystique. If we had chosen the four-course meal, we would have been handed a menu and been able to select our favorites for each course. However, the Chef's Tasting Menu was all about the mystery—inviting us into a culinary journey of epic proportions to tantalize our senses.

As we settled in, I became nervous. "What if they serve something I don't like," I asked my husband with hesitancy? Eleven courses seemed like a lot. This was not soup, salad, entrée, and dessert. They preferred to pair each unique course with a wine. We opted for two different wines—a white and a red—and the recommended champagne to start us off.

Our server asked if we had any food allergies or sensitivities. If so, the chef would make adjustments as needed. And then he explained that if there was anything we didn't like once served, the chef would prepare an alternative. That eased my mind a bit. I decided to let go of all resistance and fear and immerse myself in the moment. I chose to surrender and trust the process—trust the chef.

Each course was an incredible, mind-blowing piece of art! The aesthetic experience of colors, textures, and design was just as impressive as the aroma and taste. The portions were perfect with one, two, or three bites to slowly savor and delight in. Every dish had complex and exquisite flavors.

The service was like a well-seasoned orchestra with six to eight people gracefully and discreetly moving around our table, playing their parts before, during, and after each course. Their knowledge and expertise was outstanding. Everyone who spoke knew intricate details about the foods, preparation, ingredients, and techniques. The perfect pace between each course created a timeless and lingering enchantment that captivated all of our senses and kept us in awe far beyond the conclusion of the meal.

There was nothing I did not like. I was so intoxicated with the multisensory experience that it didn't matter there were new and unusual ingredients that at times, I couldn't even pronounce. It was gorgeous and sensual. I thoroughly enjoyed everything that was eloquently set before me.

Reflecting on the experience, I know, without a doubt, that if given the eleven courses to choose from on a menu, I *maybe* would have chosen two or three of them. My limiting beliefs, limited experience, fear of the unknown, and personal preferences would have prevented me from trying most of the "Chef's Choice" courses. In fact, my rational mind would have made a judgment and never allowed me to agree to the experience in the first place. What a powerful lesson!

Trusting a world-renowned chef to prepare a culinary feast is like trusting the Universal Source Intelligence to heal my leg, guide my life, to heal the planet, and birth a new humanity. Who am I to "think" I know better? Thoughts from my small mind simply create distractions and static in the field. Who am I to question Divine Intelligence when it's creating a beautiful, abundant life through me? Co-creation with Higher Source Intelligence makes every day, every step, more meaningful and complete. Healing from my fractured state, I no longer experience this Creative Source as "out there, somewhere," as a separate entity that I have to connect with, or as inaccessible.

I am called to walk in perfect resonance within the unified field of intelligence—the God Source within all that is. There is no separation. I am whole.

**I am nothing without Source. I am no-thing but Source.
I am only Source.**

As I learn to walk with God inside, I still stumble and fall once in a while. The dying old paradigm has a strong pull. But as a curious toddler learning to walk, I get back up and keep going. So, I must; so, we must.

God is within this evolution, within our healing, and within our wholeness. What is happening is beyond what we can imagine— beyond what we can perceive, and so much more. The linear mind cannot understand this, but we can feel it. As we surrender into the infinite mystery we are guided and we know. We mustn't reduce our understanding by trying to understand.

And this is the most profound pearl of wisdom: everything is evolving and changing at the same time. Everything—human and nonhuman, material and nonmaterial, organic and nonorganic—the whole of Creation is evolving and changing right here, right now. Plants, animals, earth, technology—there is no separation. We are part of a greater whole; we are one. We are waking, and a resonant higher frequency is calling us forward.

When we witness the impulse of Creation moving within us, we know we are in good hands. We can relax and trust a higher, divine blueprint. Christ Consciousness is in the mystery that moves the plan forward, the Intelligence that guides each step, and the Source that weaves our connective tissue. We are within God and God is within us. We are within all that is and all that is *is* within us. We are part of the Universe and the Universe is part of us. We are within the Universe and the Universe is within us. The Whole is within all things and all things are within the Whole. Marianne Williamson says we are the individual thoughts within the great mind of God. Where ego has separated us, let the grace of God heal, unite, and make us whole again.

The real you is not a puppet which life pushes around.
The real, deep down you is the whole universe.

~ Alan Watts

CHAPTER REFLECTIONS

We are all on our own individual paths with a unique trajectory. Continued enlightenment happens naturally as we birth ourselves out of the dark.

- The impulse of Creation is moving within us all. The divine spark of Creator is moving in us, through us and as us. In what ways are you beginning to trust that divine impulse? Look at ways your mind and Separate Self want to control your life and experiences. The need to control or feel safe keeps us stuck in the same patterns having the same experiences over and over again. Einstein said no problem can be solved with the same level of consciousness that created it. Yet, we dig our heals into the safe, familiar, and predictable ways of our being and can't understand why the problems persist. Look at the areas in your life where you know you are trying to control the outcome. What keeps you from trusting a higher power? Like they say in Alcoholics Anonymous, where do you need to "let go and let God?" It's time to walk with God inside and co-create your expanded reality.

- Take a few deep breaths. Imagine a divine treasure map in front of you. All you can see are the next few steps. Know the map represents a perfect higher order. Without seeing the entire map, you are invited to take your first steps forward. What do you need to be ready to blindly take the first few steps? What is your experience of trust? What is your experience of doubt and fear? This divine map is encoded within you. It's in your very DNA. Your own individual, unique blueprint resides within your being. Trust the map and trust the step as you take it. Each new step will present itself in the perfect, right timing.

- The caterpillar's metamorphosis into a butterfly is a common metaphor used to describe our own transformation process. Research the butterfly story—how the caterpillar literally digests itself and turns into "metamorphic soup" before the sleeping imaginal cells, similar to stem cells, eventually find each other and grow into the body parts of a butterfly. Imagine the genius of life in this story—the brilliance of the animating force that resides within that metamorphic soup. Many are feeling the effects of individual, local, and global change and likening it to that of the butterfly's journey. Meditate on the role of imaginal cells. They exist within creation, here and now. How are your imaginal cells speaking to you? What are they communicating?

CHAPTER SIXTEEN

Creating the Conditions for Healing

Humanity appears to be rapidly approaching
the breaking point. And there are two possible outcomes:
breakdown or breakthrough.

~ Peter Russell

What we know about healing and the best-kept secret of medicine is that the body has the capacity to heal itself. Like with the healing process of my fractured bones, there's a Universal Designing Intelligence—the Creative Source within—that knows what is best to return our bodies to balance. Our job is to get out of the way and create the right conditions for healing to occur. When we stop doing the things that cause the imbalance, discordance, or illness in the first place, the magic of healing intelligence can flow in and move freely. Eventually, the system is brought back to homeostasis, balance, and harmony.

After almost two years of healing, my ankle still wasn't 100 percent back to normal; neither was my gait or leg strength. My left foot was not yet in perfect alignment with my body. I wondered whether I would ever be back to pre-breakdown homeostasis. Walking any distance was difficult; normal daily activity created challenges; and pain and swelling were an everyday occurrence. It even hurt to merely touch the outside of my anklebone and the soft tissue around it. My range of motion was compromised. I couldn't descend stairs with my full weight on my left leg, no matter how consciously and carefully I tried. I remained unsteady and vulnerable on uneven or rough terrain, always staying vigilant not to twist or slip.

And I was weak. Riding my Peloton and recumbent bikes helped strengthen my legs, and I was doing a bit of weight lifting with my arms. Yet, I couldn't climb or bend like I used to. There was a general full-body weakness and lack of coordination that became my temporary mode of operation during this phase of my healing.

My doctor assured me that I was healing nicely considering the level of trauma that had occurred. Complete healing takes time. My patience was wearing thin. I wanted to run, jump, water ski, and dance again.

Then I remembered, I was not just in the rehabilitation phase; my bones were still in the remodeling phase of healing, and working hard to return to normal bone density after the significant osteopenia. It had been only a little over a year since the fractures in my knee had been diagnosed. And there was significant soft-tissue healing that had to occur on top of the bone healing.

I began having dreams about my fractured bones and the similar fracture or "wound of separation" that has occurred within humanity's collective body. As the weeks and months went on, the parallel was uncanny. Symptoms of global chaos were mounting. We could no longer deny the cumulative signs of stress, disorder, dysfunction, disease, and breakdown as it pummeled our collective psyche through popular media. Violence was escalating around the world. Fear was increasing. Individuals were going mad. The whole system was out of balance, polarized, and in unrest. It seemed as if we all could viscerally feel and hear that dreaded "Snap!" as a deeply injured Humanity recognized itself in a fractured state of incoherence—disabled by a consciousness of separation.

While Climate Change is a symptom, the fever that our Earth has contracted, the underlying disease is the disconnection from Creation that plagues human societies throughout the Earth.

~ Interfaith Declaration on Climate Change signed by myriad faith dignitaries including Archbishop Desmond Tutu

It's time to heal our collective wound of separation. It's time to come together to transcend our limited perspective of separation consciousness and the rising cumulative fear that comes from it. Let us move into our greatness by embracing what is in the highest good of the whole.

~

Our Collective Wound

As a healing practitioner, it was easy for me to see the parallel to my situation and begin to reflect on the stages for our collective healing on the planet. How do we calm our collective psyche enough to invite the conditions for healing to occur? How do we trust the Designing Intelligence—God, Great Spirit—to heal our fractures and ease our pain? How do we get our limited minds—our pride and ego—out of the way and return to wholeness?

Like fractured bones, wounds have a similar three-stage healing process. After stabilization, both fractures and wounds begin the healing process with the first phase—*inflammation*. Blood rushes to the site, allowing nutrients, white blood cells, antibodies, enzymes, and other beneficial elements into the affected area to promote a good healing response and stave off infection. Swelling, pain, heat, and redness occur.

As I discussed in chapter two, the second stage for bones is the *reparative stage* where bone callus begins weaving together to repair the bone. For wound healing, the second stage is called *proliferation*. Here, new tissue begins to form, weave together, and reorganize in order to repair the site and replace damaged tissues. Inflammation likely continues during this phase to aid in the healing response.

For fractures, the third stage is the *remodeling phase* where your body turns the weak bone callus into strong bone material and remodels it to normal shape and size. The cell density increases and the bone is strengthened. This stage overlaps with the previous stage and could last up to a few years in adults (hence, my impatience). For wound healing, the third stage is called *maturation*, or like bones, *remodeling*. This stage occurs as the wound has closed up and also can take up to two years to remodel the newly formed tissue. During this phase, the dermal tissues are overhauled to enhance their tensile strength, and functional fibroblasts replace nonfunctional ones.

As you can see, healing for both wounds and fractures occurs in a similar pattern.

Imagine our fractured, wounded world within this same healing response. See these three phases at work as whole systems break down in healthcare, education, economics, governance, politics, environment, and so on.

> Earth has its own self-healing capacity. Imagine that the earth is simultaneously engaged in a complementary, comprehensive healing response as well. How might we assist in this healing? Many individuals and organizations are working on resources, tools, technology and practices that positively affect and/or reverse climate change and global warming. Remember, to heal, we must create the conditions for healing to occur and at the same time reduce or stop the negative behaviors that create disease, illness, wounds, and fractures in the first place. Are you willing to do your part?

All of Creation has this creative, healing intelligence. We, as humans, can assist by creating the right conditions for a broad-spectrum healing to occur. When we stop doing the things that have caused imbalance, discordance, fractures, and wounding, the healing response begins. When we effectively eliminate undue stress, the collective body can initiate deeper healing. I believe our world will be brought back into homeostasis, balance, and harmony. However, humanity is invited to wake up to this capacity, take responsibility for its actions, and create the right conditions for healing to occur in the collective body.

As I was with my injury and recovery, humanity has been in this state for so long, we can't readily see the progress we have made. We have been fighting against the systems that aren't working. We have been valiantly trying to "save the world," not remembering to focus on our individual wholeness. We have been resisting change and clinging to "the good old days." We have been working hard to hold things together. Trying to be strong, we have minimized or denied our pain, limping forward, yet always feeling like we're getting nowhere. We are tired. We are weak, uncoordinated. We feel broken.

But there is hope.

　—

The Inflammation Stage of Healing

Humanity has been lingering in the initial healing stage of inflammation. No longer can we deny our pain. Many are feeling the heat, redness, pain, and swelling in the wounds of our social body and environmental crisis. Indeed, as systems break down, there's increased chaos, outrage, fear, anger, violence, polarization, and drastic imbalance. Yet, if we look closer, with every system breakdown, natural disaster, act of terrorism, and large-scale crisis, the heart of humanity has rushed in with compassion to serve, like "planetary blood cells" offering much needed aid, stabilization, and a healing response to our collective wound.

The swelling of love, compassion, service, and yes, outrage, in many cases, has been overwhelming. Our collective heart is waking up more with every injustice and every symptom of our aggregate pain and suffering. When we recognize the needs of the marginalized and underserved, we rush in with resources. When we see those at risk, we reach out with the basics to stabilize. When we feel the gravity of large-scale trauma and mass destruction, we flood the area with first responders, triage, and emergency care.

Sometimes inflammation comes in louder forms like social activism, drawing attention to a collective wound that is ready for an organized healing response. As we wake up as a species, we will no longer sit idly and allow wounds to go unattended; and we will not tolerate reckless behavior that puts the collective, greater whole at risk of further injury.

Activism, as an inflammatory response, has played a major role in initiating healing for humanity over the past couple of centuries. Activism prompted the end of slavery, challenged dictatorships, protected workers from exploitation, brought awareness of the environment, promoted equality for women, protected children, opposed racism and sexism, ignited campaigns for justice, fought for basic human rights, and ignited a healing response to many other important issues. From the Civil Rights Movement to the Occupy Movement, activism has opened our hearts and minds, calling us forward to repair what's not working for the good of the whole.

Activism generally challenges broken policies, procedures, and practices, trying to make healthy systemic change and evoke transformation for the greater collective. Through peaceful protests (and unfortunately, at times, those which devolve into violence), activism rushes attention to places the whole system might not see, feel, or experience as broken, whether leaders, systems, and governments are ready to respond or not.

Yet even activism, itself, is evolving with higher consciousness. We have raised our inflammatory response an octave to align with our deeper spiritual truths, authentic compassion, and integral wisdom. This evolved "Sacred Activism" has become a conscious, spiritual practice. Andrew Harvey writes:

> *A spirituality that is only private and self-absorbed, one devoid of an authentic political and social consciousness, does little to halt the suicidal juggernaut of history. On the other hand, an activism that is not purified by profound spiritual and psychological self-awareness and rooted in divine truth, wisdom, and compassion will only perpetuate the problem it is trying to solve, however righteous its intentions. When, however, the deepest and most grounded spiritual vision is married to a practical and pragmatic drive to transform all existing political, economic, and social institutions, a holy force—the power of wisdom and love in action—is born. This force I define as Sacred Activism.*

Humanitarian efforts and mutual aid also provide relief in times of emergency, crisis, and disaster. These are other expressions of humanity's inflammatory healing response. The collective body pools resources and rushes aid to the site of people in need until the long-term help by governments and other institutions can begin the reparative stage.

Natural disasters, extreme poverty, migration issues, disease, homelessness, war refugees, terrorism, and famine are events that call forth our collective inflammatory healing response. The list of emergency situations receiving humanitarian efforts over the past several decades has grown exponentially. Material and logistical assistance help to stabilize the area, while additional resources flow to those in need in order to save lives, alleviate suffering, and maintain human dignity. Humanitarian aid, as a first response to healing, is easy for our hearts and minds to embrace and employ.

What is needed now, more than ever, is leadership that steers us away from fear and fosters greater confidence in the inherent goodness and ingenuity of humanity.

~ Jimmy Carter

The Repair and Proliferation Stage of Healing

After an initial inflammatory response, the body moves into repairing what's broken or wounded and proliferating new healthy cells. The body creates brand new bone and tissue (form and structure) to replace what has been damaged. Proliferation is the growth or production of cells in a rapid, and often excessive, spread or increase.

In the collective body of humanity and our planet, this reparative and proliferative stage has already begun. Sadly, we are not often aware of the vast movement of self-organizing groups, organizations, and healing initiatives already in formation on our planet. Yet, new and emergent social forms and structures are popping up everywhere, available to replace old, broken-down, fractured, and outdated social systems.

As consciousness shifts, the collective body is evolving toward systems of greater complexity and higher order. We are aware of our awakening and conscious of our evolution. Science and spirituality are demonstrating our interconnected reality and we are responding. Inherent unity and the innate universal intelligence within humankind move and inspire us to find solutions and provide healing to systemic issues.

The creative impulse drives us to work together, share resources, and weave a stronger connective tissue that supports and sustains us as a whole. Each and every sector of society is being infused with more consciousness, greater connectivity, and our collective genius.

Solutions for climate change, poverty, the environment, peace, clean water, hunger, social justice, economics, health, conservation, human rights, and more are emerging every day. New healthy cells of like-minded, like-hearted individuals are working together to reform, evolve, and revolutionize different systems within our social body. And now, networks of networks, organizations of organizations, and communities of communities are coming together. And the Reparative/Proliferation Stage is becoming more visible.

Paul Hawken spent over a decade researching organizations dedicated to restoring the environment and fostering social justice. He wrote a seminal book, *Blessed Unrest: How the Largest Movement in the World Came into Being and Why No One Saw It Coming.* In his book, he describes how "a movement, created by billion-dollar nonprofits and single-person dot.causes" alike, is defining a new future for humanity. Hawken says, "the movement has no name, leader, or location, and that has gone largely ignored by politicians and the media. Like nature itself, it is organizing from the bottom up, in every city, town, and culture, and is emerging to be an extraordinary and creative expression of people's needs worldwide."

In a popular speech in 2012, Hawken listed 130,000 organizations in the world that work toward social and environmental justice. Those were only the ones he was aware of. Likely there are many, many more. He said there may be 200,000 or 500,000: "We do not know how big the movement is." And he acknowledged, "It's so new, we can't recognize it."

Beyond Hawken's identification of organizations serving environmental and social justice, myriad others exist that create solutions for education, economics, healthcare, and so on. We are seeing solutions that bring higher consciousness into every realm and function of life on the planet. We must create new, whole-systems change, better reflecting our humanity—our shared values—our inherent undivided wholeness. As consciousness evolves, we are evolving and healing in response. Institutions, organizations, and systems refusing to adapt, change, or upgrade their operating systems are no longer viable or sustainable.

This is humanity's Reparative/Proliferative Stage. The response is everywhere. There is no center. There's no leader. There's no organization. It is in every country on Earth as the Creative Impulse works within the collective psyche. The reparative response is present and active—right here, right now—in every tribe, ethnic group, and culture. We have demonstrated the capacity to respond to our crisis and we have all the resources we need to heal and be whole. We know what to do and we are doing it. Yet this stage takes time and sustained effort and commitment to maintain the conditions for healing to occur. The whole collective body is invited to cooperate and participate.

Often resources and attention get diverted back toward crisis and a continued inflammatory response—the stress response. But also, many resources are invested in trying to maintain, preserve, and conserve the old systems that are breaking down. Not wanting change, the old guard tries to preserve the Golden Years and "business as usual." Yet, that's proving to be like administering CPR (cardiopulmonary resuscitation) to a dinosaur. The old, wounded structures control a lot of our collective resources. Instead of competing for those resources, we are learning to focus our attention on possibility and potential, being just as creative with our energy and limited resources.

Buckminster Fuller said, "Don't fight forces, use them." His encouraging words have inspired many to step into a call to be architects of the future, not its victims. He said, "You never change things by fighting the existing reality. To change something, build a new model that makes the existing model obsolete." We are seeing this actualized in the proliferation that is a natural part of this stage of healing. Alternative economies, intentional communities, and sophisticated barter systems of all types are responding where people and public good come first. New models are emerging. There are millions of people around the world working for the greater good.

> *"The first rule of sustainability is to align with natural forces, or at least not try to defy them."*
> ~ **Paul Hawken**

The Maturation and Remodeling Stage of Healing

We have yet to reach the final healing stage. There are numerous initiatives and movements gaining momentum and visibility. Individuals, organizations, and communities continue to create new, healthy forms and structures to replace those no longer serving our highest good. Gaining strength, stability, and sustainability in the reparative stage is imperative before we mature into the remodeling. We are preparing for wide sweeps of whole-systems change and global coordination. Efforts are now being made to coordinate, synergize, and streamline our progress. The Maturation Stage will depend on how well we are willing to work together as a single, global *whole* living system.

Relax into Healing For now, we must relax into our healing response and remember our undivided wholeness. Fear, anxiety, and despair are not helpful and do not serve us in this time of healing. Feeling anxiety and fear are understandable as systems break down. This is a scary time. Yet, these feeling responses cause constriction, resulting in even greater tension and anxiety within the larger system.

Research has demonstrated that psychological stress can have a substantial and clinically relevant negative impact on the healing process. Furthermore, psychological and biological stress can actually promote health-damaging behaviors and delays in healing. Compromised health and/or compromised healing due to stress increases the risks of further complications, magnifies discomfort, and slows the return to normal activities of daily living. The relationship between stress and health and healing is more than significant.

Our current planetary crisis is causing stress (and lots of it) on many levels. The stress response is causing even more chaos, pain, and suffering. We mustn't allow the stress to interfere with our healing response. We mustn't allow fear to constrict the birth of a new humanity. We are in need of one big, collective, unified breath (before the unified push in our birthing process). It is time to elicit the relaxation response to assist our efforts as we evolve and heal what is no longer working or serving us. Let us breathe. Let us breathe together and shift our focus from the stress of our crisis to a healthy, self-organizing, self-regulating, innate, healing response, trusting the Cosmic Physician is always right here with us. Barbara Marx Hubbard says our crisis is our birth. Remember my stories of being stuck in the proverbial birth and death/rebirth canal? This is us.

Let us celebrate our inherent unity and wholeness while we acknowledge the impending birth. As we dispel the illusion of separation, we allow the Creative Impulse of our innate oneness to emerge naturally and organically, rather than continuing to obstruct it with our fear and need to control.

Good of the Whole We can celebrate our collective action and shared practice of taking responsibility for the whole. This is a new consciousness. We are shifting our awareness and experiencing how our actions affect the greater whole. Global cooperation, mutual tolerance, trust, and respect have become regenerative acts. We are empowering a social-potential movement for the global good. Humankind, as a whole, is now being represented and finding a collective voice. Intention, action, and devotion to the greater good are enabling solutions that bridge artificial and dysfunctional boundaries and beliefs. We are unfolding a future story and making visible what's working.

Celebrate humanity's strength through our indivisible wholeness. Working together, we are one great, coherent force for good. Separate, we are weak and vulnerable. We have yet to see the full magnificence of our own collective capacity and human spirit. Let us relax into our greatness and astute capacity to co-create change.

Like my recovering body, our collective body lacks strength and coordination right now. That will come but it depends on us to develop and implement new social architecture. We are the connective tissue. As the self-organizing capacity of Creation repairs and rebuilds, knitting together a stronger humanity and new world, we will move into the maturation and remodeling phase with whole-systems coordination. We are connecting, reorganizing, and rebuilding. We are learning to walk a new way and birthing ourselves anew as we heal our collective wounds.

And let us not forget our individual wholeness. This is our time to remember and return to both our individual and collective wholeness. We are whole beings within a greater whole. When whole beings contribute to and serve the greater whole, the whole can serve and support the individual.

Living for the "good of the whole" is more than just a nice phrase or good idea. As an idiom, the meaning of the phrase is so much more than "good" and "whole." Good of the whole is the foundational principle for living a healthy, interconnected, interdependent life in unity, harmony and exuberant vitality. It's a powerful prescription for ultimate quintessential health and oneness. It's an ideology, creed, ethos, doctrine, and belief that can guide us individually and collectively back into our innate genius. It's a polity, a worldview, and a vibrational frequency that returns us *home*. Both ancient spiritual traditions and modern, leading-edge science point to the unified nature of reality, so living for the *good of the whole* brings us back into right relationship with all things.

A Healing Prescription The etymology of the word *heal* means to cure; save; make whole, sound, and well. To heal is to make whole again. Our healing elixir begins within the recognition that we are not separate—there is no separation—we are all part of one living, dynamic system—a sacred whole. When we resolve the illusion and great myth of separation, we dissolve fear. When we dissolve fear, we relax into our higher creative potential, our regenerative capacity to create the conditions for healing to occur. This invites our natural creative intelligence to come forward. Experiencing inherent unity inspires us and calls us to serve the greater whole.

When each individual human takes full responsibility for his or her unique purpose and steps forward to serve the greater whole, the whole takes care of the individual in that person's fullest expression. Herein lies peace, freedom, and prosperity—a beautiful prescription for creating an abundant and healthy future for us all.

⁓

Levels of Consciousness

I was sitting outside at the lake on one of our comfortable aqua-blue Adirondack chairs, having early morning coffee with extended family. I love that time of morning as the sun comes up, the birds begin to sing, and the world wakes up. We all had our smart phones and occasionally scrolled through news, email, social media, and the like as we listened to the birds and talked about the sunrise and the change in weather. At one point, I chuckled and made a comment about a Comedy Central skit about US politics. After a brief exchange of polarized opinions, one family member said, "That's why we don't talk about politics or religion—we just don't."

The exchange between us bothered me more than the differing opinions or levels of consciousness. If family members can't talk about what really matters, then who can? I thought, *This conversation doesn't need to get polarized or thrown into the terminal taboos of politics and religion, if we can instead talk about common values and shared purpose.* I tried to speak from my heart and share how I was feeling. However, the conversation just dwindled. No one followed my enthusiasm, responded to what I shared, or addressed the emotion that presented as tears rolled down my cheeks.

After having Richard Barrett on my show, I recently posted a graph from his work on my Facebook page. The Barrett Values Centre works with levels of consciousness and gave a great description of personal and national consciousness at the differing levels. Moving through self-interest to the common good, Barrett described the fears we face in the developmental process. I could see our conversation was coming from both ends of this spectrum.

I took a deep breath and moved on with my day, focused on compassion. Yet all day, I felt the real experience of separation that occurs when people come from differing places, beliefs, and consciousness, and don't move toward understanding. I ached for common ground and mutual agreement. How can we resolve this collective wound of Humanity in this reparative stage of healing, if the "translation" of issues is coming through different levels of consciousness and cultural lenses? How can we move toward reconciliation and peaceful solutions if the rendering of ideas can't be seen, heard, or held respectfully with common agreement?

Later that night, in my sleep, it felt like I was working on the issue all night long. I was seeing structures and graphs and geometry in motion. I was seeing differing boundaries and beliefs moving and connecting like an old-fashioned erector set. I was seeing the flowering of consciousness coming through nature like a tight bud that blooms as it reaches for the light. Cycles and seasons and dimensions all coexisted in harmony as each expression worked its own magic in service to something greater. Beautiful strands of light held the structures together like Indra's Net. Every individual parcel and part had pieces of beauty and truth, and moved toward a collective whole.

Religion, politics, and culture were structures within the net that represented and held a repository of common values and shared purpose. There was no room for stagnation rooted in individualism and isolation. Within the net, everything was moving from birth to death to rebirth, from idea to policy to new idea and changed policy, from value to behavior to refined values and new choices. Religion, politics, and culture were evolving in proportion to the maturation of the individuals within them, and along the same layers of shifting creative energy. Myriad common threads permeated and pulsed throughout everything, as transient as the changing seasons in nature, yet leaving a beautiful tapestry of diverse and rich textures and designs.

Common values became shared purpose. Shared purpose organized into systems. Everything was moving toward higher order and more complex systems simultaneously. As individuals and systems grew, facets within these would jump freely in perfect timing. Every individual, system, and structure was moving toward greater wholeness as divinity wove magic through the veins of this superstructure. Polarity and duality were simply tension rods of simple, but incomplete, truths that held the net together within the superstructure until they bent back around in an inverted fashion to reconnect. Varying thoughts, words, and deeds moved fluidly between the rods. Like a continuum of hot and cold, high and low, smooth and rough, or light and dark, the multifaceted net was a complex design, too sophisticated to render in three dimensions. Yet, it was purposeful and perfect when seen through this cosmic lens.

I first experienced this superstructure as a blueprint of the Universe—a cosmic design. And then it became clear that it was the same blueprint or design as within us. The blueprint represented the same thing. Information in-forming the universe within us was the same process in-forming the greater whole. It is the same thing. Crystal clear but hard to put into language.

A microscopic lens cannot capture the vast design of the cosmos. A telescopic lens cannot capture the intricacies of a microorganism. And the human eye cannot see either extreme perspective. That doesn't mean they don't exist. We trust they do. Our human minds may limit our understanding of the great mysteries of life, our three-dimensional orientation may restrict our view, and our level of consciousness may preclude our full awareness. But in the quiet space within, there is a knowing. Let us rest there.

When I woke up the next morning, I had a new appreciation for how random things appear. They really aren't random at all. And on the transverse, I had gratitude for the simplicity of things even though the universe and the evolution of consciousness are incredibly complex.

Levels of consciousness appear like simple stages or steps we transcend as we go and grow through life experience. Yet, every individual has a trajectory that is attached to a complex set of threads, which are then pulled through the net accordingly. Just because we are waking up as a species, and aware that we are waking, doesn't mean we can rely on our limited intelligence and mortal understanding to solve our perceived collective problems. We can't see the entire perspective yet. Like my favorite professor in counselor education always used to say, we must "trust the process!"

A Call to Wholeness

So, what is our prescription? What is this resounding call to wholeness? What process might we trust? I have shared my healing journey with fractured bones as a reflection of my experience of living into my wholeness and mirroring the greater whole. I hope this bold expression of relaxing into resonance, aligning with the Divine, and serving the greater good by co-creating with others will inspire you to welcome deep self-reflection and this healing prescription.

When we look at nature, we see the Designing Intelligence that creates wholeness. We see a pattern that helps realign our individual separate lives with a greater unified whole. The wisdom of nature's interconnectedness creates a blueprint for mutually nourishing relationships. And, nature's wholeness design creates beauty, peace and healing for ourselves and the world. We must harness the wisdom of nature and living systems in order to understand the master plan available to us in these times. Whole systems change is our call to Wholeness. Now is the time. Here's what nature teaches us:

1. **We are unique, individual, diverging parts.**

    David Bohm said, "Individuality is only possible if it unfolds from wholeness." We are each unique, valuable, and diverse parts of a unified whole. There is unity in our diversity and the more diverse we are, the stronger and more resilient we become. Our diversity gives us greater clarity, exceptional creativity, and complex beauty. As separate, intricate parts, we are called to be adaptive, self-organizing, self-governing, and self-correcting. In our authentic, autonomous and unique expressions, we literally create a greater whole. We have a valuable role and vital responsibility to contribute to, and serve, the good of the whole.

2. **We are a unified, harmonious, converging whole.**

    We are a holy, whole system comprised of interrelated, interdependent parts. This unified whole cannot be understood by simply looking at and seeing the individual parts. As each individual part converges to create a coherent, resonant whole, we become much greater than our individual expressions. Together, we create a clear, concise shared purpose that's difficult to comprehend when we're identified with our individual selves. We bring harmony by putting our deep, meaningful purpose into action on behalf of the whole. In return, the whole engages the individuals, creating a network and infrastructure that generatively serves each and every individual part. This unified WHOLE ecosystem experiences all of the parts as NOT separate.

3. **We are the expression of an interdependent, co-creative, mutually nourishing relationship.**

    Saying all things are connected is inaccurate, as the oneness of the whole isn't about separation or separate parts as mentioned above. We are in a living, dynamic relationship with all things. This relationship extends both internally within and externally throughout the cosmos. This open, free-flowing relationship is a vibrant, generative network. This supports self-organizing teams and assists us in developing methods to practice resonance, establish co-creative coherence, and tap into collective intelligence. The relationship cultivates meaningful conversation and supports thriving communities.

4. **We are the Impulse of Creation—the Designing Intelligence of the Universe—in motion.**
   The animating life force in nature is the same animating force within us. The same impulse of creation moving through the cosmos, oceans, trees, and mountains, moves through us. This is the designing intelligence of the Universe. This is an organizing, creative power.

5. **We are the recipient of loving, benevolent grace.**
   According to Mirriam-Webster online, grace is "unmerited divine assistance." This divine assistance asserts a new way of looking at our unity within diversity. It teaches us that the Universe has our back. Grace is the magic and the mystery. Grace is the sweet nectar of life. It is the unmerited divine assistance within our healing.

Nature's design for wholeness enables life to thrive. Every level of life is patterned, designed and organized for sustainability and abundance. We are governed by this same design. It's a healing blueprint and treasure map that can take your life to a new level. So, follow the blueprint. Grab your treasure map and go places.

Live into your wholeness. As we shift our perspective from fractured to whole and adopt what Jude Currivan refers to as a "WholeWorld-View" (www.wholeworld-view.org) of inherent unity and unitive consciousness, we grow our capacity to foster and experience our unified wholeness. We expand our capacity for compassion. Living into this wholeness, we also recognize and respect the divinity within all humans, creation, and ourselves. Let us love ourselves—from our bifurcated nature of unique, individual expression to our inherent value as integral parts of a greater whole. Trust the sacred orchestration within this whole. Trust the whole within the parts—we are all whole beings within a greater whole. Trust the Divine Intelligence. Creation is creating through us. Once we stabilize this essential part of our nature and identity, we relax into a greater essence of whole and our highest future potential. Let us surrender and BE the love and divine expression we were created to be!

Relax into resonance. This sounds kind of funny. Relax into resonance? Reversing the stress response by intentionally activating the relaxation response, we open to our creative, healing potential. This is the path of least resistance, where we come from a place of full presence—equanimity—and activate the qualities of harmony and coherence. Full body muscle relaxation is one thing. Resonance is another. Resonance is activated within the heart space. This deeper sense of relaxation and wholeness induces a state of internal resonance and supports external, authentic connection and resonance with others. A relaxed, resonant field directly affects the environment and people around us, creating the best conditions for healing to occur.

Relaxing into resonance expands our awareness, optimizes problem solving, creativity, and intuition. It induces a state of acceptance, open mindedness, and open heartedness. Be mindful, let go of fear and cynicism, and stop judging—it only causes more undue stress, pain, and suffering. Embrace what comes. Love what presents. Relax into the resonant field and trust that the Universe has your back—our back.

Align with the Divine (and the design). As we create more resonance, we directly experience the sacred flow of all Creation. We are called to align with our highest, creative potential and manifest an expression of life filled with respect, reverence, and awe. We trust that Divine Intelligence is always present, always right here, right now. Trusting this new multidimensional existence and emergence as our new normal, we weave the worlds and realms together as the unified body of Christ.

As God/Creator/Source/Divine Presence pulses through all creation, we experience divine synchronicities and trust that the process of change, healing, and transformation is moving through us, in us, and as us, waking us to a higher creative potential. Let us collectively relax into this greater plan, for it is our emergent future. Allow the inherent wholeness and wisdom to in-form our path. As we co-create with the Divine and join with others aligned with this higher potential, we co-create a brighter future—a greater whole—more than we can imagine. The vast wisdom and infinite grace will carry us and sustain us.

Boldly express your divine nature. As we step into our fullest potential, we embrace our unique gifts, affirm our soulful mission, and honor the sacred whole and divine purpose that's aligned with our True Self. Valuing authentic, resonant connections with God, others, the earth, and ourselves, we begin focusing on what's creative, meaningful, and purpose-driven. We must be bold and express our creative, divine nature, and take action from this place of purpose and meaning. The world needs our clear voices of hope, healing, and wholeness. The world needs our unique perspective and intentional service. This is a time for a world of integral participation, cultural diversity, and radical inclusion for the good of the whole. And obviously, we each are a valuable part of that whole—remodeling and shaping our new highest expression and functional worldview.

Come together, connect, and co-create. As we wake to our inherent unity, and begin our unique service, we find and attract others who share values, common purpose, and who want to come together in synergistic work and play. Connect. Practice the art of authentic connection by taking responsibility for the quality of all your connections. And trust the process of co-creation. Co-creation with other like-hearted, like-minded beings is so much more than simply cooperating or collaborating. The social synergy thus created brings gifts and insight beyond our imaginings. We are stronger together. We are greater than the sum of our parts. Let us self-organize to bring forward greater coherence and our magnificent co-creative genius for the greater good.

Serve the whole. To create sustainable health, peace, and abundance, we must collectively step up to serve the greater good. Trust the benevolence. As individuals serve the whole, the whole serves each and every individual. We will be taken care of. Live into the miracle zone of synchronicities within the quantum field. It is a sacred, co-creative roadmap toward prosperity. We are always and forever stronger together and will create "greater works than these." Let us come together to transcend, and to include unique individual expression. The Universe has our back as we lose ourselves in this sacred call. Creation will continue to co-create through us. This divine, interdependent, whole-system welcomes our singular gifts of service.

Each of us carries the prescription and coding for wholeness and a healthier world within. The divine blueprint is accessible in those quiet moments of deep recognition when we're not looking, searching, striving, or wanting. Remember, as I mentioned in Chapter Two, by providing hospice for the passing of broken systems and structures built on a consciousness of separation, we are also midwifing our future potential and creative capacities of a universal humanity united in love.

As we each make a commitment to live into our wholeness, align with the Divine, and boldly express our sacred purpose in service to the whole, we co-create a healthy, sustainable, prosperous, and peaceful world that works for all. We are truly differentiated expressions of oneness. When things appear broken in our collective realm, we are called to come together, create resonance, and allow the unified field of consciousness to in-form us. We are so much more than the sum of our parts. Let us make ourselves visible as a vast, diverse, and co-creative sacred body invested in a peaceful, just, and healthy world for all. We are destined to heal the wounds of separation.

CHAPTER REFLECTIONS

It seemed as if we all could viscerally feel and hear that dreaded "Snap!" as a deeply injured Humanity recognized itself in a fractured state of incoherence—disabled by a consciousness of separation.

- Our return to wholeness—healing the wounds of separation—is an individual and collective imperative. Reflect on your own personal wounds of separation and healing journey. In what ways are you still in the actual wounding? Relational? Mind, body, spirit? Vocational or financial? What areas of your life are breaking down? Where in your life are you experiencing the pain, swelling, and inflammation? Where in your life are you experiencing the reparative stage? Remodeling stage? What stage of healing most resonates with you? Write out the six healing prescriptions from the chapter. How are you doing within each? Pick your weakest area and do some purge journaling. Allow the process to give you a booster shot of insight and wisdom to move you into your fullest healing response.

- Your personal health and wholeness is part of our collective health and wholeness. Your healing response is part of our collective healing. Your return to wholeness is our return to wholeness. The world needs YOU in your fullest expression as a whole-being. Take a whole-being inventory. Where might you need a little more attention and love right now? Ask for help. Just as first aid rushes to the site of a wound or fracture, allow yourself to accept aid, assistance, guidance, and support. We can't do this alone. We are designed to work together for the greater good.

CHAPTER SEVENTEEN

Remembering Wholeness

We are at a vital threshold in human history. While our fragmented perspective of the world has brought us and our planet to the edge of catastrophic breakdown, the newly emerging holistic perception of the cosmic hologram and the essential unity of consciousness offer us the choice for a transformational breakthrough.

~ Jude Currivan

Ready as I was for sustained change and definitive healing, something shifted in my resolution. I returned to Dr. Sheen to address alignment, strength, and coordination as muscle weakness and poor range of motion had limited my progress. I prayed, trusting the simultaneity, that the answer exists within this moment: *If I am called to 'walk a new way,' what final layers of mending, weaving and proliferation are needing my attention; what adjustment, technique or therapy will align my will with Thy Will; and what consciousness will clear the field and regenerate my physical constitution, so I may leap into my next highest evolution?*

As we worked with this shared intention, it was as if every familiar chapter of **Fractured Grace** was written in that eternal moment of now—my childhood, development, family, experiences, the war with my body, shame, stories, and energetic blueprints—things I had already written about were being presented and wrapped in a bouquet of final closure. We cleared unconscious programming and incited cooperation between muscles, nerves, ligaments, tendons, and bones. Toward the end of an extra-long, tedious session, where it felt like all of my neurological wiring was either crossed or short-circuited, he made an enlightening proclamation: "The first time you felt like this—where you were struggling to move and take a step—was when you were nine months old, learning to walk."

A remembering broke through my consciousness. A familiar visceral response grabbed my curious psyche and pulled me straight into my heart. I was that nine-month-old baby girl! I could feel her heavy feet. I could remember the fear, frustration, and confusion that grounded her spirit and challenged her freedom. I got in the car to drive home and released liberating tears of mixed emotion. Compassion flooded my being as I relived the experience along with the sadness and grief of the helpless child. I was *her* standing there wobbling, alone and unsure, not wanting but wanting to take that step, not sure about how to navigate or even be in this world. I felt her and I lived her awkward paralysis.

And then I saw her young, scared, teenaged mother feeling the same fear, overwhelmed and frustrated, as she tried to manage two toddlers under twenty-one months, among other life challenges. With grace, I saw a teen mom, hamstrung, unable to take her own steps. Next, the vision evolved and expanded into the experience I'd had in Colorado decades earlier. Once again, I saw the generations and generations of women lined up in an inverted triangle, looking at me, wearing their drab clothes and flat affect.

From my having seen that nine-month-old wobbly toddler, to my teenaged mother, to generations of women past, and now to the millions affected by and speaking out through the #MeToo movement, empathy soaked deep into my bones, igniting a peculiar strength and piercing the thinly veiled marrow of my soul. This was a transpersonal experience of women healing the Feminine Wound—our experience in our bodies, within our culture, and with the Divine.

The shift opened to a deeper, more meaningful experience of the Divine Feminine. I felt, as if for the first time, the nurturing, infinite love and presence of a Divine Mother-God. I saw the feminine face of God, and she washed away my tears. I also saw the young child, Julie, not wanting to be on this planet—not feeling "at home" in her body—and wanting to return home to the Divine Mother's bosom. Empathy melted my fractured soul like a sunrise warms the landscape. I opened to a feminine experience of God—to the Mother. I yearned to be held and cuddled and comforted, and the Divine showed up. She was God.

Later that night, in my quiet repose, another layer revealed itself. Mother Earth. She was calling and crying out to me. The Mother— my home. Why have I lived decades on Earth and denied myself the feeling of being "at home" here? I looked closer at this disconnect and my relationship with Earth—*our* relationship with Earth. I was invited to heal this wound of separation and change my story. I am a living being, born of, and sustained by a living earth. This was momentous and an essential connection in this recent healing step. I could see why creating a beautiful, harmonious, and loving home was so important to me. I am a divine feminine transducer of the home frequency, and I long to co-create nurturing, safe spaces of peace and harmony, realizing heaven on earth. In this tender layer of healing, I embraced the feminine aspects of a *whole* God, with the feminine aspects of my *whole* self, and the feminine nature of our beloved *whole* Earth mother. The Mother energy and the Divine

Feminine was fully present deep within my hungering soul, and she had a peculiar sweetness that wanted to be tasted.

The structure of my universe shifted as quickly and unexpectedly as that dreadful "Crack!" years prior. As my heart broke open again, I was challenged to look deeper at my own fractured worldview, which lacked the expression of a *balanced and whole* Divine Mother/Father God. I was invited to live no longer disconnected or separate from my masculine/feminine being and becoming. If I were to live as a reflection of this Mother/Father God, that meant it was time to fiercely move into my power and occupy my body, my life, my masculine and feminine expression, my divinity, and my Earth-home more wholly.

From a young age, I saw this time as one of great transition on our planet. I experienced the macrocosm and understood our evolving consciousness from a *whole-world* perspective. I saw templates and blueprints and systems and codes. I saw breakdowns and breakthroughs. I saw systems and structures and laws of nature. I saw energy and regenerative patterns. I saw life with a multidimensional view, yet wore great blinders.

With the aperture of my lens wide open, I was eager and rather impatient to do my part. I was stepping forward to cultivate an ethos of wholeness and help advance a "WholeWorld-View," from the grass roots to the evolutionary edge. I enthusiastically looked for ways to support and provide opportunities for others to experience, embody, and express their inherent wholeness. I held the vision of a conscious world where every individual would feel valued, connected, and fully expressed as a whole being within a greater, unified whole. And yet, I failed. I failed *myself.*

For all I had been doing for others, I fell flat in affording myself this same opportunity, and quite frankly, I was missing the point. First, while I was looking "out there," projecting the need for wholeness onto a world in crisis, and people in pain, fear, and disconnection,

I was busy overlooking or excusing my own disconnection and disembodiment. I didn't feel valued, connected, or fully expressed as a whole being alive within my physical body. I had yet to come home to my body; to "re-member" all the parts of me within my wholeness. I had yet to remember the I AM Intelligence of Life lived and loved within my physical body. I had yet to learn that I am the steward and custodian of this separate, individual body, just as I am of my home, my community, and this beautiful Earth.

Second, I wasn't seeing deeply enough into how the conditions of consciousness on the planet were affecting me personally. We have been socialized into a culture that perpetuates deep, deep separation and "othering." We have been raised within a worldview of mechanistic, consumerism and separation. Without really seeing, we have assumed that democracy and our patriarchal systems of governance were designed for the highest good to take care of us and create liberty and freedom for all. And now, in the United States, as the two-party system, in the midst of chaos and corruption, crumbles around us, we are seeing that it never really was a true democracy in the first place. The founding fathers (wealthy, white men) created a system that allowed wealthy, white men to vote. Now I had to wake up to truth, the reality, and my responsibility within the broken system. We cannot heal the deep wounds of women and all our endemic injustices, while the system keeps perpetuating more of the same. We can't heal any injustice—racial, religious, political, gender, or otherwise in these conditions. The wound is festering, inflamed, and calling for intensive care.

———

Inflammation Response to Injustice

We need the loud, angry voices born of injustice to show us our ignorance. We need the rage and alchemical fires of activism to show us what hides in the shadows. We need the absurd, irrational, and painful actions of the "old guard" as they fight back—the broken systems trying to remain in power—to enrage us and catalyze the transformation more quickly. This seemingly endless barrage of painful breakdowns is giving us fuel for the work ahead.

> It is time to allow and nurture the conditions for this radical healing and evolutionary transfiguration to ignite, emerge, and come forward for our individual and collective health. Herein lies our new, enlightened social architecture—designed with balance, respect and inclusivity for the good of the whole.

Now more than ever, healing the deep feminine wound, and balancing the masculine and feminine is essential. We can't tend to Earth without embracing the Mother. We can't live into our wholeness without embodying both masculine and feminine energies. And we can't step into our authentic feminine power without healing the wounds of misogyny, sexism, sexual assault, abuse, harassment, and discrimination. Our political landscape and the plethora of recent events is bringing more light and depth of insight to such matters as the scandals revealed by #MeToo, and the horrific realities within our cultural story. From the Catholic church to Olympic athletes, to Hollywood moguls to the Supreme Court nomination process, gender inequality, abuse, and downright disrespect in the treatment of women is everywhere—now visible in epic proportions.

Many are being pulled into the drama as it triggers recollections of their own experiences of abuse. Women are gathering in voice and activism—choosing to fight back with fierce feminine power. Others are scratching their heads, feeling helpless and frustrated. The gravity of comprehending just how deep and wide this societal dysfunction is dug in— systemic, and buried in the recesses of our collective psyche—can be rather overwhelming. Simply asking men to be nice, play fair, treat women with respect, and step down from the archaic patriarchy to make room for women at the table isn't going to fix the problem. Women have to evolve into their fullest feminine expression and step into a new, clear power that honors both masculine and feminine. This is our only roadmap to wholeness. It is time to let go of the oligarchy and the patriarchy. Let go of the old systems and structures, and allow the new to emerge by taking our feminine power back. Women need to learn how to bring their full, feminine genius into expression, balanced with a healthy dose of their own masculine energy. Not to compete with men in the existing patriarchy, but to create the new, feminine models and to ground the force of love.

Remembering My Personal Wholeness

With all the injustices being exposed in the world, deep, deep layers of my personal experience emerged to be composted. In a compost pile, if you layer scraps and debris and don't tend to it, it will eventually break down. Left unattended, anaerobic bacteria set in and begin breaking down the organic matter. It takes a long time, and the pile gets slimy, gooey and begins to stink! However, if one tends to the compost, stirring the pile regularly, oxygen gets worked into the layers. With oxygen, aerobic bacteria come in to break down the matter. The process happens much faster with tending, as the pile heats up. The choice is to leave it alone and allow the trash to pile up, get slimy, and stink. Or tend to it, stir it with care and intention, and allow the burn—a speedier progression toward a more favorable outcome. At this point on my healing journey, I chose to go in with care and intention, and begin stirring the unconscious pile of old repressed memories and emotional debris.

My life experience has been similar to all the brave women coming forward in the #MeToo movement. It's funny. As a psychotherapist, I had done so much of my own personal healing work on childhood sexual abuse and sexual assault, that by comparison, the effects of sexual harassment didn't seem to me to be all that big a deal. I minimized it. I ignored it. I suppressed it. And then, that first big stir of the harassment pile induced a flood of memories, emotions, and heated healing opportunities.

In my early professional career, I had four different male bosses—all with their own signature style of misogyny. The first was incredibly sexist and overtly inappropriate. The sexual harassment in which he engaged was so blatant and obvious that it was not only painfully uncomfortable, but profoundly confusing. He hid behind the guise of "Clinical Supervisor." It was his "job" to desensitize me. It was his "responsibility" to teach me about transference and countertransference. And it was my job to tolerate and weather the storm of his daily barrage of sexual remarks and harassment. By today's standards, this man would be considered a serial perpetrator of sexual harassment.

After the birth of my second child, I worked hard on maternity leave to lose the extra pregnancy weight and get my body back in shape. One day after I had returned to work, we had a staff meeting in the basement of our office. After the meeting, he was behind me as we climbed the stairs to get back to our individual offices. I was wearing a cute, fitted, soft-cotton navy dress with small white polka dots. As we moved up the stairs, I heard the most shocking, descriptive comments about how my backside looked in that amazing dress and what "any man" would want to do in that moment.

I was horrified, humiliated, and triggered. Speechless, I didn't acknowledge his comment. I calmly went back to my office and got to work.

Don't get me wrong. I liked this boss. I thought of him as my friend, a close friend. And yet, he could act like a jerk at times!

My learning from boss number one: **hide my body**—it wasn't safe for me to be sexy, sensual, or show my fit, feminine body. Dealing with this daily flood of sexual innuendo initiated my treacherous journey of not owning my body—not embodying my feminine power. Out of shame, I began hiding behind conservative, professional clothing—business suits—and began gaining weight. Peeling back the layers of this enervating experience from my early working years proved liberating. Living with this chronic sexual harassment had been genuinely traumatic. Yet I had minimized the effects, and assumed the responsibility, thus beginning my thirty-year war with my body.

Boss number two was more mild-mannered and polite. Steeped in professional integrity and wrapped up in the good-ole-boy network, he maintained appropriate boundaries and impeccable decorum. Yet, when he hired me, there was a condition that I didn't learn about until months later. I was a test case. This organization had never hired mid-level practitioners, let alone female practitioners. I was his experiment. I was recruited for my impeccable decorum and astute professionalism. I was the perfect candidate to demonstrate to the CEO that women could compete and produce like men in the industry. I was expected to leave my feminine power and working-mother identity at home in order to pioneer a new breed of female professional pedigree. Could I manage and maintain a full, lucrative caseload? Could I bring added value to the organization? Could I juggle the responsibilities of home and children without encroaching on work time and responsibilities? The experiment worked. Not only could I play in the good-ole-boy network, I could win. I succeeded.

Again, I liked this boss. He was a friend, and I deeply respected him. Yet he was entrenched in the masculine paradigm, and that was the status quo back then.

My learning from boss number two: **deny my feminine power.** I learned to operate in the masculine world of patriarchy by embracing my masculine energy. I learned my feminine energy was a weakness and being a working mother, a liability. I played the masculine game so well that I was promoted and invited to climb the patriarchal corporate ladder. Looking back, I can see how much these subtle messages influenced my psyche.

Boss number three was demanding, dismissive, and power-driven. He was very self-centered and expected his staff to make him—not necessarily the bottom-line—look good. He was on the fast-track to greater success, and I became his guinea pig. I was running a new department in a new position. In this role, I was expected to build referral relationships with professionals of great influence and status. I was a natural. I enjoyed the job and the new relationships. I was a master communicator and developed great professional etiquette and rapport. I became a great negotiator and trusted colleague to many. As the number of referrals continued to climb steadily and the success of my new department was evident, I was being considered for yet another promotion.

Due to our success, the organization was considering expanding my department and scope of practice to serve the entire system, while implementing a new critical program and service. My boss didn't want to lose me or my department. He didn't want to share with the rest of the organization. He was responsible for bringing the department to the organization and didn't want to lose control over the process. In one of his emotional, self-centered rants against the proposed changes, he told me that the only reason I was successful in my job was because I was an attractive, young female.

Why wouldn't our referral sources want to see me show up in their offices? Ugh.

I liked this boss. He was my friend. And he was horribly self-absorbed.

My learning from boss number three: **my intelligence and skills don't matter as much as my appearance.**

The proposal went through, and I received the promotion. I began building a new department with expanded responsibilities under a new vice president. I talked about this boss—male boss number four—earlier, where I was climbing the corporate ladder and it was leaning on the wrong wall. This was the emotionally and verbally abusive boss. In fact, he was so abusive and out-of-control, most of the time, that I didn't even comprehend the misogyny and sexual harassment, per se.

This boss really liked me. He leaned on me emotionally and professionally. He asked my opinions and respected my professional vision and ideas. He allowed me incredible freedom and independence. He also depended on me to fulfill many of his responsibilities, such as board reports, projections, and negotiations. Again, I was good at my job and demonstrated measurable success.

I liked this job. I liked this boss. He was my friend. However, he was my friend only in private. Publicly, he had an arrogant persona and was dismissive, condescending, and belittling. As a department director, I was expected to be at monthly board meetings to give a monthly report. Yet this boss expected me to be seen and not heard. He saw it as his responsibility to deliver my reports. Often, when I was asked a direct question, he would give me a stern look, interrupt my response, and answer himself. This was the status quo for me, but not the other department director under his directive, a male.

Toward the end of my tenure, we were sitting in an executive planning meeting with only the top administrative executives and a few department directors. I was asked a question by the CEO and began to respond. I was abruptly interrupted and publicly scolded in an angry outburst. In an ugly, verbal attack, he said, "I will tell you when it's okay for you to talk. Shut up and don't talk unless I tell you to talk."

After my resignation, I sat down with the VP of Human Resources for an exit interview. I had never complained about his behavior, as that was my conditioned response. However, she asked me whether I would consider filing a lawsuit of sexual harassment and discrimination against him. I was shocked. I said no. She asked me to reconsider and encouraged me to do so. She had witnessed this ongoing public treatment, but needed complete documentation to deal with disciplinary action.

What did I learn from my fourth male boss? **My voice is to be muffled.**

As I continued to stir the compost pile, many of these long-forgotten stories, memories, emotions, and patterns of misogyny, abuse, harassment, and discrimination emerged to be transmuted. I'd had a successful journey of climbing the patriarchal ladder, competing in the man's world like a man, and playing within the good-ole-boys network. Yet, the personal consequences of this feminine wound were grave. I learned to **hide my body** in shame and fear—not wanting to be misunderstood as seductive, to **deny my feminine power** and the things that mattered most to me, to **muffle my voice** because it wasn't safe to speak up or speak out, and sadly, that my intelligence and skill-proficiency was overshadowed by how I looked—that **being attractive was more important than my innate genius and ability**.

As things began heating up in US politics with the hearings of Judge Kavanaugh and the allegations brought against him, I became obsessed. I watched the same good-ole-boys network at work in our world on public display—angry, divisive, and disrespectful. The abuse of power from all sides was sickening to me. I was aware of how many women were triggered by this spectacle, feeling helpless and hopeless. And so was I.

I stirred and stirred the compost pile. Yet a heavy cloak of shame clung to my psyche, like peanut butter to the roof of my mouth. I couldn't get the picture of me walking up those stairs in the blue, fitted dress out of my mind's eye. I intuited this was a critical piece of my ultimate, universal healing and I knew I needed a little extra help. I reached out to my friend and skilled, energy practitioner, Teresa, to clear whatever was lingering in my energetic field. I knew she was the perfect person to help me lift this layer of shame.

The energy session was truly transformational. With her prompt, I described the heavy cloak of shame. She worked within my energy field and created the perfect conditions for deep transmutation and clearing. Toward the end of the session, I was laying comfortably relaxed and peaceful on her treatment table, when I physically felt and experienced the magnificent release. My energetic experience of the heavy, dense cloak transformed into what I experienced as a "cape of light." It was so cool, like a superhero cape. I felt liberated, tingly and powerful. I chuckled and mentioned it to Teresa.

She continued to work within my field and a few minutes later I felt a tingly, broad band of light wrap around my waist. I experienced it like the belt, or body armor of the superhero figure. Again, I chuckled and mentioned it to Teresa. She chuckled with me. I had no expectation of the session getting any better. The cape and belt felt like a huge, benevolent gift. I felt complete. However, settling back into the resonance, I soon had an inconceivable sensation. The same pure light source began tickling my toes and then moved up through my feet and wrapped around my calves in a spiral motion. My boots—I had boots! I was given a pair of superhero light boots. I laughed out loud and reported the experience. Both Teresa and I shared a moment of playfulness as well as reverence and awe.

I was set. The shadow of toxic shame was fully integrated in the light. I now had a new superhero outfit: a cape, body armor and boots all made of cosmic light! The boots really touched me. It felt like a significant closure in the epic story of my fractured leg—a final missing piece in my healing was complete. And the spiral energy of light that wrapped around my legs was peculiar, mimicking my spiral break. How perfect that the cloak of shame was transformed and elevated into this superhero status. Healing this lingering feminine wound moved me into a new sense of feminine prowess and a new relationship with my body.

The Fierce Feminine Momma Bear

Back to U.S. politics and the relentless process of patriarchal antics, I realized that this, too, could be composted in a rapid, heat-induced alchemical transmutation, or these chronic, archaic patterns could remain stuck in a stinky, slimy pile of cultural neglect. I asked for guidance.

How can I help women move into their fullest feminine expression? How can I help women take back their power and step into a new, balanced relationship with themselves, men, other women, and the world at large? How can I help change the cultural narrative and prevent these crimes against women and children permanently? How can I help the feminine energies to rise up and meet the masculine as an equal, balanced partner? Remember my bottom-line message? *We are better than this. We can do great things. Anything is possible.*

The next morning in my meditation, I had a powerful vision. I called it, "Waking the Momma Bear."

The vision began with a *yin-yang symbol*. The yin-yang symbol represents the complementary forces that make up all aspects of life—two halves that, together, complete wholeness. The black yin side represents the feminine and the white yang side represents the masculine. A small circle of the other color is contained in each. Neither Yin nor Yang is absolute. They are interdependent.

In my vision, the yin and yang were dancing a beautiful, sensuous tango, much like the day flows into night and the night flows into day. There was a tension that attracted the two together and a freedom that allowed each half to express and morph and play. It was an exquisite dance.

At one point in the tango, both yin and yang morphed into two whole circles. The dance ended. The yang half was elevated, hovering above a horizon line and shining bright as a single white circle. The yin half—a complete black circle—lay down horizontally, fell asleep, and became the shadow for the yang. I hope to draw or paint a picture of this. It was such a powerful image!

Next, the sleeping yin circle morphed into a momma bear that had gone into hibernation. This was so interesting. A momma bear is a quintessential example of a mother's love. Her fierce, protective nature is revered and feared. Many say the most dangerous place to be is between a mother bear and her cub. In my vision, she woke up and began circling around beneath the elevated yang circle for some time. She occasionally pawed upward, as if trying to get his attention. She was agitated. She got up on her hind legs, stretched upward, and gave out a huge roar. But the yang circle couldn't hear her or see her. She retreated back and became more agitated. She was angry, not dangerous—but definitely angry.

Then the momma bear sat down and laid two eggs—one white circle and one black circle. She lovingly sat on the eggs until they hatched. At the moment the shells broke open, the black-yin-baby circle and the white-yang-baby circle fused together and began dancing, which created a new yin-yang symbol, this time without the small embedded circles.

This yin-yang baby began to grow, probably ten times the size of the momma bear. She just sat there resting on top of the whole yin-yang baby, and smiled.

All of a sudden, the floating white yang circle that had been hovering over the momma bear gently popped like a soap bubble and turned into a pink heart symbol. The heart gently floated down and landed on the momma bear's chest. When that happened, the momma bear morphed back into a small black circle and moved into the larger white yang half of the yin-yang baby—back into the greater whole yin-yang.

Another "soap bubble" popped open from that space and became a small white circle. This circle moved into the larger black yin half of the yin-yang baby. All was complete and whole again, and the yin-yang tango resumed.

That was the end of the vision. I'm still pondering and learning from the vision's symbolism and deeper meaning. But the most important catalyst of the vision was how the momma bear woke up and redirected her attention, anger, and agitation toward laying the eggs and nurturing them. This was teaching me about my own internal balance, as well as our innate, dormant feminine powers that are waking. It seemed to be a prescription of how to heal the WHOLE of us. For me, it was an invitation to turn my attention to healing the rifts in the masculine/feminine balance in a loving, peaceful, yet fierce feminine manner. It's all about balance and the dance of masculine and feminine. Healing the dance will return us to wholeness and help us re-member who we are. Embodying the balance will once again give us an authentic feminine voice and genuine feminine power.

Developing Custodianship

Instead of waiting for a new normal, amongst all the chaos of a world falling apart, a friend encouraged me to look for or create a "new natural." That was a wonderful suggestion. It pointed me back to the Designing Intelligence of Life and the in-formation at the center of my being. It suggested I return to the womb of Creation and allow myself to listen deeply for guidance and my next best steps. It reminded me of the stewardship and guardianship of the life I had co-created and brought me back to the laws of nature and the allowing, surrendering, and emergence of not just my new natural, but our new natural—not my will, but Thy Will.

This past summer my husband and I had been away from home a lot. The beautifully landscaped koi pond in our backyard was being neglected. Several weeks into the summer, I was frustrated with the overgrowth of weeds and went out with my gloves and tools to begin pulling and cleaning up. We hauled out loads and loads of weeds, branches, and pruned debris. The pond looked good again, and I was pleased with the progress. We talked about it and decided it would be best to let go of our beloved pond and the many fish we tended to over the past fifteen years. Times have changed, and now our summers are spent at the lake. We are not home much on the weekends or weeknights to tend to the garden, let alone enjoy the fish pond.

Weeks passed. Again, we were not tending the garden, and neither had we closed the pond down. Part of me thought that if we could just wait until fall, all the perennials would go dormant for the winter and all the weeds, just die. Surely that would make it easier to deal with? By the end of the summer, the garden around the pond was in complete chaos and disarray. Not only were the weeds growing rampant, but there were volunteer trees sprouting up everywhere and invasive plants choking out the flowers and bushes that I wanted to keep. It was a horrible, pathetic mess.

My garden reminded me of how I was neglecting not only my body, but my function within the larger collective body. I remembered the months before I broke my leg—when I'd discovered an unfamiliar, new love for my body. How I was tending to my physical health and wellness out of that love. How I was feeling so peaceful, whole, and free in my body and in my life. That became the prescription for my new natural—a love relationship and deep custodianship with my body and my responsibility to the collective body. This kind of love is a daily practice—a continual tending. It's a directive to "stay home" in my body and "stay awake" in my guardianship of our collective body and the earth. We all have been entrusted with responsibility for the safekeeping of the beauty, truth, and function of the undivided wholeness that we be.

The garden reminded me of other systems and structures undermined by the neglect of my/our collective love and attention. It brought to life my custodianship responsibilities for governance, education, healthcare, religion, media, and every other system that has and could support life. Healthy, evolved whole-systems will support the abundance of life. Neglected and broken-down systems diminish the potential for health and wholeness, allowing invasive entities to take hold and choke out our truth, beauty and goodness. This is what was being demonstrated in the news, daily.

This quest to love my individual body as aggressively and radically as I love our collective body was real. If truly I held the vision of a conscious world where every individual feels valued, connected, and fully expressed as a whole being within a greater, unified whole, I had to begin with me. I needed to remove all barriers to my feeling valued, connected, and fully expressed as whole. Pursuing my "new natural" taught me many lessons on being a whole being, contributing to and in service of a greater whole; many lessons on in-forming healthy structures; and many lessons on conscious, nurturing custodianship. The embodiment of my wholeness shifted how I experienced *our* wholeness.

The subtle shift into custodianship changed everything.

> The Designing Intelligence of Life uses us to be the custodians of the cosmic garden. God, Creator, Source uses our eyes, ears, hands, and feet to serve a higher purpose. The microcosm of life in a body is, indeed, reflective of a cell within the macrocosm of the Universe. Tending to that cell is part of the plan, and every single cell has a job to fulfill in service of the whole. Embracing our wholeness is embodying the responsibility of the individual and the collective, the micro and the macro, the body and the Unified Field of Consciousness.

Everything is determined, the beginning as well as the end, by forces over which we have no control. It is determined for the insect, as well as the star. Human beings, vegetables, or cosmic dust, we all dance to a mysterious tune, intoned in the distance by an invisible piper.

~ Albert Einstein

Embracing the dance of this "mysterious tune," we move into an enlightened flow state. Not abdicating responsibility for our lives, but listening even more deeply to the organizing guidance and moving fluidly with the brushstrokes of Designing Intelligence. Mahatma Gandhi put it this way: "There is a force in the universe, which, if we permit, will flow through us and produce miraculous results." The invitation is to surrender and allow the force to create through us, to weave our individual wholeness into the tapestry of the greater whole. And that begins by being and becoming a healthy, generative, whole being—listening to that creative force and moving into action. We must move into conscious action in service of the greater good.

This missing feminine piece had been huge. I finally felt home in the Mother and home in my body. Another black wrought iron cage was lifted, and I stepped out into the expansive mystery of grace, knowing and experiencing the epic love anchored deep inside. I was this love—this grace. And this love that dwells within was ready to be unleashed into the cosmic dance. This bright point of love and light was quickening as the divine blueprint for everything. I now felt equipped to reclaim my body and rebuild a connected, whole, and free life. With discipline. With structure. With fierce love.

Ram Dass said, "Healing does not mean going back to the way things were before, but rather allowing what is now to move us closer to God." This is a powerful quote. We have been living in a world that perceives itself as profoundly separate, fragmented, and broken. And all the systems and structures built in this consciousness, including patriarchy, are dismantling themselves. Yet, like the compost pile that heats up and burns quicker, we often feel the heat of alchemical fires and try to avoid the transformative process of change. We want the healing to return us to the way things were before.

It's a funny paradox. As we remember our wholeness, we're made new. We allow *what is* to move us closer to God and the divine expression of who we really are. To return to wholeness, we leap and shift and evolve, becoming more of who we are and yet never have been before.

Remembering the Mother—the feminine face of God—is a powerful, evolutionary catalyst. Experiencing that nine-month-old child who struggled to take those early steps broke me open and brought me home to my feminine power and my beautiful, neglected, sensual, abused, sexual, feminine, powerful human body that had a voice, intelligence, and gifts that made a difference. I moved closer to God.

I invited that lonely nine-month-old to "walk a new way," promising her we would walk together. I promised the eleven-year-old little girl inside that I would not only walk with her, but wholly embody our fullest incarnation, highest creative potential, and boldest divine expression. And I surrendered to my higher self, knowing there were to be no more cautious baby steps walking down the same old hill over and over. This evolutionary leap is imperative. I've fallen for change and have landed within the benevolent flow of grace.

CHAPTER REFLECTIONS

The subtle shift into custodianship changed everything. Who's tending your garden? The Designing Intelligence of Life uses us to be the custodians of the cosmic garden. God, Creator, Source uses our eyes, ears, hands, and feet to serve a higher purpose.

- Have you ever thought about the process of learning to walk, or learning to walk a *new* way? As systems and structures break down around you, you are called to break out of your habitual, conditioned life and explore how you are being called to grow and change. I love the saying, "If you always do what you've always done, you'll always get what you've always gotten." Take some time in your journal and explore what areas of your life are calling for change. Take an inventory and make a list. And then prioritize just one area where you might be able to begin being a better custodian.

- Do you feel at home in your body? This is a difficult one, especially for women. Use this custodianship model to focus on your embodiment. What does your body need from you? How might you feel more whole in your body? Reflect on your past experiences. Have there been times of sexual harassment that you've brushed under the rug or minimized? Allow yourself to unpack it and look at the effects. What did you learn? What needs to be composted? What is new and beautiful that can come out of it?

- Who's tending your garden? Have you ever thought about your life and what you create as a garden you are responsible for tending? What happens when you neglect areas of your life and your creations. You are uniquely gifted with talent and purpose to serve as a custodian of the larger garden—the whole of Creation. While everything is breaking down around you, what areas of your life need tending with love and care? What's your new natural when it comes to consciously evolving your life?

- What does being a *"whole being"* mean to you? What does being in an enlightened flow state mean to you? Allow the higher Designing Intelligence to in-form you at the very core of your being. Surrender and allow entry to what wants to come through.

CHAPTER EIGHTEEN

Fractured Grace

The only way to transform the world is to rethink it.
It's not about one of us. It's about all of us.
It's not about money, it's about love,
And it's not about out there, it's in here.
Such thoughts are miracles, and they change everything.

~ Marianne Williamson

Moments of grace—they usually appear in the most surprising places. Sometimes in a small, insignificant conversation; sometimes when you're stuck in a dark place and just want out; other times in huge, life-changing events. Often, they pass without recognition if you're not paying attention. That's the beauty and magic of grace. Pay attention. Open your heart and pause. Everything will be okay. Tune in and allow your fractured sense of hope to break you open. Feel the resonance: a peculiar, coherent joy in that space. The grace will be hiding in the afterglow.

Those are the moments that shape us and carry us forward. Those are the moments that deliver us to ourselves and remind us to walk a new way. Andrew Harvey writes, "If you're listening, if you're awake to the poignant beauty of the world, your heart breaks regularly. In fact, your heart is made to break; its purpose is to burst open again and again so that it can hold ever more wonders."

It is at the bottom where we find grace; for like water, grace seeks the lowest place and there it pools up.

~ Richard Rohr

Now on the precipice of great change on the planet, I prepare once again for another great change in my life. I'm feeling another big leap coming. I don't know what it is, but I'm ready to say yes when it presents. I trust I will be prepared, as all things *are* connected.

My life experience and all those moments of grace have prepared me. The universe has my back. No more baby steps or walking carefully downhill. No more cautious, calculated moves. I will show up and dance with the Divine—the nameless. I feel called to wildly co-create beauty and greater connectivity on the planet. As I leap forward with joy and reckless abandon, I will follow what presents and tune into those moments of grace. I will lead with my heart, creating more resonance and weaving the connective fabric of conscious love and creative potential. The ultimate healing prescription is to live into my wholeness and walk a new way.

You can't wait for your healing to feel whole, you can't wait for your abundance to feel wealthy, you can't wait for the mystical moment to feel awe.

~ Joe Dispenza

No more waiting for change, for healing, or something outside of myself, for I AM whole. I experience my wholeness with a new sense of joy. Through our surrendering, grace leads us; grace allures us into our unmanifest potential and the unknown future.

Remembering that Louise Hay said bones represent the structure of the Universe and bone fractures represent rebelling against authority, I guess, in a way, I *was* rebelling against authority. Rebelling by breaking away from the governance of a worldview contrived on separation; the ruling empire of ego; the power of old social forms and patriarchal structures; the dominion of faulty belief systems and artificial boundaries; the injustice of "othering" and the segregation of the "wrong" race, gender, religion, political party, class, or sexual orientation; the tyranny of a fear-based mythology; the oppression of the divine, feminine face of God; the devastating war against our own Earth-body and individual bodies; the death-grip of all that no longer serves the good of the whole.

As I reflect on the deeper meaning of my experience, everything has changed, including how I experience the structure of the universe and my personal sovereignty. I am no longer a finite individual on a planet or a single cell within the collective human body. I *am* the flowing presence in the infinite, cosmic web of all Creation, showing up as Julie. I step into a *whole* new way of being with more grace.

I am thankful for the breakthrough—to be released and free to express my highest potential. More than that, I am thankful for the breakdown—my fractured sense of grace—that allowed my broken heart to merge with the sacred heart and propel me forward in service of a cosmic heart. I experienced an intimate, benevolent, and compassionate Creator within the fracture, in the healing process, and with each new step I have taken. I now walk on the sacred land of *my* Mother Earth with the sweet salvation of walking in union with the Mother/Father-God/Goddess within. I move at the speed of resonant guidance, poised to co-create a world that mirrors our highest creative potential. My healing is our collective healing and my journey is our collective journey; our collective healing is my healing and our collective journey is my journey. There is no separation. Together, we are social change artists rising up to co-create positive health and healing, ground the creative force of love, and live into our wholeness with love, compassion, and peace.

This is my direct challenge to you. Let us stand up with grace and grit, find the courage to speak up with fierce conviction, and take inspired action to manifest a global shift in consciousness. There's work to be done. Together, anything is possible and we'll create greater works than we imagine.

Breaking through, let us rest in the awareness that love stays whole and grace is infinite. Our humanity is the connective tissue of the soul. Our inherent wholeness is the only true medicine for our times. May we breathe into our connection. Feel our interdependence. Experience beauty, peace, healing and our holiness as healthy cells within the unified whole body of humanity—of Christ. Sourced within the heart, this innate wisdom will lead us home.

CHAPTER REFLECTIONS

Breaking through, let us rest in the awareness that love stays whole and grace is infinite.

- We've all felt quiet whispers of grace in our lives. Grace shines even more light in life's darkest moments. Grace lives in every shadow. It lifts us when we fall and points the way when we are lost. Grace transcends suffering. Is there really such a thing as a "fall from grace?" It's time to rethink all our myths and stories. It's time to co-create a new story and create a positive vision for our future. And that begins with grace. Find some quiet time and ponder your own personal moments of grace. How does grace fall on you? What does *fractured grace* mean to you? How has grace been a healing elixir for your soul? How can you use the medicine of grace to heal the wounds of separation?

I am wishing you an elegant, graceful return to wholeness and I'm sending you a world of love! ~ Julie

If there's no breaking then there's no healing,
and if there's no healing then there's no learning.

~ One Tree Hill

Acknowledgments

How do I acknowledge all those who have been a part of the journey through *Fractured Grace?* The narrative began in my early childhood and continues through today. When my first grandchild was born, I developed a deeply poignant connection with future unborn generations. Thank you, Kooper. I dedicate this book to you and all my future grandchildren. In fact, it is for all children around the world, that I wake up each day committed to cultivating the seeds of change for a global culture of peace as we learn to live for the good of the whole.

I am deeply grateful to all those who have supported me and this book. I first thank my husband, Kevin, for the myriad expressions of love and support during my healing journey and the subsequent birthing of this book. Thank you to my children and their spouses for being the joy that buoys my life, and my sisters for sharing this day-to-day journey in meaningful ways. I thank my healing practitioners who are treasured friends and thought-partners: Teresa Bushnell, Sherryl Lin, and Jim Sheen. You have literally been there for me inside the entire process and between the lines of each page. I want to acknowledge the deep wisdom and generous spirit of Shelley Ostroff, who lives, and models, wholeness. I am nourished by our friendship, blessed by your guidance, and honored to co-create with you. There are many others who have supported me, my journey, and this book—friends, mentors and teachers—Andrew Harvey, Jude Currivan, Monica Sharma, Carolyn Anderson, Kurt Johnson, Katharine Roske, Anneloes Smitsman, and others too numerous to mention by name. Thank you. I hope you feel my sincere love and gratitude.

Finally, I deeply honor and want to thank my fellow GOOD of the WHOLE Stewards—in particular, Shelley Darling, Linda Linker Rosenthal, Glenn and Marian Head, and DiNahma Machado for living the mission with me every week over the past several years. Your generosity and friendship have become the ingredients in my *"Fractured Grace Stone Soup"*. A very special thank you to cofounder and friend, Shelley Darling. Your perennial commitment to develop resonance and play with me in the Unified Field of Consciousness, have truly in-formed my life, vocation and this book in profound ways. Thank you. Your friendship is a precious blessing.

About the Author

D r. Julie is a steward of the new earth, midwifing the evolution of consciousness and a whole worldview. Her 30-year career as an intuitive, integrative health practitioner and psychotherapist has influenced her work with evolutionary thought leaders and change-makers—co-creating connections that inspire and create the conditions for individual, collective and planetary healing. Her authentic, down-to-earth approach invites others to embody their highest creative potential while shifting from the ego-centric challenges of separation to a healthier soul-centric flow of resonance and coherence. She is a mentor for leaders and influencers who are dreaming a new dream and working toward whole-systems change. Dr. Julie is a popular speaker, teacher, Founding Steward of GOODoftheWHOLE.com, radio talk show host of The Dr. Julie Show: All Things Connected, and author of Fractured Grace: How to Create Beauty, Peace and Healing for Yourself and the World.

71397854R00167

Made in the USA
Columbia, SC
25 August 2019